NICOLE DAEDONE

Jailbirds in Flight

Everything You've Wanted to Know About
Enlightenment in Prison but Were Afraid to Ask

soulmaker | PRESS

First published by Soulmaker Press 2025

soulmakerpress.com

First edition

ISBN: 978-1-961064-43-0

Dedication

For my sister-inmates who serve to power the transformation of the world
The anointed officers who serve as Guardians
Topeka, Cynthia, and Marcus serving as strength in the fight
Emmett serving flow by working with the words
My Drupon and Roshi who serve as wings
And my Lama who serves as the waves of inspiring strength on which I fly.

May we all take and remain in flight!

This book is drawn from journals, letters, and dispatches I wrote during my time at MDC. Everything about my own experience is, for the most part, taken word for word from those original writings. Many of the biographies come directly from my sister-inmates and have been woven into conversations to preserve the texture of life inside. A handful of pieces, to protect the innocent (and the not-so-innocent), are what I call essence stories —accounts where certain facts and details have been fictionalized, while the lived truth remains the same. To enhance the narrative flow, thematic resonance, and overall storytelling, some elements—including characters' actions, dialogues, timelines, and events—have been dramatized or reimagined based on real inspirations.

For an interactive experience of this book,
visit book.jailbirdsinflight.com

Contents

Definitions

Jailbird:

A woman physically caged, learning to be free—flying above all circumstances.

Dakini:

In Tibetan Buddhism, a sky-dancing feminine deity who never lands on solid ground, because she is emptiness itself—flying on waves of inspiration.

1

The Ending (Almost)

For two days, women moved around Rachel and me like storm fronts around a mountain. Conversations stopped mid-sentence when we walked by, then restarted in a lower register. The same women who used to borrow our hair ties, our pens, our patience, were avoiding us. In the six months we had spent in federal prison, we'd never seen anything like this.

"Is it me?" I whispered to Rachel as we passed the laundry room.

"It's us," she said. "But I don't know why."

By dinner on that second day, the air had the pressurized feel of a storm shelter. Even Royal's usual "Hey, baby" sounded far away, like it had to travel through water to reach me.

Kiki slid up just close enough to talk without looking like she was talking to me. "They're preparing to lynch two white women," she muttered. "That's you and Rach."

My stomach dropped.

"They found some pages," she added.

Her eyes never quite met mine; she couldn't risk the association. Then she peeled off, leaving me in the wake of her warning.

Two days earlier, I'd tried to print a few pages I'd written. The printer jammed and spat out nothing. I shrugged and walked away. Just another glitch in prison life.

Except it hadn't jammed. It *had* printed. Someone found the pages. Someone passed them around.

To them, it looked like one of the hood books that circulate in dorms—the kind with thirty-two assaults, a cold-hearted pimp, and women whose pain is just plot. From where they stood, I wasn't a fellow inmate. I was an outsider taking notes.

That afternoon, Rach and I were walking the track in the prison gym, just doing our laps under the humming lights, when the door opened and a wave of seven women came in. They moved slowly and silently. No one smiled.

It felt like a scene from a mafia movie.

"Well," I said to Rach, "it's a good day to die."

They surrounded us on the track with silent, practiced ease. The lead woman dragged a plastic chair into the middle of the circle and sat down, legs wide, arms loose, the way someone sits when they know they're not the one in danger.

"We need to talk," she said.

She held up two well-worn pages between her fingers. "You writing some kind of hood book about us?"

The words hit harder than if she'd swung.

I reached for the pages, scanned lines I already knew by heart. In my hands, it was a story about a difficult, holy conversation between two women in a place built to break us. In her hands, it was evidence— another white woman turning other people's lives into material.

"Wait, that's only the middle of the story," I said.

No one moved. No one blinked. The air inside the circle thickened. In a prison dorm, your reputation is your oxygen. If a storyline takes hold, it doesn't matter what's true. What matters is what travels.

"Please. You have to read the end."

2

The Beginning, the Unf*ckwithable Phase

The first day being federally incarcerated felt like a stage dive. Stripped of everything, all I have now has been given to me—from the too-tight, government-issued bra to the roll of toilet paper gifted by my prison patron saint, Luciana. The women offer small mercies to the new arrivals—Rach and me. Commissary won't reopen for a week, so even if we had money on our books, we still wouldn't be able to buy shampoo, a toothbrush, or the insulated sippy cups everyone uses for water.

By the time Rachel and I finally arrived to the prison after a day of holding cells and transport, we were thirsty. Mariella, extradited from Guatemala, offered her Styrofoam cup of murky liquid. We hesitated. She caught our look.

"No, no—water with a little apple juice." She smiled.

It's like that here: Your instinct is to assume the worst, and then something kind—almost magical—cuts through.

It's astonishing how a few words can dismantle an entire life. Before the judge even finished her order, the marshals had stepped forward, cuffs ready. I turned to the gallery—rows of friends, eyes wide. "It'll be okay," I mouthed.

Fifteen years building the business, the community, the practice I was eventually indicted for. It had been years living under federal investigation, months of motions, and weeks of trial—all an inextricable flood that finally gathered enough force to dislodge me from my seat, earrings and necklace removed, and whisk me through a hidden door in the courtroom wall into the underworld.

If the prosecutors get their way, this is the beginning of my next twenty years. I'm fifty-seven.

The door sealed behind us with a vacuumed sigh. The most dramatic moment of my life was, for the officers, just another Tuesday. Rachel—my co-defendant, my friend—looked at me. We were certainly somewhere new.

They placed us in a stainless-steel holding cell. Eventually we'd be put on a bus, but for now, we sat filling out forms. Even here, relieved of our freedom, there was paperwork. Then intake began—the ritual undoing. We undressed, stood naked, bent over, and coughed on command; our courtroom clothes replaced by federally issued beige. My new underwear rose to my breasts; the bra slid up over them. The tan canvas pants could fit a linebacker, their cuffs swallowing the boat shoes that were a size too small for me, while Rach's shoes were a size too large for her. We looked like two children playing dress-up in our gangster fathers' closets.

The absurdity made me laugh. It was funny, but it was also the point. Identity, dignity, free will—all stripped and replaced.

We were marched again and sat on another steel bench, still swimming in our oversized uniforms. Across from us sat a woman who wore hers like silk. Black hair to her waist, Salma Hayek eyes, the body of a gazelle. She sat as if holding court.

"My name is Mariella. Mari," she said.

"I'm Nicole. This is Rachel," I said, nodding toward Rach.

"You just arrived?"

"Yes. You…live here?" I wasn't sure what the right verb was.

"Yes," she said, neither proud nor ashamed. "At MDC. They'll probably bus us over around five."

I leaned forward, trying to get a sense of where we were headed. "Is there a chapel?"

She tilted her head. "Well…kind of."

"A gym?" I'd read that exercise was the only way to avoid collapsing into despair.

"Kind of." She smiled.

"Do you work? Do people have jobs?" I was already imagining a library, maybe a teaching post.

"I clean the toilets."

"That's full-time?"

She laughed. "About an hour a day."

My mind skimmed every prison blog I'd read. "Do you get enough fiber?"

This time, she was really laughing. "You'll figure it out."

It didn't feel like the most auspicious moment of my life. I'd just been found guilty after a five-week trial, but I'd vowed not to get disheartened. To find the perfection inside the mess. My capacity, let's just say, was being stretched.

Still, Mari felt like a wind from somewhere sane, a trickster angel reminding me: Things are not as they appear.

For years, that's what I'd been teaching on the outside—that nothing is as it first seems, that the story we think we know is almost never the true one. Now, locked in a cell, life was asking if I really meant it.

They shackled us. It was time to move again through more cinderblock mazes painted in the same dull shade of disorientation. It's the same logic as putting a hood over a kidnapped person's head and driving in circles: By the time you arrive, you have no idea where you are.

5

Then the bus.

A short ride from the courthouse. Oddly familiar sights blurred by metal grating and tinted glass. We drove down a street I'd walked the day before, a ghost passing through her old life.

As we got closer, the bus began to lurch over potholes before rolling through the metal gate. Off the bus, into line, through another door. Each buzz and clank, the apparatus ingesting us deeper into its gears.

Another strip search. Every instruction felt like a threat, designed to remove you from your dignity. But you only mind the status signifiers—bending over to cough, lining up like cattle—if you don't know who you are. I watched the angular-faced guard with the cement chest deliver dehumanizing orders and felt a tenderness I didn't expect. Everyone here was doing what it takes to make it through.

Rachel stayed close. Having each other was a small miracle. Finally, we stepped through a doorway and entered 3 North, the women's dorm of the Metropolitan Detention Center, Brooklyn.

Bubblegum-pink cinderblock walls. Institutional fluorescent lighting so harsh it blurred the edges of everything with a rainbow haze. The air tasted fake—like a casino with no clocks—and the scent of bad food lingered. I thought of a sign I'd once seen on meditation retreat: *Unconditional freedom is freedom in all conditions.*

Enter Luciana.

Picture two bougie white women dressed like Cholas, blinking in the light—then a hot Latina with pre-Raphaelite curls, brown anime eyes, and an ass that announces itself. She bounced toward us like she'd been waiting all day.

"You're new," she said. "You'll sleep in my row. Two beds just opened up!"

We dug through the dark storage room for our so-called mattresses, then followed her back. She showed us how to tuck the thin sheets, then pressed toilet paper rolls into our hands like party favors.

"Don't worry," she said. "Prison is what you make it. Personally, I'm the woman I am because I came here."

She'd read Viktor Frankl. She compared herself to concentration-camp survivors: They had no food or shoes. We have everything.

She bragged about commissary sushi and her DIY face cream—vitamin-E oil mixed with preparation H. "You'll eat well and stay wrinkle-free." She grinned.

The absurd. The kind. The useful.

"And this is Nevaeh," Luciana introduced us to another member of our row of bunks. "She's going home soon."

Nevaeh was a Black woman with the timing of a comedian and the poise of a church matriarch. Her father had given her the name "Heaven" backwards, so she'd never have to be far from the Lord. Nevaeh grew up in the church and knew scripture like her own hand. Later, I'd see her holding Bible study on her bunk, two over from mine. But for someone that angelic, she also had a wicked sense of humor. Fast on the draw, key on the insight.

"MDC is just holding," Nevaeh explained, matter-of-fact. "After sentencing, they ship you where you'll serve."

She listed the options like a college counselor: Danbury's nice, Alderson has a salad bar, Philly has rats, Tallahassee's okay. It helped to hear there were differences, even inside the choiceless.

We asked the practical questions: Hair dye? No. Pillows? Contraband. Food? Expect bloating and weight gain.

She squinted at me as our list of questions began to slow, her curiosity growing.

"So what they got you in here for, anyway?" she asked.

There's no short version of my case, but I gave her the bones: that I'd spent the last twenty years teaching a practice that treated women's desire as something sacred instead of shameful; that the government had decided to call that a crime. I told her I still believed the same

7

thing I'd believed on the outside—that if you have a steady inner signal, nobody can run your life for you. Not a boyfriend, not a boss, not a judge, not this place.

"Not hard or mean," I explained. "Inner freedom—no matter what the institution throws at you, you can't be shaken from who you are. I want women to be *unfuckwithable*."

"Girl!" Nevaeh perked up suddenly. "Oh man, that's my word! You gotta see..."

She looked up, scanning across the mass of photos she had stuck to the bottom of her upper bunk, a constellation of life outside these walls.

"There it is," she said, pulling out a photograph from the corner. It was a picture of herself wearing a sweatshirt, arms crossed, and written down the sleeve in bold white text was the word: "UNFUCKWITHABLE." It was powerful to see these different sides of her. She'd gone from advisor to us newcomers in here to untamed hottie out there in an instant. She was more than could be captured in a single story. I could tell that these were not women who could be fit into a box and labeled, as much as this system might want to. I heard a quiet voice inside myself, in the midst of a day like none I'd had before, orienting me toward seeing these women as they truly are.

Later, on recall—a part of my new daily schedule when everyone is required to stand in a certain area of the dorm, by the bunks, behind a blue line on the floor—Nevaeh's voice dropped low as she told me more. How she was close to going home. How this time she wanted to do it different—no circling back, no "catching a new case." She wanted to serve the same women she'd done time with.

The shield dropped for a moment, and beneath the prison-slick exterior was something riskier: hope. Her hushed tone conveyed the sense that she was sharing contraband. I had the sense that in prison you're always one disappointment away from deciding never to feel it again.

They skipped suicide watch for us, which is two days of solitary confinement in the "Special Housing Unit," standard procedure for new arrivals and also the place women go if they break rules, step too far out of line, or get one too many warnings about their behavior. Maybe they thought we'd weather it. Maybe after years of practice, we were built for this. Everywhere can be home if you know where to place your attention.

I slept like a baby, and at 4:30 a.m., I woke up clear. The dorm hummed—fans, the TVs now silent, the white noise of forty women dreaming under indoor daylight. Rachel and I did a little yoga and a mini meditation in front of the only open window.

She asked if I had regrets.

It wasn't the usual prison question—not what wrong steps I'd taken or how I'd fallen in with the wrong crowd. I knew what she meant: Do you regret the promise you made, the mission you took on, now that you know what it costs?

"Not at all," I said. It's easy to tell the truth when you're living your worst-case scenario and still feel peace. I knew what I was taking on. I knew my work collided with the story society tells about women and sex, and I walked into that collision with my eyes open. If the worst consequence is time in prison, and the work we did turned a cultural tide, that's worth it.

Rachel nodded. The judge had offered her an exit: renounce me, renounce the work, play the victim. "Do you feel differently about that now, Ms. Cherwitz?" the judge had pressed. Rachel's attorney looked at Rachel and voiced her response: "No, Your Honor, she does not."

That's the line between freedom and comfort—the voice that promises safety if you deny who you are. They hide the cost in the fine print.

We talked about our friends on the outside and hoped they could be happy, as apart from us as we were from them. I thought of the Tibetan monk who learned to walk through the walls of a prison camp to go meditate in his cave. I understood the impulse.

My Zen priest friend Ed loves reading poems. One of my favorites begins: "Last night as I was sleeping, I dreamt—marvelous error!"

I love that line. The accidental miracle of being alive in this exact, impossible moment—the beauty hidden in catastrophe. Every disaster, a doorway.

And so, at 5:30 a.m., my first morning in prison, first prison yoga and meditation complete, Rachel beside me, the fluorescent convent humming, I saw it. The noise, the ugliness, the discarded—all of it transformed.

I turned to Rach beside me. "Rach, you see that?" I whispered.

Her head nodded slowly, quietly in awe.

Hallowed.

We made it.

3

Bran Flakes

Bran is manna in prison—neutral-to-good taste, recognizable as food, and the medicine that keeps you regular. If you're not vigilant, the whole experience can be one big bloat—stagnation. Women lie in their beds with makeshift eye masks of sweatshirts or towels to block the light. The one window with moving air sits just outside the sleeping area; the cardio machines gather dust. Lack of circulation—heart, air, digestion—leaves inmates to, as Octavio Paz put it, "kill time, kill life." For many, the burden that brought them here, coupled with the stigma, is too heavy to bear. Heads hang. Eyes drop. Hope follows.

To stay in motion—this is the how. Inside of prison, that means going against inertia. This is the beginning and end of rebirth, repeating until one wakes up, not despite being here but because of being here. The pressure either crushes you or makes the diamond.

Years ago, on psychedelics, I would open my eyes and simply *be* somewhere—consciousness landing in a new scene. Now I open my eyes inside bubblegum-pink cinderblocks, brown prison T-shirt, white boxers. Scene. Go. What will this consciousness do with this one wild and precious scene? How will I extract the jewel from this moment?

It's easier than you'd think if you've grooved the carrier signal of practice. My mind has been secured on that plane—the wisdom of "no matter what." Through sleet or snow, attraction or aversion, resignation or hope, I practiced. The muscle memory is strong: get up, kneel and pray, write, yoga, meditate, eat well(ish), a little cardio, a little fresh air, be of service. That's the recipe for portable enlightenment.

"Daedone! Miller! Santiago!" A bark ricochets off metal bunks, snapping the dorm to attention. We head to the little office where Santoro, the counselor—stunningly kind—waits with a clipboard to run the intake "talk."

Brynn, a new arrival, slides into the chair beside me, Alma to her left. Brynn's the kind of warm and funny you only find in someone who's given up even the pretense of pretense. A few teeth missing, eyes bright.

Santoro reads the script. I'm told to sign a form. If someone leers while I shower, that's on them. If I shower *seductively*, that's on me. No sex with guards, no sex with other women, no sex with myself. Systems of control see sex as kryptonite.

"That's crazy—why would they want to get it on with each other?" Brynn hoots.

"Because we all want some lovin'," I say. Even the counselor laughs, then slides the form across the desk and watches me sign.

The talk reminds me how fast rules clamp down on a body. Last night, Rach sprinted back to her bunk like a kid chased by a monster. She'd made the mistake of wearing the prison-issued (and huge) boxers into a public area. It seems those boxers are potentially too alluring for the male guards to resist. The female guard on duty would have none of this seduction. Getting barked at in prison activates your nervous system at a level reserved for life-and-death situations outside.

Much of making it through—without feeling like you're scaling an electric fence—is fight-or-flight management. One wrong move and you're in the hole—no window, no sun, no air—and sometimes everyone else pays, too. That's how conformity is enforced: If one woman "acts out," the whole dorm suffers. A climate is created where the safest thing is for everyone to flatten themselves.

Control of sex is control of women. Rename desire as danger and you can police everything, from how we shower to what we think. We should give no hint to the outside world what it feels like inside us.

Which is why, as strange as it is to be here, it's not entirely unexpected. The logic is brutal and simple: When control is the foundation of a culture, women's desire comes under attack.

When the verdict came in, the Department of Justice celebrated and called me a "charlatan" and a "grifter," as if no sane woman would choose to make sexual energy the ground of her meditation and meditation the ground of her life. In their world, women don't really want sex, and if they do, they certainly can't be trusted with it; the idea that sexual energy could be not only empowering but sacred—and not only sacred but central to a spiritual life—is anathema to almost everything the modern West believes about women. That this same force is honored and integrated in some of the most advanced streams of Eastern philosophy and religion was completely lost on my prosecutors. They were a Western, secular team steeped in a culture that first infantilizes women and then casts itself as the hero, swooping in to "save" the very infants it has created.

It would have been quite a con: More than two decades ago I founded a practice and built a company to teach it. It started small. Then the fire caught—tens of thousands of customers, a TED Talk, a book, press, celebrity endorsements—and yet the whole thing rested on one simple belief: Women's desire isn't a problem to be managed or "figured out." It is the living power that makes us alive.

I didn't come to that lightly. I came to it by trying everything else first. Be smaller. Be nicer. Be grateful for crumbs. There's a particular exhaustion that sets in when you've spent years negotiating with your own life. I believed there had to be a different way. So I said the quiet thing out loud: A woman's turn-on can be healthy, ordinary, even holy. Not meant to exist only in dark, furtive rooms, but brought into the light and celebrated.

I didn't set out to be a controversy. I set out to tell the truth I learned in my own body: Aliveness isn't something you think your way into; it's guided by something felt. For many, especially women, feeling has been treated like contraband. We're taught to hide it, hush it, or hand it to someone else for safekeeping. Desire is the inspiration to transform; it's the basis of sovereignty and intimacy. Instead, we try to package it into convenient, manageable shapes. I wanted to place that power back in the hands of women.

Simple, not easy. Daylight shows everything—the beauty, the mess, the learning curve. People brought their hopes and histories, their hunger and heartbreak. Some found what they came for. Others hit their edges and left—most on good terms, a few less so. That's real life in any family, classroom, start-up, or church.

We built a community around the truths we believed and, yes, a business to support it and a nonprofit founded on the same principles. We had rules. We had forms. We had sales goals, rent to pay, and long meetings to sort out feelings and reconnect. We also had the least reliable variables in human history—love, jealousy, hope, disappointment, money, longing, and the way memory rearranges itself after a breakup. You can craft all the guidelines you like; the heart is a wild animal. We're human, and human connection is messy. We invited people to bring the whole of themselves. Could it be painful? Sometimes. Criminal? No. Some left whole and grateful. A few left bruised or mad. I respect both kinds of leaving.

Years later, the knock came: badges, questions, case numbers. I understand the optics: Sex plus money plus community looks suspect to people who've only ever seen those things misused. When the government enters the room, everyone's memories sit up straight. Nuance gets nervous. Old lovers turn into headlines; complicated seasons turn into exhibits. If you've ever tried to explain a breakup to a friend looking for a villain, you know the sensation. The truth is many-sided and tender. The legal system is not.

I am certain of my innocence, and my lawyers are too. Much less certain was whether that truth would be able to make its way through the byzantine rules that govern a federal courtroom. People ask why I didn't just take a plea deal. Picture me in a cold government room, pen hovering over a sentence that turns my life's work into a sham. "Sign here," they say, "and you can go home sooner." Sooner to what? What's there to come back to after you've denied the truth you know in your bones? I couldn't confess to a crime I didn't commit.

If you're waiting for me to hate the people who testified, I can't help you. I don't. I know what grief does to the mind. I know what shame does to the tongue. I also know what attention and care can heal. I can hold compassion in one hand and my innocence in the other. That's not a magic trick. I know the cost of a closed heart.

Women's desire is not a crisis to be managed; it's a medicine to be practiced. I treated desire like penicillin. The prosecutors treated it like street drugs. They told their story to the court. They needed a villain. I was handy. After five weeks, the prosecution got their way.

The Department of Justice picks its words carefully: "charlatan" meant desire has no real power; "grifter" meant it was all a cynical ploy. Neuter the threat, vilify the messenger. Control moves to eliminate what might undo its system of domination.

Back in the dorm, the hum swallows us—fans blowing, TVs, women, dazzling overhead glare. Alma falls in beside me, eyes wide but fixed forward.

She jerks her chin toward my row. "See that? With Luci?" A tiny woman with translucent skin perches on the empty bed between ours, hands busy with glitter and paper. "That's Claire. The sex thing is no joke. They were talking about it in my row last night. She got written up for flirting. She gotta cool it or she gonna get us all in trouble."

Alma peels off and I walk to my row of bunks. Claire, still shaken, sits on the empty bed between Luciana and me, making glitter pictures while Rach sits on her own bunk farther down. Luci is speaking excitedly, doing her best to switch Claire's mood. "She loves airplanes, like *loves* them. She was arrested for sneaking onto runways. Did it four times! She's just obsessed." She looks at us wide-eyed. Claire smiles without pausing on her pictures.

"Wait, she's just obsessed with planes? That's what she was arrested for? Not for drugs or something?" I can't calculate why a person who would break onto an airfield to try to fly with the plane would be sent to prison and not, say, a mental hospital. Still, I'd heard Luci say her name, Dakina, as we'd walked up and it stood out to me, a mere letter away from the fierce and flying enlightened dakinis, Buddhism's female counterparts to the calm and grounded masculine buddhas.

Luci fully embodies this wild woman as she imitates her. She stands and runs hard in place with arms outstretched, a bowels-of-the-earth sound coming from her, shaking her head the way a dog might if it got wet. I am fascinated by the idea of this woman so unable to color within the lines and consumed by the desire for flight enough to sneak onto runways.

The room around us pulses within the pink cinderblock walls—the smell of yesterday's food wrestling with detergent; women braiding hair, swapping stories, laughing too loud; some trying to sleep, others watching true crime, peppering it with commentary. Some sleeping

16

through the day, others spark with an aliveness the world doesn't know what to do with. Originals. The ones who feel the system's pressure push down while their chests push back with equal strength. This is the raw power of desire—wild, unpredictable—dissolving the lines that work desperately to rein in a force they can only appease but never subdue. These women at society's edges withstand the weight of the world against them—diamonds beneath the mountain, free despite any condition. What would it take to unearth them?

"Oh I almost forgot," Luci says, breaking from her Dakina impression. She reaches under her bunk. "I got something for ya."

She pulls out a bulging plastic bag packed with bran flakes.

"Some of the ladies don't want their cereal—they only like the poundcake." She grins. "I ran a collection." Inside are a dozen boxes of bran flakes. "And watch this," she adds, leading Rachel and me to the ice machine on the other side of the dorm, now stashed with cartons of milk. "Insurance policy. If they serve mystery meat again, we eat like queens."

Abundance, just like that.

4

Janiya

This one might be beyond my pay grade, ran through my mind, as the Black girl with cornrows and no comprehension of indoor volume twerked her way past my bunk, fast-talking to Luciana.

"I *fuckin' love* watches. I just love 'em."

I poke my head out from under my "eye mask," which is really just a sweatshirt, to see Rachel doing the same from her bunk two down.

"Good for you," Luciana says, in perfect prison-etiquette language. Translation: *Get out of my row. I don't want any problems.*

Seeing she now has an audience, Janiya somehow finds a way to turn herself up louder.

"Yeah, you know me, I'm a ho—but not a cheap ho. I need them watches."

This is a new category of ho for me. Not a shoe ho. Not a bag ho. A watch ho. A Rolex ho.

"Okay, thank you for letting us know," Luciana says in the exact tone of someone politely closing the door on a religious pamphlet they did not request.

I could take a page out of this woman's book. Janiya is completely

18

unfazed by Luciana's *please evaporate* energy. If anything, she's more energized now that she's picked up two extra spectators. She's moved on to karaoke twerking, shimmying through movie soundtracks and landing on *Grease*.

She looks my way. "You know that one?"

I glance to either side as if to ask, *Are you talking to me?* Yes. She is talking to me.

"I do," I say, and somehow manage to sound like a 1950s librarian answering a reference question.

"I do that one for my baby, my son," she says. "People tell me to leave his daddy, but I ain't goin' nowhere."

Within three minutes of meeting her, I know more about her love life than I know about some of my closest friends on the outside. Most people reveal this level of detail somewhere around week twelve of therapy. Janiya offers it before I have fully sat up in bed.

Now, I might be reserved, but I marvel at the sheer social athleticism of it all. Can you really wake up a stranger with your ass in motion, not know their name, and then slide right into the kind of confession most people save for a locked diary? If you're Janiya, you can.

And if you're Janiya, you can also make a white woman in the early days of her prison stay fall completely in love with you, even when you wake her up in the middle of the night.

She is, for many, an acquired taste. I lived with a Janiya-adjacent personality for years on the outside, so I take to her quickly. Well. In fifteen minutes.

You know those cartoons where the brain and the heart talk to each other? The heart holds the brain's hair back while it leans over the toilet, throwing up bad thoughts. That's the dynamic here.

Janiya is the heart. Everyone around her is forced into the role of the brain.

Her favorite "brain" is Nevaeh.

Another day, another...Twerk, twerk, twerk—down our aisle she comes.

"Wake up," she announces, planting herself by Nevaeh's bunk. "I cooked lunch."

Nevaeh, who is very much not at the loving-Janiya stage, groans and pulls the covers higher.

"I don't like your food," she mumbles.

Me? If I cook for you and you don't go back for thirds, I spiral into a crisis about my life's purpose.

Janiya? Totally unbothered.

"Your loss," she says, and sashays away, humming.

Even in those first few days, I started to notice something about Janiya: She never stays down. She might get loud, get checked, get on people's last nerve, but she always pops back up with the same irrepressible gleam. There's an innocence to her joy that people mistake for ignorance. They think it must be easy to live like that— loud, shiny, unapologetic. It isn't.

Everyone thinks joy is simple until they try it. So simple, in fact, that they don't bother to try it but then judge the ones who do.

One afternoon I'm sitting with my plastic mug of lukewarm coffee, watching Janiya orbit the dorm. She is in rare form, running commentary on the TV, hyping up a spades game, stopping mid-aisle to show off a new hairstyle she has given herself with nothing but gel, a toothbrush, and determination.

The saviors start circling.

"Girl, you gotta calm down," one woman tells her. "You need to think about your future."

"You gotta stop playin' all the time," another adds. "You in *federal* prison."

They mean well. They usually do. They tell her she needs to get serious, start planning. Their faces hold that particular blend of concern and superiority reserved for women who have decided they know what your rehabilitation should look like.

Janiya cycles through her options like wardrobe changes: grateful student, apologetic child, bored parishioner. "Yes, ma'am." "You right." "I hear you."

We lock eyes for a second and I send the silent message: *You are very good at what you do.*

Because what she does is let people believe they've tamed her. It soothes them. They feel useful. She gets to keep being herself.

What I love is how expertly she refuses to be pinned down. She's far more sophisticated than anyone gives her credit for.

Luciana, for one, is often somewhere between exasperated and homicidal.

"She reminds me of this Buddhist line, 'tricksters and bandits of the dharma,'" I tell Luciana. In spiritual circles, the *dharma* is the truth of how things actually work, beneath the surface drama. Tricksters and bandits are the ones who refuse to let that truth be shrink-wrapped into something safe and beige. They stay a step sideways from the rules, not because they're shallow, but because they're protecting something alive.

To actually change a world that wants to iron out every edge and turn everyone into the same polite, powerless citizen, someone has to move like the coyote. Leonard Cohen was once asked what the most powerful role for a Zen teacher was. His answer was "trickster." You have to fool the ego out of itself. Even the noblest idea, once it gets fused with ego, will drive you straight into suffering. Sometimes the thing that looks terrible from the outside is actually the medicine.

I tease Luciana that maybe, just maybe, Janiya is a better trickster than both of us put together.

The heart usually is.

Janiya lives in the bunk that borders the dining area, the "front bunks." It's like living in the median of a freeway. The front-bunk women are the extroverts, the late-night TV devotees, the ones most likely to be mid-laugh when an officer walks in. They're also the first to get a talking-to when the unit is inspected.

To say that Janiya's bunk is a mess is an understatement. You know that house on the block with three dead cars in the yard from ten years ago, a Christmas tree still up in April, and so much stuff inside that it starts spilling onto the porch? The one you suspect will one day be on a reality show where someone in a hazmat suit and yellow gloves comes to clean?

That's her area.

She can absorb the reprimands. I cannot. Something about watching her get scolded turns my stomach.

I walk over and sit on the edge of her bunk.

"Do you want Rachel and me to help you clean your area?" I ask.

You would think I had offered her a fully comped cruise. She leaps up and does an entire dance routine.

"When?" she demands.

"How about tomorrow at noon?"

Noon rolls around. No Janiya. I assume she has forgotten or changed her mind. Then the bathroom door swings open.

"I'm ready, ladies!" she calls, beaming and strutting toward her bunk.

"We thought maybe you didn't really want to," I said, offering her a way out if she'd like to take it.

"No way I was missing this," she answers, a full grin across her face.

We get to work. We do not, in fact, throw away her overflowing stash of plastic spoons. We box them.

"The institution ran out of spoons once," she reminds us. "Girl, that was not pretty."

Mostly, she sits and pulls out photographs, old letters, little folded notes that once came tucked into commissary bags. She reads some aloud, sings along to half-remembered songs from the radio, tells us who is who in each picture. Rachel and I scrub and sort and fold and stack while she narrates.

There's a sweetness to it that I didn't expect, a softness about her I hadn't noticed. She is letting us into her world the way she can, and the way we can receive it: side by side, hands busy, past and present spread out on thin prison sheets.

That night, Janiya slides into a metal chair across from me without asking. For once, she's quiet.

"No one's ever really liked me for real," she says, picking at the peeling edge of the table. "They like the show. They like what I do for 'em. But me?" She shakes her head. "I don't know if people even see me." As she talks, it's as if she is removing masks that she wears. I see a wise woman underneath.

"Wait a minute," I say. "*This* is you. *This* is who is in there."

She smiles. "You knew that, didn't you?"

"Yes. But one can never be sure."

For a minute, we're two women from the same weird spiritual army, both undercover. I let her see me, too, underneath my own costume: the naïve first-timer, the middle-aged white woman they tease for being out of place, the teacher trying not to teach.

"Bitch, I knew who you were," she says finally, and the spark comes back into her eyes. "Soon as you walked in here."

We both crack up. Some kind of soul recognition—when you spot the same flame in someone else. On the outside, years ago, I brought my street-clothes rabbi to meet my Orthodox rabbi at a Torah study. When I introduced them, the Orthodox rabbi said, "Hello, Rabbi," like it was obvious. Later I asked how he knew.

He rolled his eyes. "Please."

Same principle. Different costumes.

"Don't tell nobody, though," Janiya says, leaning back. "Let them figure it out."

"Janiya, even if I told them, they wouldn't believe me," I say. "Remember, I'm the naïve one."

She grins and gets up, mask sliding back into place as easily as lip gloss. A second later, she's at Nevaeh's bunk again, stirring the pot, making jokes, ignoring the volleys of "girl, shut up!" that greet her.

And before long, the whole row is laughing. Even the ones who swear they cannot stand her can't hold back their smiles.

One of my favorite books is *The Book of Laughter and Forgetting* by Milan Kundera. The title alone has always felt like a teaching. Laughter and forgetting arrive together. Myth says laughter gives the mind wings; it lets us lift off the ground of our lives for a moment. Angel's wings, dakini's flight. It doesn't erase what hurts, but it loosens its grip. It makes a little space.

In a place like this, space is everything.

When the officers walk through, they see a loud girl who doesn't know when to stop. A problem. A disruption. A write-up waiting to happen.

What I see of Janiya is a kind of jailhouse jester. The trickster in lashes and cornrows. The Rolex ho with the wide-open heart. The one who chooses, over and over, to risk being ridiculous rather than let any of us sink completely into the silence.

She's not here to be nice. She's here to make sure we're still alive.

5

Retreat

A few months before my indictment, I was traveling in Mongolia with my Lama, who had spent decades in Northern India and Nepal studying with Tibetan monks until he had become an accomplished lama himself. I said out loud something I had always wanted. "I want to do a three-year retreat." Three years of structured practice and quiet, no life-multitasking, no performance. He gave me a warm, amused look, as if saying, *be careful what you say, they hear you.*

I understood what he meant; thirty years prior, I'd had a similar interaction after watching my first demonstration of the practice that eventually became Orgasmic Meditation.

I get it now. The road to the real thing looks nothing like the polished moment. It's harrowing, grueling, mostly dark with pinholes of light. You're tied to a bucking bull until, for reasons beyond you, it stops. That's why I laugh when people accuse me of *luring* people into spirituality. Please. The part of you that wants the real thing cannot be seduced. It has its own key and its own lock. I've spent years at the gate shooing away the tourists. The real ones keep coming anyway.

After I was indicted, I contemplated what it would be like to go to prison. I worried about comfort: Would I be able to eat the food in prison? Have bathroom privacy? Exercise? A few days in and I was surprised how little those things mattered. Only one restroom locks. The water runs hot, not cold. The food is...fine. And my digestion, sleep, and overall well-being are the best they've been in years. Also, Mari slipped us enough tea to make it to commissary day, which felt like winning the lottery.

The restrictions here serve the same purpose as in a meditation hall: The very limits make you free. Certain times of day require specific behaviors. Twice a day during the week, three times a day on weekends, you must be in a bunk area of the dorm, behind a blue line of tiles on the floor for "recall." Movement becomes even more restricted. "Count" happens after recall and you must stand by your bed. I know the schedule for "main line" meals. All my other time I spend meditating. Sometimes there's a disruption—a visit, medical forms—then I adapt and go back in.

I sit meditation about four hours a day, do various breathing techniques, including tummo which heats the body from the inside, a little yoga (not enough), walk the track, and write. I want to get to seven hours of practice. I think I can.

What I am finally understanding is this: If you want the deep quiet, you have to let go; you can't hedge your bets. You can't say, "Yes, I want freedom—but I also want a picture-perfect partner, rock-solid finances, and the same public life." That's how freedom ends up last in the race, still in the gate with its saddle on.

A woman wants a man who can hold her up—a partner she doesn't have to prop. I think that wish points to something deeper: the soul's desire for a happiness that holds *us* up, instead of the endless managing—the shell game of if-I-just. If I just make this meal. If I just get this outcome. If I just get through *this*. Before being remanded, it was the next interview, the next legal report, the next call.

I feel my purpose shifting. Maybe it's energetic, not logistical. Maybe my work isn't interviews, teaching, and designing programs anymore.

All that is gone. I used to wake and scan the horizon for bad news— or, just as unsettling, hopeful news of something that might somehow extricate me from my situation. But either way the news came, it was still oriented around fear. Fear that I would end up exactly where I am today.

It's funny how long I taught that inside what you most fear is what you most want. And here I am: I ate my demons. They're in my belly now, not the other way around. My teachers would talk about the dakinis—sky-dancer women, embodiments of wisdom—who devour fear, shame, ego-clutching. She doesn't banish it; she chews it up and turns it into fuel for flight.

In truth, they're not ethereal dancers in red silk, floating across temple murals. If you really want to find them, you go to the charnel grounds—the cremation field of burning and decay where everything you cling to as "me" and "mine" is stripped away. The dakini doesn't show up to flatter you or fix your life. She appears where life has already blown your cover and sits with you in the ashes until you stop pretending you're in control.

What makes her dakini is that she's always in flight—not escaping, but refusing to land on anything solid and pretend it holds any truth. The ego wants to create comfort by creating some solidity, some identity to cling to: I'm the good one, I'm the ruined one, I'm the one who's got it handled. The dakini is allergic to that kind of certainty. She'll tear it out of your hands, cut it out of you if she has to. One minute she feels like fierce love, the next like total abandonment, but underneath both is the same invitation: Let go of the fixed identity, stay in the open sky.

Had it occurred to me that a modern charnel ground might be a pink cinderblock prison dorm? But that's what this is: a place where bodies age, illusions die, and every role you've ever played—teacher, lover, mother, villain, victim—gets ground down to powder. To be a dakini here isn't about being mystical or special. It's being willing to live in this fluorescent charnel ground without numbing out, to keep your heart bare and your feet off the fake safety of a fixed story, even when every instinct begs you to land.

I'm being rearranged at a breakneck pace. Humbling doesn't cover it. I don't want a phone anymore. I don't want constant communication. I want a uniform and a bare face. Some women smuggle in the old life to rehearse for having it again. I don't. For me, this is the next level of sobriety—being sober *from the world.*

I read a line last night that stuck with me: A true seeker is an *insider,* someone who realizes happiness is an inside job. The opposite is the *outsider,* always hunting for meaning "out there."

Prison, at the soul level, sobers you up from the outside hunt. Maybe I was too entangled with the world to hear what the heart wanted, so life called me home. If "home" came with a bit more silence, I wouldn't mind—but I'm working with what I've got. I redesign my days, not as an activist tallying shortages (whether the ice machine is broken one day or the commissary is thin on stock), but as a curator: What are the few jewels we *do* have, and how do I place them so they shine?

What I have, and can barely put into words, feels like a blessing. On Saturdays I get to talk to my Lama for about fifteen minutes. As strong as I know I am, those fifteen minutes work like a time-release capsule; they keep dissolving through the week, lifting me when I might otherwise just trudge through the mud of this experience. It's not even about what we say—how much can you really cover in fifteen minutes?—it's that we meet and laugh and, without my noticing, I am suddenly filled with light. I'm so brimming with it that I want to tell him how much I love him, but instead I try to show it. After our calls, I walk through the dorm and share the surplus, looking for the corners that most need it. I do my best in his name. That is what I know love to be: a love that invites you into your own greatness. I pray that every woman has this kind of love at least once in her life, in a world that keeps telling us love means selling your soul.

If I am lucky, that is what I am most lucky for. I know love can be a hard-fought commodity, and without that basic need met, it can be near impossible to see what's available here in prison. I also know these are women who haven't done retreat. What's "unbearable" in here is a normal day in a meditation hall. No one's thwacking you with a stick when you nod off. Most officers are civil; a few are downright kind. My favorite looks like a stern drill-sergeant version of a church minister and runs a tight ship. My nervous system settles when he has us in our aisles instead of the all-night block party free-for-all that reigns at other times.

In here, I don't have to lead anything. I'm *at effect*—not the decider, not the knower. Decision fatigue is real. Those first few days before my email account and phone were set up were a particular kind of life-quiet: no updates from friends, no updates on projects. A kind of hermit's life: simple, steady, quiet.

It can be uncomfortable if you're not used to it, but it can also feel like a great relief. Most of the enemies you're fighting live in your own head. But when you rest in the clear, steady part of you—the one that exists underneath the weather stirred up by the everyday happenings of life—the attacks have nothing to land on. That's been my method for years. People may ask you to be a warrior-queen swinging a sword but honestly, most fighting is just shadowboxing. Still, I had to fight long enough to see fighting wasn't helping. And I refuse to grant manufactured conflict the dignity of a duel.

I thought I came here to be broken. Maybe I came here to be *simple*, stripped of any last tethers to the ground beneath me.

6

Anything a Man Can Do

Rach was sitting cross-legged on her bunk next to mine, air-drying her one pair of socks on the safety rail, when Mari called us over to show us pictures of her son. Her bunk was ultra-feminine, like a European princess had been dropped into a federal dorm. Most beds had the same Mexican-market-looking blanket—grey and blue stripes like a checkerboard—but hers was covered in a white bedspread that caught what little light there was and softened it. A small haven inside here.

In the same way her bed stood out, so did she. Not just her beauty, but the way her spirit and grace changed the air around her. Rach and I perched on the edge of her mattress, thumbing through glossy photos of a little boy with her eyes.

"You're Italian, yes?" she asked, looking at me.

I glanced up from a picture of her son grinning at the camera.

"Your last name. Italian, right?"

Entering a new world, even a simple question can feel loaded. For a second I wondered if I was answering for more than my bloodline.

"Half," I said. "My father's side is from Sicily."

Mari's face lit up. "I knew it," she said, stepping in like she had always belonged there. "I lived in Italy. My nonna there, she would sense you coming home when you were still down the street and start cooking."

I felt a sigh of relief wash through. "You said yesterday you are from Guatemala?" I asked.

"Guatemala City." She nodded. "But the first people who really raised me were my grandparents in Italy. They were old already when I was born, but they gave me everything. Love. Food. Discipline. Stories. My parents were busy, very young, trying to be adults. They did what they knew. Still, I grew up like a little suitcase passed back and forth. Never fully unpacked anywhere."

"How did you end up in Italy?" I asked.

"Guatemala was a hard time." Mari shrugged with a grimace that suggested a longer story. So often we practice these stories of our lives, we know the way to dip and weave, avoiding the more difficult parts. But here, living inside the worst of it, the usual barriers of "polite conversation" have already been taken down.

"A cousin," she said. "He did things to me. It went on for years. And when I finally said it, nobody believed me. That is when my world flipped. I stopped trusting my own body. I got very quiet outside."

She looked down at her hands. The skin at her knuckles was dry and faintly raw from the institutional soap.

"But inside," she went on, "I decided I would make myself too valuable to ignore. There was this voice that said, 'Anything a man can do, I can do better.' That voice took over. It was my path forward."

She glanced up at us, like she was checking whether we understood the cost of that kind of vow.

"That same path," she said, "is probably why I'm sitting here inside these pink walls with you."

Her eyes stared out beyond the physical space we sat in. There is a kind of nakedness to sharing. I could feel us slipping into that quiet chamber all women carry, where the knots that want to be unwound wait.

"They arrested me at the grocery store," she went on. "I had my baby in my arms. One minute I was buying food. The next minute, my baby was gone and I was on a plane."

I felt it land in my chest, that image of a woman standing in the aisles of a grocery store, infant on her hip, circled by officers, separated and taken.

A woman appeared in front of our bunk, clutching a crumpled sheet of paper. "Mari, *por favor.*" Her eyes flicked toward the officer's station. "*No entiendo esto.*"

Mari took the paper. It was a form dense with legalese, all caps and tiny boxes, the kind of writing each of us had slowly grown more familiar with through our interactions with "the law." We stood to allow some privacy.

She skimmed it, then switched to rapid Spanish, her voice dropping into a softer key than I had heard from her so far. The other woman nodded, shoulders lowering as the anticipation relaxed. She said her thanks and took the pages back, their meaning now conveyed.

"They do not give these in Spanish," Mari said, almost apologetic. Then she turned back to me, like she was returning to the thread she'd left hanging. "Anyway. I wanted to say hello, my new Italian friend. Don't let this place convince you your worth comes from what they say about you. It comes from what you keep doing with your heart."

I felt something in me rearrange, just a little. "Thank you."

She smiled, the sideways smile of a woman who keeps going despite the worst of it.

"And for the record," she said, "I still believe women can do anything men can do."

We said our goodbye, a funny thing to do when you live within a single room, and made our way back to our row of bunks.

7

Prison Women

I don't know that anyone, least of all these women, needs "help." Maybe they do. But I can tell you this: The women in here are more capable than many of the women I knew on the outside. They're alive, hilarious, tuned-in, fast. On Sunday a minister came to preach for the dorm—a charismatic evangelical, the real kind. Genuine, powerfully faithful, perfectly attuned to the room. She said prisons are her favorite place to preach because people actually *receive* the message. "Not plastic Christianity," she said. I knew exactly what she meant.

We got a survey for the First Step Act—a new federal law that lets people earn earlier release if they complete certain "rehabilitation" programs. With the possibility of home confinement in the balance, everyone rushed to fill it out, huddling over "agree" and "disagree" like it was the LSAT.

One question asked something like: "Do you like criminals more than everyday civilians?" As if the risk is we'll fall in with a "bad crowd" and go shoot things up. I picked "no response." What I wanted to say was, *Have you ever been to the Upper East Side? West L.A.? Marin County?* In here, every woman has a story—rich, textured, outrageous, devastating—and the way they tell it is art. It's like the difference between American tomatoes and Italian ones: minerals and sun so vivid you can *feel* the food humming in your cells. That's what the women in here are like—nutrient-dense.

For years I called myself an introvert. I think I was just bored. I was listening to the same muzak loop: breakups, calories, a thousand beige complaints. The air in those rooms felt recirculated—no wind, no weather. Then the trends turned to a wave of Instagram diagnoses, the pharmaceuticals to handle them, and a gospel of perpetual trauma.

But these women have punched through the membrane into the wilds. Their lives have real stakes—actual harm, actual consequence, to self and others. What's missing is the drone of self-pity. Instead: humility, humor, and genuine curiosity about how cause and effect actually works in a life. How do you circle that on a survey? I love these women. One of my closest friends, Topeka, is a pardoned formerly incarcerated woman. Nuance doesn't fit multiple choice. Honesty gets you in trouble.

It registers first like a pressure change in the room: the tiniest lift under the heaviness, a sense of air where there shouldn't be any. The dakini never really lands—she takes *flight*. Not escape; BOP owns the fences and the keys. Flight is what happens when the story you've wrapped around yourself loosens its grip and you stop insisting life match your picture before you agree to be here. Same bunk, same case, same powdered eggs—but something inside sits up, looks around, and says, "Okay. I'm still alive. Now what can I make with this?"

It's a controversial kind of freedom, especially when you're talking about women in prison. We're supposed to be broken, remorseful on cue, grateful for every scrap. But the flight I see here isn't denial of harm or consequence; it's the refusal to live as *only* the harm and the consequence. A woman comes back from a bad day at court and somehow she's the one making everybody else laugh over ramen

34

that night. Another gets denied bail and spends the evening braiding hair, plotting someone's reentry plan like it's a group science project. They're not pretending it's okay. They're just not waiting for the outside to change before they let their insides move. These are the hearts I wish the world could see behind the headlines and indictments that try to proclaim who these women are.

I don't mean these women float above the pain. They cry, pace the floor, rage into their pillows like anyone would. But over and over I watch them choose movement over collapse: one more joke, one more favor, one more tiny act of generosity that keeps the air flowing. Their charges are fixed on paper; they are not. Maybe that's the deepest form of flight—when the world has you nailed to a story and you quietly, stubbornly refuse to stay pinned.

The conditions here would take out a lot of people. I manage not because this is my natural habitat (for some women, it is), but because I've lived in similar ways: communal housing, little privacy, few possessions, navigating personalities and power structures, going invisible when needed. What we all share is iron will.

At first they didn't know what to make of me and Rach. We were tested. Officers sniffed our perimeter. Inmates tested us too. I have found the key is to walk in a quiet sanctuary: You can't move me. My body will comply with the rules, but my center won't budge. Then it got better. The women christened us The Real Housewives of MDC—as in the TV franchise. There was real affection in how they told us. "Actually," one woman said, "it's more like *Real Housewives of Atlanta*—not as bougie as Beverly Hills." High compliment. The unit counselor was surprised we weren't getting "worked" more intensely.

MDC is different from most prisons. In the federal system, once you're sentenced you get shipped to the place you'll actually do your time. Before that—while court dates are still rolling and your case is in motion—the Bureau of Prisons parks you in places like MDC, close to the courthouses and lawyers. Women sometimes wind up at MDC at the end of their sentence, released through the same courts they came in through. So the dorm holds a constantly shifting mix: women newly indicted who couldn't make bail, women already convicted and waiting to be sentenced, women who've been parked a few weeks while a prosecutor leans on them for names, and women on their way out, with only parole hearings between them and home.

At any given time there are maybe thirty-five to forty-five of us in the women's dorm. The other fifteen hundred bodies in this place are men, scattered across two buildings and various security levels. In our room, the severity of the charges all get tossed in one pot. Faces appear and disappear—off to court, to meetings with lawyers, or to the prison where they'll serve their bid; sometimes home.

Unlike many prisons, there are almost no jobs here, beyond the chores that keep the dorm as clean as we're able. There aren't many programs or classes either. It's an odd mix of transience and stagnation, waiting for whatever's next.

And in this purgatory space we share, the women take care of each other. Past the circling-and-handout stage, there's a moment they invite you in. You get a seat at the feast: spicy crab cakes made from commissary cans, Doritos for breadcrumbs, Velveeta-jalapeño drizzle. The other women start including Rachel and me in their circle as part of the "we"—the inmates of the MDC women's dorm. It feels like a blessing.

What still amazes me is the lack of complaint in the face of steady instability. You never know which way the wind will blow. What's fine for one officer is forbidden with another. You learn to lower your head without shrinking your spine. Honestly, the years of being canceled were a gift. They burned out my old reflex to manage other people's opinions—that compulsive "be nice, be smaller" training that would get you eaten alive here. Now it's muscle memory: You don't like me? Okay. I don't have to fix you or fight you. I go on, grateful the commissary had cocoa butter, grateful it's Chicken Thursday—the best meal of the week.

Here's the paradox I didn't expect: Prison is a hidden shrine to free will. People who insisted on exercising it, wisely or not, end up here. The body language that works is spacious. Move through the dorm with an air that lets people take their own readings, make up their own minds. Don't sell yourself. Don't grovel for belonging. Play your role without becoming it. That's another form of freedom.

When you're free inside, the caricatures of prison start to fall apart: color of uniform, rank of crime, guard vs. inmate. The real logic is simpler. We're all in the same pink cinderblock room with cockroaches and windows that barely open and air that is either swamp hot or meat-locker cold. That includes you too, Officer. Different jobs, same human weather. Since we're all here together—in this intense little theater of being human—we might as well make the best of it. I'm an extreme-sports person when it comes to life, so my version is: We might as well have a rocking good time. And honestly? Most days it's a street party in here. We just don't say it out loud; it breaks character.

The last question on the survey was the easiest and somehow the trickiest: "Do people who commit crimes deserve to be treated like everyone else?" It seems they want you to answer no. But the answer is yes. Equal dignity isn't a reward for good behavior, it's the ground floor of being human. If you need a source for that, you don't have to crack open some obscure mystical or philosophical text. Just open the Bible to the Sermon on the Mount. Jesus says the quiet part out loud: Treat people with mercy, turn toward them instead of away, love your enemies, do unto others as you'd want done unto you. The entire sermon is a blueprint for baseline dignity—especially for those the world says don't deserve it.

8

Royal

"Five-thirty evening stroll for anyone who wants to join!" I call out through the dorm. The first time I did this, the guard laughed and told Rach I sounded like a suburban mom power-walking in yoga pants. I just smiled and said, "Well, except we're in here, aren't we?" There's a kind of stereotyping that happens here—they see "white woman" and think they already know the story. I don't bother correcting them. I just pray they'll encounter me directly.

Rach and I had started a new practice, walking the indoor track. I invite the ladies to join in the walks because Royal—a respected "OG" in our dorm who's had two strokes and a heart attack—sat behind me saying her legs hurt from never leaving her bunk. She's scared one day they'll stop working. My plan is indirect: Get other women walking, ask her friends to invite her, and let pride step out of the way. Then one night there she was, joining the herd like a retired mare turned out to pasture again.

I like her a lot. She strut-shuffles the aisles murmuring, "Hey, baaaaby," with a warm baritone that reminds me of Maya Angelou—love concentrated by pain. It took time before I made her "baby" list. She'd trade her cereal for our morning cake and offer me a steady, curious look, but that flood of sunlight was reserved for others. I pretended not to care. I did.

I told Rach I'm drawn to the apex in any field and agnostic about which field that is. I'm bored by the middle. People who've gone the distance carry an added dimension—robber barons and innovators, special forces and lawyers who actually win, the ones carved by the river all the way to the ocean. Royal is one of those. She has nothing to prove, which frees up all the proving energy other people spend. She pours it into love. She'll talk about disappointing her grandkids with a humility that almost hurts. She doesn't try to look cool; she is cool. She reminds me of my friend Ed, a lifelong Zen teacher whose goal is simply "to be a pretty good Ed," and then he tears up. Those are the real ones.

But 5:30 this evening, no one shows. I tell Rach, "We started the walks; it's not our job to chase anyone. But it is our job to hold the frequency." We lap the gym alone for fifteen minutes...and then, like an alarm across the dorm, the walkers begin drifting in.

Allison arrives first, then Brynn. They join me and Rach. Royal and Janiya, her "granddaughter," come in shortly after. They do a few loops and puppy-bright Janiya gets distracted and peels off, leaving Royal solo. I can see her angling back to the dorm. She walks for the company. I wave our little gaggle—Rach, me, Allison, and Brynn— over to her. Then I speed up to meet her and it's Royal and me, stride for stride. We're both big planets: warm to everyone, cautious with each other, orbiting to see if the other is actually paying attention.

Royal is a storyteller, and she has stories. A full-on OG from the eighties and nineties.

Out on the track, she talks the way some women pray—somewhat to me, mostly to God, the rest to herself. "I always wanted to be a lawyer," she says. "First grade. Teacher go around the room, everybody saying nurse, ballerina. I said, 'Lawyer.' I wanted that briefcase. I wanted to walk in the room and know more than everybody else." Her voice is matter-of-fact, like she's reciting a file she knows by heart.

She tells me about Bedford, her first bid Upstate. "I studied law the whole time. State law, not this federal shit." She chuckles. "It's not if we did it or not. It's if they can prove it."

"I was in my twenties," she goes on to explain. "A kid. And one day I just said, you know what? Fuck it. I'm not getting no job, I'm not going back to school. I'm gonna be a criminal. I made a conscious decision. I decided this my life."

It started small, she tells me—"simple things," walking into banks and walking out with money that wasn't hers, paper games that felt like magic tricks. "We all teach each other what we good at," she says. "One girl good with checks, one with IDs. I'd be amazed at the shit I could get away with." Her eyes gleam, remembering. "It's like an orgasm. When you hit it, it's good, then it's gone, and you want it again."

She tells me about the crews she ran with—mostly men, always talking like they were the brains. "They think they slick. Think 'cause they the ones with the gun or the suit on, they in charge." She snorts. "Half the time they running on what a woman taught 'em." She glances at me. "I ain't never let no man run my show. Not the ones in the street, not the ones in my bed."

"God said, 'I make men.' And I said, 'Me too,'" she says, tapping her chest. "I carried them in my body nine months. Fed 'em, wiped they nose, taught 'em how to walk in a room." Her hand goes instinctively to her belly, then drops. "Everybody act like these men just appear or like these men made us. Nah. They come through us.

"I make men. My sons, my grandsons, my dudes. Whatever man I'm with, I'm making him. I build him up, talk life into him, show him how to move. He walking around in a body that came through a woman. He can't never be better than his maker." There's no brag in it; it's doctrine, an honest evaluation. "Lotta these girls shrink theyself so some man can feel big," she says. "Not me. I make men. I been like that my whole life. I don't care how many mistakes I made, I'm the best."

Abandoned at birth, her mother resurfaced after this most recent arrest—sixty years later—and told Royal she needed to eat salad instead of her daily meal of wings and ribs and potato salad from Shop Fast. Shame, regret, a long ledger of hard choices.

Listening to her spill it out while we walk the track, I think of all the invisible women who have been "making men" their whole lives—the mothers and aunties and girlfriends who packed the lunches, wiped the faces, said the one sentence that shaped how a boy would see women for the next forty years. We talk about "the system" like it fell out of the sky, some neutral machine. But every system was once a boy in a kitchen absorbing a woman's tired story about power, about who matters and who doesn't. Standing with Royal, it's obvious: She's been making men and making the world, and then getting punished inside the very world she helped make.

"May I offer you another read?"

She gives me a small nod of assent, a conversation between equals.

"You walk through this dorm giving love to everyone," I tell her. "That's the real work. Beating yourself up hasn't helped—you said it never stopped you after any arrest, it just took you away from your kids. What if you gave yourself the same love you give these women, the kind that makes them stronger?"

She stops mid-stride, considering the option.

"You're smart," she says, picking the pace back up, an extra glint in her knowing eye.

We keep going. Ninety minutes. She doesn't want to stop. By the end she's agreed to drink two glasses of water a day—another huge step toward "healthy." Royal tells me she's never done more than seventeen laps. I finally have to laugh and say we'll pick it up tomorrow because I'm the one who's tired.

Real-deal love finds itself in the most unlikely places.

9

Outside the Trap

In all the spirituality and religion I've studied along my way, there's always been something that rubs me wrong: the suburban, comfort-version of enlightenment. The float-above-it-all vibe. The spiritual shopping—collecting practices like status symbols—so long as no one chips a manicure or witnesses real pressure.

Plenty of people romance the idea of "sexual energy" and the path of desire, right up until it means bringing women's real lives and bodies into the room. When it's time to climb out of the dream and into the mud—*boo hoo, too harsh*. Everyone wants the benefits of the practice; almost no one wants to shovel.

Prison has pressure. Encoded in that pressure is a right response. Light pressure? You reach. Heavy pressure? You open. It isn't about bowing to anyone's barking. It's the opposite: knowing who you are so fully that you can offer people what *they* think they need—respect, a yes-sir, a nod—without losing your center. I remember a nun once explaining that she could bow to a roomful of men and still keep her feminism intact. "Because *they* need that," she said. Exactly. I know who I am. My dignity isn't for sale. I can still offer courtesy.

That's the move in the face of inhumanity: *You* supply the humanity, even in tiny doses. Talk to people in the language they understand. Give them a way to feel decent in a job that often makes them feel the opposite. Cruelty doesn't feel good, no matter which way it's pointed. Someone has to be the place where dominance isn't required—where aggression has nowhere to land. The only way I know to do that is to be like water.

There's an old exercise: Two people press their hands together. One is told to push. The other gets no instruction. Almost every time, the second person pushes back, and they lock up. Rarely does the second person think to simply give. But when they do, it ends quickly.

So what, exactly, is there to assert?

What is there to protect?

What do any of us "win"?

For me, the answer is simple: I protect inexhaustible peace. I can add kindness where it's scarce. That's the infinite game—the one where the point is to keep the goodness flowing, not rack up trophies. In the finite game, the company I founded got taken down and I landed in prison. Dramatic. But in the bigger game, it's just one scene. If you can't feel that wider frame, things will hurt for a long time.

There is no "them." There's only the clumsy momentum of ignorance. If you fight ignorance on its terms, you become it. The most subversive thing I can do is refuse to become what's ugly in front of me. As Martin Luther King, Jr. taught: Darkness cannot drive out darkness; only light can do that.

And I don't dismiss Malcolm X, either. He drove rage into strategy. He turned fire into clarity—discipline, dignity, purpose. That's the road I intend to walk: Take the raw surge of energy and send it where it can do clean work.

My instinct has always been to build the whole ecology so there's no enemy position to push against. Turn toward what's been rejected instead of away from it. That's where the real power lies. When you stop flinching, healing begins. From there, contribution follows.

Underneath all my big visions, I still worry for my friends and community outside these walls. My being remanded was a sudden altitude change for all of us. So I ask them what I ask myself: Can you *use* this—not despite it, but *because* of it—as the wall you push off from? Can you get smarter, stronger, more precise, more determined to be what the world is missing? It's the same question inside and out.

The most radical act I can take is to show that I can, and do, take pleasure in doing the work, even here. To be a small pocket of ease and refuge for whoever crosses my path. To not take it personally, because none of this is personal.

The success of my work won't be whether anyone knows my name, my résumé, or my rates. Success will look like this place hurting less because I was here.

I want people to know who I am by how they feel around me, not by my titles. That's why I chose stigmatized, controversial work over a safe set of robes. People who rely on uniforms to command respect are negotiating with fear. I want the message to be carried by who I am in any room.

During my trial, the expectation was for me to either fall into shame and exile or defiance and attitude. I chose a different option, the only option that would work for who I am: warm dignity that would not be moved by projection.

Here, it's different. Here, being "no one" is the default. The system tries to strip identity and make you reactive—either defeated or combative. My job is to stay human and step outside that trap.

No one has to know my kindness is deliberate. They can think it's automatic or weak. That's fine.

I will know.

Personal agendas blind us. You can miss what's available here—the sophistication it takes to navigate an endless slalom of shifting rules, man-made laws, and moving targets. The art is to live in a fear-built system without operating *from* fear.

Now *that* is gangster.

10

For the Woman in the Bunk Next to Me, Part One

T he woman in the bunk next to me told me she's ashamed that she's such a sexual woman. It was passing in conversation, the kind of admission meant to register as a simple, obvious moral failing—as if having that much current in your body is a defect, not a pair of wings the world is terrified you might actually use. These are the confessions the world trains us to believe are right and moral: that we, especially women, should be ashamed of our sexuality. Free from so much of the world outside, these rules still run deep here, even stronger. There is little room to say what I wish I could say to her:

I believe that for those who have been chosen to carry it, sex is a grand responsibility—equal parts burden, capacity, and honor.

Do not listen to the grim, tight-lipped women full of scorn and judgment. They are frail from lack of power. Just as the expression of the sun is light, the expression of powerlessness is fear. Fear shows up as judgment, comparison, fixing. And if the first two don't work, they will resort to the third. "Fixing" is garden-variety envy, the hobgoblin of a sexless mind. It masquerades as superiority. Remember that the best that unhappy people can hope for is *position*. Their anthem: "I may not be happy, but I am right. I am in control. I am on top." They know not the delights of being at the bottom—of being on our backs.

That position is for a person of noble birth, a person with not superior position but superior *constitution*. We all enter the world as an expression of sex, and just like a real, bona fide orgasm, constitution cannot be faked or feigned. It holds up irrespective of condition.

The difference between those who can and those who cannot climb to the top of Mt. Everest is not determined by money, fame, status, appeal, or intellect. The one who plants her flag at the peak has the *constitution* to do so—an invisible, unalterable quality given to those meant for flight at higher altitudes than the others gawking from below.

This is why I'm asking you to recognize yourself now, to see that you are not cursed but chosen to carry the crown with your head held high. Others lack the spine to wear it without crumbling, without letting its weight push them into the ditches and gullies women fall into: holding themselves as victims, romanticizing men, criticizing women. At the root of each woman is truth—the truth of her inestimable power—resting on the source that animates all power: sexuality.

But in this world, it is not true sex or power that is displayed. It is their impostors: aggression and greed. We grow suspicious of sexual expression after having been so often deceived. The deprived and the depraved dare to extract, bastardize, and desacralize sacredness herself. They have no idea what they do, these women who would use this force to sell themselves like chattel to men—Buy me! Buy me!

They think they can trade their souls for the enlightenment, the enlivenment they seek. They put on a show of "offering" themselves and "surrendering," but it's a ruse—extorting unwitting men who have bitten the hook and been dragged below. The *real* communication happens under the table: "I own you now. Give me what I want, or I will use sex as a weapon to destroy you."

The Princesses of Powerlessness believe they should never have to be overt, direct, honest. The world should read their minds. Never mind that they are entirely ungratifiable.

I digress.

But you—my dear—with the slings and arrows in your chest, who continue despite yourself to pour and offer the sex that caused them to exile you, tomato stains on your dress: I'm sorry to say it, but you take it because you can. And because you can, you must, because you know it is the path your soul has laid out. Just as they are not meant to climb the mountain, you know you are meant to strive for its summit.

Sure, you could take yourself out of the game. You could marry the "good and decent guy" and descend into suburban slumber. But we both know that life would be built on a fault line, with the chronic, nagging fear of the trembling quake calling to you. Sooner or later you will need to feed—whether it's the guy at the gym or your husband's friend. You know a moment's lapse in the hypervigilance guarding your tenuous peace could invite its collapse.

Again, this is not your curse. It is the gods' challenging endowment to you, the command to take your mantle. You are not permitted to play small in this life. You were born with a largesse, a grandness, a generosity that must be released from the cage of propriety. For a woman like you, being "appropriate" is stinginess. You were born to pour onto this desert what they are not yet conscious they thirst for.

Answering this call does not immunize you from consequence. It brings me no joy to say it. But I am here, next to you, in a Brooklyn prison, facing the consequences of being a sexual woman who taught others to free themselves from the shackles of projection—from the belief that there is something wrong with being sexual women at all. The world would rather condemn us as dangerous, conniving, manipulative. But sexuality is a primal force that exceeds the bounds of any confinement. It is not manipulative; it is ordered by natural law. As you take on your mantle, they will be frightened of you and will threaten you in response. The threats will not be idle. I am forced to undress, bend over, and cough for the prison guards, and still I must see them with compassion while dignity is, shall we say, not made a priority. You, too, will get no worldly protections.

This does not mean you are unprotected. In fact, you are well protected: Your humanity, compassion, and dignity remain untouched. Your eyes keep their X-ray vision. You can see them while they cannot see you—though somewhere deep down they know you are not taken in by their antics. They know, too, how desperately they crave and yearn for what they hope to find in their baby-girl movies and books about shades of grey. They long to live by the nature they sense in you, to feel how you feel, to break free. Anchored to what exists within, you remain impervious to the world's cruelties.

The realization of the sex within you is clear-eyed compassion—the antidote to ignorance. It is equal parts peace, increase, power, wrath, and activity, and it carries the wisdom to know which face to wear in the moment. The road is hard, but the result is invaluable.

In the end, you are given the ability to make love itself. No longer do you simply *trade* in love—you *make* it. You will make it out of the snide comments, the poison, the smog; from injustice, ignorance, and cruelty. You will have the resilience and capacity to transform it into love. Neither bowing nor retaliating, you will love those who would destroy you in a third way: understanding. They will not have the final say, the satisfaction of taking you down—not because you fought, but because if they were to win it would be a loss for everyone, including themselves.

In the end, you will make love of, and to, a loveless world. Please continue. We need you.

I'm writing this and not speaking it to you because whenever two

50

women gather to speak of sex—real sex, the sex that liberates—danger is near. We have enough of that now. I pray the day will come when we are free, not just from this place but free to express our deepest gifts in the world, free to fly the way we were made to.

11

Miss Wu

It's a whole mix of people in prison, old and young, white, Black, Hispanic, Asian. Some loud, some quiet. Some people come right up and introduce themselves with their full life's story, some take more time to get to know.

Two weeks into our stay at MDC, Rachel and I began to attract the attention of an older Asian woman who had been cool toward us until that time. She would watch us meditating in the rec area while she stood by the partially open window, tossing crumbs to birds through the metal grating. Eventually the day came when she broke the ice. With the authority of someone catching a burglar mid-window, she asked, "What are you doing there?"

"Meditating," I replied without leaving my seat.

"Where you learn that? That is real. You do it the real way. People in U.S. do not know that."

"We do." I smiled, turning. "Yes—it's real."

"Okay, okay, you know what you are doing," she said, half confirming a theory, half deciding what to do now that we had passed the invisible test she apparently proctors.

After that day, we exchange nods at dawn in the rec area as Rachel and I go to meditate and she to her birds. Other Asian women cluster around her, chirping about one thing or another while she stands as the reference point. People call out, "Morning, Miss Wu," and every so often, "When are you making sushi again?" She waves it off. "Too much work. A lot of work."

Watching her, it is clear she is the don of a quiet empire. Cool, scanning eyes. People come to her; she does not go to people. I can see her in a basement with five hundred mahjong players, the banker with all the chips.

Wednesday rolls around and nine of us are called for visitation, including Miss Wu. She slips into line behind me after flashing a look that leaves an afterimage—like a camera flash that lingers on your retina. It feels like contact, recognition—immediate and intimate— like we are POWs who'd known each other before the camp and can't let on. I offer a careful smile back, but not so warm that I'll look foolish if she hasn't shared the same experience I have.

We are waiting for the elevator. I rarely speak on that walk from the dorm to the visiting room; I'm still learning how to interact with the officers. Sometimes a guard will drop a line like, "It's cold in there," referring to our dorm air-conditioning that is colder than Siberia, and I have to surface like a submarine, consult my internal handbook on How to Respond to a Human.

"I know," I'll say. "I wore two sweatshirts last night." I never quite nail the banter. There's a particular "at the mercy" feeling with guards—you don't know where they're coming from, so you must not "over" or "under" do anything. I often think this is how people of color feel with white people, only here it's which shade of beige uniform. My spidey sense stays lit: Does this one want me to walk ahead or fall behind? Quiet submission or total invisibility? Chatty or stone silent? How do I dance the exact shape that will not inflame any tensions? I hold the intention to be a model inmate the way I hold the intention to be a model student of the dharma: to respond precisely to what is required without abandoning myself, my dignity, or my principles.

But right in the middle of those calculations, Miss Wu lights up like we've just come off silent retreat and she's been saving a story.

"Ah, yes. I need to tell you," she begins, as if we're picking up a conversation midstream. "I grew up in China, close to Tibet. I know what you are doing. Very famous Rinpoche—the head of tradition in the biggest temple on the edge of Tibet. My mother..." She searches for the word. "What is the word—surrender there."

"Surrender?"

"Not the word. Like Americans—accept Christ. She do that with Buddha."

"Your mother took vows in Tibetan Buddhism?" I ask, wanting to be sure I'm hearing correctly, mindful of the politics braided through identity and geography.

"Yes. Exactly." Her moon-bright face beams. "We went on big tour with Rinpoche. He took us to special ceremonies in Nepal. Ceremonies for the dead, in between life and death." She lowers her voice as if we share a secret language.

"You did a ceremony for someone who died? For someone's spirit?" I ask.

"Yes! Exactly. But it have very strong effect on me. It made me remember. Past life." She taps her forehead and opens her hand—an explosion. I see it: the flash of light, the sudden memory, the Buddha meditating under the Bodhi tree—only in a too-bright hallway with a correctional officer two steps away.

Then she winks—ancient, cosmic. "I know who you are. What you do."

She'd been waiting two weeks to tell me.

I've felt this before. When I was twenty-seven, I wandered into the "drug den"—the warehouse where people lay tripping on mismatched sofas—and met Ada, the gatekeeper. Everyone was intimidated by her. I was too—starstruck, but not by celebrity. More like a comet had entered my atmosphere and I could already feel the heat of it burning across the sky.

Ada tested me. Left cash scattered about, wads from a grand to ten grand. Everyone else took some. I didn't. When she left the room, I stayed put, oddly reverent. The test was the lesson.

I spent two years with Ada. The main thing I learned from her, and then saw again in every tradition I studied, is that things are not what they appear. I took my vows in Buddhism not too long after. They teach to see it all as a dream. Ada said: See it all as play, as theater. Same same, only the latter arrives with an eternal wink—which I quite like.

And now I'm sitting in prison. This isn't a deviation from that vow. It's a continuation. Through Ada, through Miss Wu, that same eternal wink peeking through, just this time it's breadcrumbs scattered on a windowsill instead of money across a desk. That same actor in new costume, now dressed as a Chinese auntie feeding birds. In prison. Telling me how Jesus teaches the same thing as in Buddhism. Of course.

Back in the dorm after visitation, Miss Wu picks up our conversation again as if no time had passed. She asks what I'm in for. I say, "Conspiracy to force labor. But I'm here for teaching about sexuality and meditation."

"You taught tantra meditation?" Her eyes nearly leap from her face. "In the United States? American women could not understand. Even in Asia, only advanced people understand that." She laughs hard enough to fall off the steel stool.

"Well, yes. I figured that out when they convicted me."

Her face flickers between amusement, concern, and awe. "I am here for conspiracy too," she says, now the very image of a laughing

Buddha. "But mine is from past life. I overspent my karma." She tells me about conferences she organized—five hundred monks, sixteen monasteries, all the top lamas and teachers. Then she says we'll do the next one together. I do the math with the unknown variable of my sentencing and, honestly, my entire future.

The mystery opens, as it always does. I have the same flash I had with Ada when I chose her wild ride because what I saw with her felt hyperreal, stronger than anything I'd known, like stepping through the curtain from the simulation into the real. Potent enough to dissolve my fixed ideas about what it should look like—the robes, the solemnity, the candles, the dharma books.

I'm in prison with Miss Wu, and we both know the only secret, the one that keeps her laughing so hard I want to sit close, just to catch her if she falls off that little metal stool.

12

Flow

After Miss Wu, I kept thinking about a line I once heard: Throw a stick and a dog chases the stick. Throw a stick and a lion turns toward the one who threw it.

Most people watch the stick arc through the air. A few track it back to the thrower. Inside that few is an even smaller group who keep going—past the hand, into whatever moves the hand in the first place. They're loyal to the source rather than the shiny object.

Ada was like that. Miss Wu is like that. They're not hypnotized by the "stick"—my charges, my reputation, even my meditation practice. They look straight at whatever is throwing all of this, and they recognize their own.

I grew up around people like that. Los Gatos, near Santa Cruz, the cradle of flow: curly-haired surfers, punk skateboarders, roller skaters on the boardwalk. The meditators in town left over from the San Francisco Summer of Love found calm in stillness and breath. The rest of us needed motion. We were extreme monks. The elements were our teachers. Keep the lungs pumping and the blood bright until sight gives way to vision.

I drove an aqua Volkswagen Rabbit because it matched the surf sticker I wanted for the back window. We met at the Pruneyard: tough girls in torn black jeans and Doc Martens, boards under their arms. I was the one on roller skates. I didn't want the identity; I needed the movement.

A therapist once told me dysregulated people get regulated on wheels, that the brain balances when the body glides. I told her we are all dysregulated. Some of us are just blessed to find the thing that steadies us, and it feels like a miracle when we do.

Decades later, there are bestsellers about the neuroscience of these misfits, explaining that skaters and surfers had located the holy grail of attention. Not just the stick or the thrower, but the electricity that makes the throw possible. Scientists arrived to validate what rink kids already knew in their bones.

Our freestyle athletes moved from the fringe to the Olympics because the thing we touched did not create slackers; it created superior minds. We could have told you that, if you hadn't been distracted by our cigarettes and our parties. We drank, we danced, and found a channel no amount of discipline alone could open. Fidelity to that dimension was easy because the dimension was passion itself.

I learned early the frustration of tasting the source uncut, only to watch people dilute it with rules and judges. The source doesn't need to be cut with baby powder, gentlemen. Humans invented croquet and then congratulated themselves on their tidy boredom. Meanwhile, motion wrote its own art on concrete.

To be moved by motion is to travel in an invisible dimension with others who can feel it. You ride the edge without tipping. You make beauty out of ordinary matter while the rule-keepers wrinkle their noses at the smell of burned rubber.

In every tradition, there are quiet practitioners who keep this route secret. They know how the mind chases the stick—money, property, prestige; the badge of being "good" or "bad"; the backward math that confuses virtue with performance. Often the loudest defenders of justice are not just at all. I'm writing from a federal penitentiary to report the obvious.

I could have practiced the tentative sin of omission. Instead I chose the explorer's path and decided, as Jacques Cousteau put it, "When one has the opportunity to lead an extraordinary life, he has no right to keep it to himself."

So I wake in the MDC Brooklyn dorm before dawn and feel the same truth I felt on a pair of skates. This place is a meditation hall for extreme minds. The obstacles are the practice. I've never had so much intensity to work with, which means I've never had such clean access.

I've always been a rough-and-tumble type at heart. Fluffy halls and perfect cushions felt like padding. The ordinary world isn't different from life in here; it just offers prettier distractions. Once you're done believing distractions will satisfy you, the stripped-down version here is a relief.

Skaters and punks were called reckless. We threatened order. No one paused to ask whether that order was any good. The greats had to break through the membrane of artificial limits, the wild that threatens to overtake our finely manicured reality. It's human arrogance that calls nature a problem to control.

But once you see the distinction between the lines drawn by man and the trajectories of desire, you recognize it everywhere. In sport and mind, in cities and deserts, nature knows. Civilization usually arranges itself against that truth. This is why the Buddha taught that he was going "against the stream." He was going against man-made convention in order to follow deeper laws.

If we only chase after the stick, we'll never trace it back to the source. Further, systems of control will cloak the source, obscure it behind dogma or danger or shame. But let go of the distraction and turn against the stream, and you can follow the flow back to its source.

Those wild geniuses who make that turn aren't trying to please the second-tier class of convention. They tapped the current. They paid for it—outcasts at times—but they didn't stop. Genius is not a compliment; it's a responsibility to continue. I told a very young woman here that her gift will either make her or destroy her. She has to practice harder than an Olympian, because she's refining a fire that is already blazing.

That's what I see here: raw wildlife. Real eruptions. Real storms. Nothing supernatural—wildly natural. Life that didn't get tamed, mesmerized by the seemingly endless options.

Once you know there is only one option wherever you go—to face yourself—abundance starts to feel like punishment. Fewer options, better results.

This is why prisons feel like the frontier of awakening to me, verdant with life in a way that makes the world outside seem arid and lifeless. The women in here are geysers. Too much at once on hardened soil can rush to flash floods or landslides. But, if harnessed, their flow could irrigate whole deserts. The insights that take me decades to draw out from law-abiding women are common sense in here. These women live at a level of presence that classrooms try to approximate with endless talks and careful guidance.

Most of them don't know it consciously. They know there is something they can't cut themselves off from but they think it's the guy, or the drug, or the "life." They don't realize it's the dimension itself—the source the lion turns toward.

If you were recruiting people with the ingenuity, stamina, vision, and humility to change the world, I wouldn't start in pristine meditation halls or courthouse corridors. Those spaces can only go as far as the rules allow. Collective freedom needs something wilder.

My guess is that when real change comes, it will rise from the very places we've used to try to confine life. The only force strong enough is already here, in the bodies of those who would not be tamed. These women—armed with meditation and self-inquiry—have what others will spend lifetimes trying to access. They already carry the direct line to the source. The horsepower is here; what's missing is a steering wheel.

13

The Lines Shift

Kiki's birthday was a black-tie affair by MDC standards. We were honored to be invited. There were "crab cakes" made from whatever seafood the kitchen had that day, sushi, rice balls, and a ridiculous Chips Ahoy cookie cake with two whole Hershey's bars pressed on top like jewels.

What I didn't realize was that it was an "opps day." I thought I was being neighborly when I walked a couple of loaded plates over to Janiya and some other women. But there was an invisible electric fence running straight down the middle of the dorm. The moment my foot crossed whatever line only they could see, the air shifted and I felt as if I'd been zapped.

As I walked back across the dorm, the glares from the women spun my head around. Nevaeh met me halfway, clucked her tongue, and said, "We do not share with opps."

I blinked. "Huh? What?"

"Opps," she repeated, like the word "bitch" should follow. "Opps, opps. Janiya not cool and if you over there you ain't neither."

"That makes no sense," I said, still operating under a more flexible code. "You and Janiya were friends just yesterday."

"You need to read the headlines," Nevaeh said. "That shit is over."

"Oh dear God. Okay, got it."

Nevaeh went back and explained to everyone that it was an error of the uninitiated. That did not stop the gossip from flying. It floated up and over the dorm like laundry on a line.

Nevaeh and Janiya, up to their usual antics as the heart and the brain on Monday, and on Tuesday they are "opps." In a place where eye contact can be a threat, their volume reads like safety: If they're yelling, at least you know where you stand.

Later that week, I found Janiya on her bunk, knees up, watching *What's Love Got to Do With It* on her prison tablet, mouthing every line like scripture. Angela Bassett and Laurence Fishburne acting out the drama of Ike and Tina Turner's tumultuous relationship on-screen.

"You really love them," I said, taking a seat next to her.

Janiya's eyes stayed on the screen. "That's my couple. Ike and Tina? That's my shit. People only see the beatings. You gotta read between the lines."

"What do you see?" I asked.

"Ain't no Ike without Tina, and ain't no Tina without Ike," she said. "She was stronger than him. You can tell. He had to keep her down 'cause he knew she was better. Without her, he never would've been Ike."

She tapped her head. "That's how it is with my man. My mind, my sense, it stabilize him. He don't do nothin' without me. My man can't live without me."

There was no brag to it, just simple facts.

"First job I ever had was being a prostitute," she added, like she was telling me her major. "I wasn't supposed to be no ho. I finally got the kid I wanted, and the Feds came kickin' the door in. Now my kid got neither of us. If I never met that man, I'd be in the medical field or some shit. I wish I never met him."

She shrugged. "But I can't walk away from him. And I ain't gonna lie on him either. When it's needed, he there. We grew up together in this shit. Love is difficult."

She said "love" like a scar.

"I hate pimps," she went on. "I only like him. We had a different relationship. I learned the game. You gotta know who's gonna rape you and who's gonna pay you. Game is chess, not checkers. I watched how everybody moved. Once I got comfortable, I got more money. I became his bottom bitch, the one closest to a wife. I built his business. He know that."

On the screen, Ike was in the studio, Tina on the other side of the glass.

"At first it was romantic," she said. "Then the honeymoon over and he hit me. First time was 'cause I talked to one of his friends. Second time, I talked to another pimp, he wanted my money. My man snatched my phone and smacked me twice on the gate in front of everybody. Third time he raised his hand, I blacked out and beat him back. Treated him like any dude on the street. I was taught to protect myself. I can fight."

She said it with pride, and there was something raw under it, a small girl in boxing gloves who refused to sit down.

"So what do you love about Ike and Tina?" I asked.

She thought for a second. "I love that kind of loyalty. She stayed, even when he was on drugs. Women can change a man. She made him. I feel like that. My mind keep my man from spinnin' all the way out." She paused. "Only part I hate is when he raped her in the studio. That's your woman. Don't do that. That part hurt my heart."

"You ever heard that chant Tina recorded, 'Nam-Myoho-Renge-Kyo'?" I asked.

As if she'd been waiting her whole life, Janiya bolted upright, eyes closed, hands pressed together, and launched into a pitch-perfect imitation of Tina Turner's chanting, strong enough to overpower Angela Bassett's impression on the screen.

"You know that's how Tina finally left," I said softly. "For good. She broke the whole pattern."

"Yeah, after he broke her all the way down first," Janiya said.

"It was that mantra," I kept going. "Nam-Myoho-Renge-Kyo. Over and over. To change herself, not just her man. I did that chant for years. It roughly means 'the lotus rises from the mud.'"

I could see her version of Tina's chant hiding under all her goofy bravado. There is a way to turn poison into medicine that doesn't depend on whether a man ever changes.

Janiya looked down at the screen, now the real Tina Turner dressed in white singing for a whole auditorium of people. Then she looked at me. "So you think women can really change a man?"

"I think they can," I said. "But I think the only change we can count on is our own."

She rolled her eyes like it annoyed her to agree. "Yeah. Maybe we supposed to change ourselves first," she muttered. "Look, I'm a Leo. I want a man-man. Provider, in control. I wanna chill. But female lions do all the work anyway." She sat with it a moment before offering a quick grin. "Maybe it's our job to be greater."

That always seems to be how it works in here. But in this place, nobody gets to walk out on Ike. The state does the leaving for you. Sitting on that bunk, listening to this so-called "problem girl" talk about bottom bitches and chess and a love that hurt like hell, I could feel it: The part of a woman that knows she's stronger than the man who's breaking her, and that one day, whether by chant or prayer or sheer fighter's will, she might choose herself.

"Game is chess, not checkers," Janiya said again.

"Exactly," I told her. "But you choose how you want to play." For a minute we just sat there, the glow of the screen on her face. We would never be in the same room on the outside, but here we were, stitched together by a mantra about a lotus growing out of mud.

Later that evening, I walked toward the back of the dorm, where Royal usually held court in her bed with a book.

Royal looked up as I came over. Before I could say anything, I caught sight of them: Nevaeh and Janiya at a table near us, recently reunited, playing cards and eating banana pudding, telling the new girl they both did not like, "You better get yourself a shower 'cause your ass stank."

So much for eternal opps.

I pointed at them, eyebrows raised. "These are the mortal enemies I almost got in trouble over?"

Royal laughed, deep and warm, and squeezed my shoulder. "I know, baby, but you gotta learn. When it's real, it's real, and don't get in between."

"Royal, you know I am not a real opps kind of woman," I told her. "I think we need to change that. We have more in common with each other than ninety-nine percent of the world. You don't think it's ridiculous for us to waste our energy on that?"

"I know, baby, but that's the way it is." She rested her warm, soft hand on my shoulder. "This ain't like outside, this is MDC."

"Well, Royal, we are going to be changing that." I smiled.

"You different, Nicole," she said. "I kinda like that. But be careful."

She did not have to tell me twice. "Respect the opps" went into my mental prison manual that night, written in block letters. "Still talk to everyone" was the rule I wrote right underneath.

Over time, Janiya became a sort of steadiness for me that helps me make it through. She is loud and goofy and drives everyone crazy, but her willingness to play the fool makes her oddly nonthreatening. If I am disoriented, I make eye contact with her. That is no small thing in a place where women not only withhold eye contact, but where that withholding can mean danger is on the horizon. In a world where things are rarely what they appear, those clownish personas are just avatars. Underneath, both of them run on a serious love frequency that makes sure no one is ever completely isolated.

At the table, Nevaeh and Janiya cackled at their own joke, heads thrown back, shoulders leaning into each other like they'd never heard of opps in their lives. The lines shift. The love, when you can see past the mud, is what stays.

14

Visiting

Visitations are on Wednesdays. I was learning the rhythm. The dorm takes on a clucking, bright-eyed energy. Even women without visitors move differently, a little more aware of themselves. Locker doors bang open; tiny commissary mirrors flash; hot combs and curling wands appear from the office; dumpy sweats become date-night outfits. We go from finals-week sorority to first-date hopeful.

Diamond has Lisa do her hair in a sweeping ponytail. "Lisa did it," she says, proud.

"Well, it looks like Lisa knows what she's doing," I say.

Diamond lives out in Row Four—the far neighborhood, so we rarely interact. But, on visitation day, all borders blur and doors open. Every woman is for every woman because now there's an "outside" that is bigger than the outside we've been living inside.

Luci's been going through it. She's the glee-club overachiever—don't let 'em see you sweat. Her "happy" can read like a flex. I care about her, but I don't break down anyone's reality by force. Still, you can hear the argument inside her; even her tennis shoes land loud.

"You okay?" I ask, just that. The dam cracks. Tears.

Most people have been sold a single story about this place: wall-to-wall misery, a morality play designed to make the outside feel righteous—*See? They're suffering like they should.* But the stranger truth is that sometimes life shows up here bright and unfiltered. There's laughter that knocks your shoulder, kindness that sneaks a seat beside you, a sharpness to the moment that the outside world, for all its choices, keeps dulling down.

A lot of folks picture "heaven" as nothing but love-and-light, no mess or noise. I've learned there's another kind of heaven for the rough-and-tumble angels who show up in disguise. It's not clouds and beams of light; you get harsh overhead lights and concrete floors and seven women sharing instant coffee—and somehow, there's something more real to it. You stand next to legends and nobodies, saints and screwups, free for a second from who you were "supposed" to be. And for an entrance fee, all it costs is your reputation.

But now Luciana is looking at the other part of her journey, the return. You go out on your adventure into terror and delight and then have to squeeze back into the shape of "good civilian." There aren't enough shapewear brands in the world. Even with the "best" of a normal life, how do you survive dullness after you've seen the sky on fire—even if that sky sometimes casts its own strange shadows?

She started counting down her days, starting the transition from "in here" to "out there." The past sings loud. It wants you back. Luci asks how to walk forward. Point your body where you're going. Drop the tab you think you're owed and the tab you think you owe. Those ledgers keep you shackled—the second you turn to settle them, you're yanked off your feet.

She wrestles. I pray. I don't want her stepping into her next life with the old story clinging like static.

She nods like she's listening. She isn't. I know the drill. The lures offer something sweeter than I can. But if she changes her mind, she knows how to find me.

They call my name. Then Rachel's. Then Janiya's. Then Miss Wu's. Five o'clock. Time to go down.

We enter together—eight women scanning for prom dates among blue plastic tables. I spot Matt and watch Rachel swim over to him. Emmett, my consort—less "boyfriend," more training partner in love— stands behind, steady as a metronome.

When I reach him, the breath he's held all week leaves. We're allowed a hug at the beginning and at the end. Thirty seconds. I pull away— model inmate instincts. Rach is still hugging Matt, last to let go.

Emmett and I are built for a different destination. We train to become the signal—to find each other anywhere, any time. The eternal hide-and-seek of love. We willingly endure the ache, even impose it, to strengthen the signal.

It's a surgeon's kind of love—nothing extra added or the procedure fails. Warm, bordering on neutral. Less ownership or performance; more *for the other*. Emmett is more troubadour—expressive, romantic, music to the beloved. My way is the psyche's clean cut.

I usually allow his love but don't take it personally. I let it wash through. This time, I let it in.

He's just a man in a visiting room asking me to feel his love. No reassurance needed. Just receive. So I do. His devotion is cathedral-quiet. For once, I'm simply woman, warm and present.

"You do," I say. "Love me very much."

"With everything I am," he answers—raw, insistent that I know it's him. He can joke about neutrality tomorrow. For now: *See me.*

I soften. I don't regret holding the line; he loves me because I don't waver—until the signal is blade-sharp.

Then the river reroutes.

Somewhere between his voice and my breath, the dial clicks into a station. The image he's been holding stops being a picture and

70

becomes presence. The room doesn't change, but my skin does—gooseflesh, a tug behind the breastbone, air thickening like before a storm. It isn't *as if* I'm there: I am.

Sitting across from each other, the wall between here and there thins. We sit upright—hands visible, feet flat—and the tuning fork hums on its own.

"Cherwitz, Daedone, Wu..." The hour is up. The guard is almost gentle. The goodbye hug before they are escorted out the door. We line up. Into the search room. Strip. Bend. Cough. It seems a world away—and not really.

This visit had been different. In the first weeks at MDC, my trips down to the visitation room had been sporadic—meetings with lawyers making sure I was settling in, the next steps in my case, assurances and appeals, details that overflowed from my mind. Rachel and I had been remanded on a Tuesday so it wasn't until our third Wednesday that Emmett and Matt were approved for social visits. That first visit, we'd tried to cram a week of meaning into an hour—rations for the week. But tonight, devotion did the work tuning the signal to a frequency that can penetrate through these walls, connecting to something outside time and place.

By the time the guard walks us back upstairs, I'm relieved. The visiting room smells like the outside—so many choices dressed up as freedom, the insistence that consumption equals joy. In the dorm, the dial is quieter. I know where to place my hands, my voice, my eyes. There isn't anything I need that I'm kept separate from. He knows my coordinates now. He can find me.

I can finally say it: I love where I am right now. There's nowhere I'd rather be. With what we found, I don't worry he'll feel abandoned. He can reach me. My body can stay housed and fed, ringed by women I've grown to love—whether or not they know the secret.

In the elevator, I usually keep quiet, but I ask the six women and the guard, "Is it strange I feel relieved going back up?"

A couple laugh—the newbie gets it. The "prize" can be an ordeal.

"Yeah," Diamond says. "A lot of anticipation—during the visit, too."

"You mean you don't look forward to bending over and coughing after seeing your folks?" I deadpan. A few stare—Housewife has jokes. Janiya nods: "Alright, Housewife. Not bad."

When the big metal door buzzes, I breathe. I don't run. It feels like taking off too-tight pantyhose after a long day. Home.

We pause by Carrie, Morgan, and Rita—Morgan crocheting while half-watching TV; Carrie sitting with the grounded calm she radiates, the kind that steadies the air around her. These are the women who welcome us. Carrie's presence says, *Come in from the cold, darlin'.* Morgan would pour whiskey if she had it; instead she offers Wyler's limeade for our water.

"How'd the visits go?" they ask.

I need to tell someone. They're as good as it gets.

"Do you ever feel...so glad to make it back? Like—I love it here."

Without missing a beat, Carrie says, warm as a mother, "We love you, too."

Morgan adds, "I'm glad you feel that way. Not everyone does." I hear: Not everyone recognizes they've stumbled into heaven.

It's simple. Just love everything.

15

The Prison Monastery

"Girl, you were on TV."

Luciana said it like she was handing me a cupcake. Sweet, a little wicked. Nevaeh stood behind her, arms folded, eyes sparkling with trouble and delight.

"Bill Maher," Nevaeh chimed in, emphasizing the name, apparently impressed. "He did a bit. Your picture. Rachel's too."

They reenacted the segment from the night before, Bill Maher sneaking an easy joke on the recent verdict and the spiritual practice I taught, Orgasmic Meditation.

"'Orgasms and spirituality'?" Luciana quoted. "That's what they got you in here for?"

I swallowed. There it was—the pop of the bubble Rachel and I had been living in. We hadn't gone into specifics about our case or about ourselves.

I pasted on a smile, the kind you wear when you're not sure if the floor is about to give out. "Well," I said, aiming at lightness and landing near it, "I like Bill Maher."

Luciana waved it off. "Don't worry. We're on your side."

"Yeah." Nevaeh's eyes locked onto mine. "We got you."

Relief flooded in. Things are subtle in prison; it's not a place to let emotions out. But she had meant it. Luciana too.

It wasn't the first recognition we'd had since arriving at MDC. A few days ago, I saw a guard point us out to another CO. "That's them." Not hostile. Just...interested.

My lawyer had confirmed it later. "You and Rachel are designated 'high profile.'" She shrugged as we sat inside the glass-walled attorney rooms that line the visitation room downstairs. "It's boring in here. They read things. They Google. You're interesting." I'd felt my anonymity evaporate, my mind running through the calculations of what they might have read, what they might think of Rachel and I.

Those calculations started up again as Luciana gave a wink and she and Nevaeh headed back over to the TV, leaving us to wonder who else had seen the show.

We knew the gossip was about us by the looks in women's eyes on main line, waiting to get our lunch from the prison cafeteria. There was a felt shift in their glances—from curiosity about these strange women with Upper East Side style to warm eyes looking to someone who might be something more.

The loss of our precious anonymity turned out to be a good thing. In their newfound intrigue, some of the women realized I was the author of *The Art of Soulmaking* book they'd read.

"I heard that you're famous. I won't tell anyone. But I heard you have a book," T whispered to me.

"Shhh, don't tell anyone," I whispered back with a wink.

Word spread and others came asking for copies.

During recall, as we waited to be counted by our bunks, Nevaeh broached the subject.

"T said you got a book," she said, like we were making a drug deal—the implicit question being, "Can I have one?" We slipped into conversation as I looked for the copy of *The Art of Soulmaking* that I'd hidden in my locker. She told me more of her story, her dreams. "I think about how I'm gonna take care of these girls from outside," Nevaeh said, her eyes scanning the room but seeing something more, all the women she had come to know in the three prisons she'd spent her sentence between. She was counting down her days until she was out, but there was a sense of love in her voice, love for the women she'd served time with. Vulnerability like that is a precious offering in prison, letting the shield come down to reveal hope in a hopeless place.

Her pastor wants to ordain her when she gets out. It tracks. She was built for a flock. She moves people. When she's not doing that, she's playing poker or watching football. God, family, football. She plays poker as hard as she plays life.

I told her my vision—repurposing incarceration to be something greater than just punishment. The original vision I saw for *The Art of Soulmaking for the Incarcerated* and the book I wrote for the officers, *From Guards to Guardians*, was to transform prisons to monasteries, an experience that would actually be beneficial for the individuals within it and for society as a whole.

"I suppose it's ironic that now I'm an inmate," I joked to Nevaeh.

"Maybe." She paused. "But that's how it works too. You shake things up, they come for you."

I thought back to when the indictment against me first came out. Until then, the vision had been coming into form. What began as a correspondence course with pen pals on the outside writing back and forth with inmates at Central California Women's Facility—the largest women's prison in the world—had grown to over a thousand jails and prisons across the country. We partnered with our local jail in California, teaching classes and creating a garden that produced vegetables, eggs, and honey for their kitchen, all tended to by the inmates. CCWF invited us to develop in-unit programming for an entire dorm at the prison, introducing meditation and yoga into their daily schedule along with monthly training programs.

The indictment stopped that cold and we were removed from CCWF without explanation to the inmates. The prison cut them off from even participating in the correspondence course. Still, the program keeps growing with over 200,000 incarcerated people participating across the country. It's powerful to see the impact a book can have in the under-resourced environment of a prison.

"I started writing a new book," I told Nevaeh, "not just for inmates but for women outside too, for anyone locked in an inner prison. Anyone who feels at the mercy of anything."

The problem most women face is they don't recognize their value, so they sit out. We're told the best a woman can be is the untouched virgin. But women who choose to engage fully with life—leaders and warriors—get dismissed or derided. These are the women who have a real experience of life and have met the obstacles that come with that. And they have not shied away from those obstacles, nor shrank back into quiet submission in the face of them.

The systems of the world like to reward those who bend to their force and hand over their power. Act out, and they'll threaten to take it all away. But freedom's just another word for nothing left to lose. Incarcerated women, shackled and led into these prison walls under the scornful glare of polite society, are set free from those threats and expectations. The wisdom and power they hold is their own, beholden to no one. This is the unseen gift, the jewel hidden under lock and key of a federal penitentiary. This is what I hope to share.

As the guard came by to count us, Luciana got her attention. "Oh hey, Miss Q," she said, addressing the armored officer like a schoolteacher. "Yeah, that's Nicole—the one who made that guards program you did."

Recognition clicked across Miss Q's face as my eyebrows popped. "Oh, you're the one who wrote that book?"

She remembered doing the Guards to Guardians program I'd built for correctional officers years before becoming their ward. She asked if I was teaching meditation to the women here. I could feel the stirring begin.

16

Nevaeh

When we first arrived, I thought Nevaeh was a bit dozy given the amount of time she spent napping in her bunk, until one day, as she walked by, she said to me, "I overheard that conversation you had with Monica. You were right. I told her so." She'd been keeping one eye open, vetting the newbies to see if we matched her metrics.

Since then, she's offered the kind of protection that can only be earned. She's always looking to answer her question of, "Are you for real?" As in, are you who you say who you are? Do you talk one way with these people and another with those? She vets hard but once she gives the thumbs-up, you know you're in good company.

I watch her the way she watches me. My closest friends are scattered around the globe; many I've never met in person. We ask a different question: Do you have what it takes to change the world? The fearlessness, compassion, skill, grit, humor, intimacy. The ability to follow your compass, no matter what.

A few days after Nevaeh started *The Art of Soulmaking* workbook I'd lent her, I thought of some questions for her. The book is structured with readings followed by integration exercises to have readers uncover parts of themselves they don't always look at. Since we'd both passed each other's vetting process, I decided to go for it. I walked over to her bunk and handed her a paper. "You might not speak to me after reading this, but here."

You said twice that someone said that you are brilliant *and* lazy. What is the source of your laziness if you follow it back to the origin? What would your life look and feel like if that quality were lifted? I don't know the rules about such things but if you made the vow, "no matter what," I'd back you.

She came over to me a few minutes later with tears in her eyes and said, "I'm not gonna cry." Then mouthed the words, "Thank you."

Later that day, I found her response on my bunk.

1. The laziness comes from my college professors.

2. If laziness went away, my life would be more structured and disciplined. I was spoiled growing up the youngest in my family. My mother emphasized education but I didn't have to do any chores. I was intellectually smart, exceptional. I could get A's without working hard. I cut corners a lot which led to my destruction.

It's always a risk to touch those vulnerable places. You can hear the sensation as you get close, the extra acceleration in how someone may mention a topic before glossing over it without going deeper. But Nevaeh had played back. I left her another note:

And if you were more structured and disciplined?

I was sitting on my bed when she came over this time, paper in hand. It stayed folded as she took a seat next to me.

"I'd be working on Capitol Hill," she verbalized her response now. "Maybe a senator or a congresswoman. I have a degree in Criminal Justice. I wanted to be an attorney, a prosecutor actually. I did an internship at probation and parole. But then I saw how bad felons were being mistreated, and that the majority of them were African American. Then one day they're bringing in somebody for a probation violation report—it was my cousin who was addicted to heroin. I was the one who had to write up the report. I was devastated. I left not too long after, got a sales job instead."

She continued on, telling me about growing up in the church, how it was her whole childhood. She became church secretary as soon as she could hold a pencil. All-day Sunday services, then cleaning the sanctuary on Monday, choir on Tuesday, Bible study Wednesday, board meetings on Thursday, missionary work Friday, choir again Saturday. She loved God, and Jesus, Mary, Joseph, Peter, Paul. Really, she loved everyone in the Bible. But then her body started waking up.

"My hormones were racing out of control and no one at church explained what to do about any of that," she said, rolling her eyes. "Other than don't kiss a boy because if you do you're going to end up pregnant. And don't kiss a girl or you're going straight to hell with gasoline drawers on. No forgiveness for that."

I could imagine her, 15 years old, burning in a church pew. I could feel the intensity in her sitting across from me, those two forces aimed against each other: desire, and everything the world does to try to force it down.

"My favorite verse is I Corinthians 13:4-8: 'Love is patient and kind, love does not envy or boast, it is not arrogant or rude. It does not insist on its own way, it is not irritable or resentful, it does not rejoice at wrongdoing, but rejoices with the truth. Love bears all things, believes all things, hopes all things, love never ends.'" Her eyes closed, chin nodding in time with the rhythm. "And, here I am, an impatient, erratic, arrogant, boastful, proudful, irritable, resentful woman who rejoices in wrongdoing and all in the name of love. I'm enduring a lot of bullshit in the name of love. Love for who? Love for what?" Her exasperation looked around for an answer. "Like really, what the fuck? Love is within and it moves through me, but it took me a long-ass time to realize and recognize love."

"What's it feel like when you recognize it?" I asked, grateful for the river beginning to pour out from behind the door she had kept closed so long.

"Oh, you know what that was like." She smiled, settling into the flow. She went on to tell me her love story. "Everybody sends a stand-in to the first date. I sent in my 'sweet Southern church girl.' He sent his 'quiet provider with a strong backbone.' Time goes by and the real ones arrive. That was my toilet-bowl boyfriend."

"Your...wait, what?" I asked, laughing, not quite sure I'd heard her right.

"Oh, he hates when I call him that," she replied, laughing along with me. "He's always saying, 'I have a name!' It was when I was locked up in Philly, it's an old building. People talk through the plumbing. You flush first so the line clears. Then you lean in and sound carries through the pipes, cell to cell. At first all you get is a voice and a tone. You can lie about the facts but you cannot fake that electricity. That is how I met him.

"Eventually, we got to know who we really are. I cuss and yell. Turns out he's soft and tender. I yell at him but he does not yell back. He says, 'Okay, baby, calm down, I got you.'" She laughed from low in her throat. "Tender. Tender like dough."

"He's a good one," she said, "they're not all like that. I'm in here because of another man. My first love. It was a whirlwind romance." She paused, remembering. "But that whirlwind ended with an indictment."

I nodded. It wasn't the first story I'd heard like this, a wayward romance that ended up somewhere those first innocent flirtations couldn't have guessed.

"My lawyer comes in with that indictment and it says in bold letters *United States of America vs. Nevaeh Chris.* All I could think was, *How the fuck the whole U.S. government versus me?* I got convicted. Sat in court while the judge called me a 'master manipulator.'"

"You get remanded to prison on the spot?" I asked.

"Nah, they gave me some time before I had to turn myself in." She heaved a sigh. "My daddy was scared to be late. We drove in days early and waited in a motel like we were catching a flight we could not miss. We bought toiletries I couldn't bring in with me. We took shots we should not have taken. Still had tequila on my breath when I turned myself in. They put me through the drill and parked me where they could keep an eye on me until I sobered up. The women made space, told me it would be alright, and it was. Not easy, but alright."

Nevaeh shook her head at the memory. "Last time the Feds came, I acted like I did not care. Told myself I was camp status, easy road. Pride talking. God does not love that version of me. I do not either." She paused, letting it sink in. "County held me. Philly held me. None of it broke me. It did scrape off the shine in the places that needed it. I realized I was running from charge. Not the kind on paper. The kind that flows through you when you are supposed to stand in the front and take the heat. Leaders get looked at. I didn't want the eyes. But the eyes came anyway."

"You still carry that charge," I said to her, my voice steady. I could feel it sitting with her, listening to her story. That same undeniable charge that coursed through her from that little girl at the church all the way to now.

"I tell people I do not like women. Truth is I love women. There is a difference. My spirit mama told me there was oil on my head."

She caught herself and translated. "Anointed. She meant I have a responsibility on me whether I sign up or not. When I do what I know is right, I can sleep. When I run my own hustle, the night grows teeth."

She looked down at the paper she was still holding in her hand. "If I tighten the bolts, the lazy knot loosens. I know exactly what happens. I get structure. I get discipline. I make the speech I have seen in my head for twenty years to a room full of women I did not think I even liked. Turns out I am a popular loner," she added, amused. "I can be quiet in a crowd and still hold the room. I can walk into any yard and be okay." She met my eyes and let the words land without decoration. "I can be or do anything." She said it as fact, not charm.

Her hand went suddenly to her thigh. "I keep feeling like my phone is vibrating in my pocket. I haven't had a phone in almost two years. But suddenly, I feel it all the time."

"It's almost like home's calling," I mused. If I'd been talking to someone else, they might think I'm crazy. But I knew she'd know what I meant.

"Yeah," she said. "And this time, when I answer the call, I do it the right way. I submit to what I know is right, not just whatever is loudest." She slipped the folded paper into the pocket of her sweatpants and stood, steady and unhurried, like she had already begun.

17

The Undercover Trinity

I cannot overstate how much MDC Brooklyn feels like an inner-city elementary school. The women have an outsized fear of being "sent to the principal's office," the principal being a forty-something Black woman who, out of uniform, could just as easily be featured in an MTV music video instead of working security. She has the presence for it. In a different life, she'd wear a sexy knockoff cop uniform, bark a few orders, and people would both swoon and behave.

Here, the role is real and the presence is sharper. When she walks in, everyone snaps to attention. That's not a suggestion. Her baseline expression is permanent exasperation, but there's a wink under it for the women who have learned to read her. First you see authority; only if you're brave enough to keep eye contact do you see "beautiful woman."

My first run-in with her happened when I wasn't even in the room. I'd hung my towel on the end of my bed, like the other women do, so it could dry. What I didn't know is that they do that during the day, not at night. When I got back from the gym, my towel was folded on top of my mattress.

"Smith came in, pulled it down, and left it on the floor," Nevaeh told me. "You don't wanna be drying yourself off with that. I just picked it up."

Lesson number thirty-two at MDC: it's not personal. Fortunately, I'd already learned that one. When the women looked to see how I'd respond, I let it go.

"It's all like sorority hazing, isn't it?" I said, laughing it off. I knew that if I took it personally, even a little, I'd carry a tiny charge of "againstness" into every future interaction. That is not something you want in a place where, as one guard told me, "We have to notice down to a hangnail because everyone's life is in jeopardy constantly."

Not long after that, not yet hip to the rules, Rachel and I made a bigger mistake. We didn't realize you can only wear your grey sweatsuits on weekends. So on a Tuesday, there we were, parading down the hall in our greys like we were flaunting a dress-code violation.

"Where is your uniform?" a voice barked from an office.

We stopped like we'd been tased, then bolted back to the dorm. Luci was standing in the aisle, laughing at something I didn't understand yet. Breathless, I blurted, "Oh God, we got in trouble. We just got yelled at for not wearing our uniforms."

"Oh yeah, it's Tuesday," she said, like, *Oops, forgot to mention that part.*

"It's Tuesday," I repeated, dragging the word out like it was a federal charge all on its own.

"Don't worry," she said. "No biggie. Happened to all of us."

You don't realize that inside your five-decade-old body lives a perfectly intact twelve-year-old, terrified of being told to "stay after school." Only here, "after school" is solitary, where the water is rumored to run yellow and the toilet isn't even behind a door.

Luci later told me she'd told Smith about our near heart attack, and that Smith had howled with laughter. I didn't bother to hide my *harumph*. What I did try to hide was my reflex to hide, period. Any time I heard the jangle of keys that meant an officer was entering the dorm, I felt like a dog diving under the couch. I'd race to my bunk, pull out a book, and try to disappear.

That worked until destiny walked in wearing hot-pink lipstick. Topeka was coming to the prison.

Before MDC, I knew Topeka K. Sam as one of those women who escape the zoo and then go back with bolt cutters. She had done time at Danbury women's federal prison, taken full ownership of her part in the whole mess, and turned that reckoning into a calling. After she came home, she founded The Ladies of Hope Ministries (LOHM), a web of housing, reentry programs, and leadership training for women coming out of prison. She can move from pulpit to policy meeting to corner stoop without changing her voice, carrying both a pastor's heart and a hustler's stamina.

Topeka is my twin, if my twin were a hot-pink-lipstick-wearing, formerly incarcerated, force-of-nature activist. Our souls are cut from the same cloth. Two women who have always been "too much" in any room found "just right" in each other.

There was going to be a resource fair in the prison gym, a lineup of organizations that support justice-impacted people. Of course Topeka would be there with LOHM. In my old life, I would have been set up at the next table with my nonprofit, the Unconditional Freedom Project.

But no. This time, I was on the inside of the fence.

I took a breath and asked the officer who was signing women up for the event if I could go. He's the kind of man you'd define entirely by his eye twinkle. I don't know how he's done this job for two decades—listening to our stories of woe—and still manages to make you feel like you're walking into an amusement park when you see him. It was solely because of his warmth that I had the courage to ask to go. His kindness softened the intimidation of deliberately walking into the principal's office.

He was genuinely sad to tell me no. I nodded like it was fine, because I had expected it. Then I went back to my yoga mat while the other women, excited for the candy they'd get for attending, lined up to go see *my* friend.

There I was, yoga-ing away on the dorm floor with Rach while Topeka set up her table in the gym, when a fierce, funny guard burst in, yelled our last names, and jerked her thumb.

"Come on," she said.

She marched Rachel and me down the hall and into Smith's office. We stood there like two snot-nosed kids who weren't sure what we'd done this time.

"You know this Topeka?" Smith asked.

"Yes, ma'am," we said, in unison.

"I looked at your case," she said. "Doesn't seem to have anything to do with this woman. You wanna go?"

I couldn't help it—I lit up. If I hadn't been in prison, I might have actually levitated. Instead I tried to keep it to a human level of joy. Topeka is my oxygen. I was about to get to breathe for the first time since I arrived.

Smith watched me ride the edge between hysteria, laughter, and tears. To protect my dignity, she put a firm lid on the moment.

"Well, alright, go on now," she said, catching my eye just long enough for me to give her a nod that meant, *You just saved my life.* She received it with her own small look that said, *I got you.*

One of the biggest challenges I faced walking into MDC was that, before I ever got here, I had spent years building Unconditional Freedom, the nonprofit I started to test a stubborn belief: that people are not the worst thing they've done, and that the places our culture throws away—prisons, jails, encampments, the food-insecure corners of our cities—could become monasteries in disguise. With programs like The Art of Soulmaking for incarcerated people, Guards to Guardians for corrections officers, and Free Food for folks who are hungry in both body and dignity, we tried to give everyone on both sides of the bars real practices, real responsibility, and a real way to contribute. My job on the outside was to see the best in everyone and build systems around that faith.

So at MDC, my challenge is different from many of the women around me. I have written books, designed curricula, stood on stages talking about the inherent goodness buried under all this mess. I didn't want to be wrong about people—not about the women, and not about the officers. Sure, the women here give me a run for my money. But I had assumed if anyone, it would be the officers who would finally break my worldview, that they'd be the ones to prove my faith naïve. What I've discovered instead is that some of the deepest confirmations of that faith have come through them. They are, in fact, hidden jewels in uniform—people whose real care runs underground, beneath the role they have to play.

And it is moments, flashes like Smith's nod, that confirm all of it.

Walking into that gym to see Topeka was like coming out of anesthesia and remembering who you are. You wiggle your fingers and toes, realize everything still works, and feel a ridiculous, overwhelming gratitude just to be alive and intact. We met in the middle of that gym and both started crying. It didn't matter that we were under fluorescent lights next to a folding table stacked with pamphlets. For a few minutes, it felt like the world had snapped back into its proper shape.

Apparently, word traveled fast. I introduced every single woman I could to Topeka as if I were showing off my sister and my hero at the same time. I told her what they were up against and what they needed to succeed. Nevaeh needed a correspondence-ministry program for when she got out. Allison needed transitional housing, not just a bus ticket. It's rare to have a hero and a sister in one person. I was so proud to share Topeka with my new friends.

Of course, the tears came right when I'd have preferred to look composed.

Later that afternoon, the twinkly-eyed officer walked into the dorm.

"You have a good time?" he asked, a little smile hiding in the corner of his mouth.

"Yeah," I said, trying not to cry again. "I really did."

"Well, good," he said. "Smith did you right."

Without thinking, I did what I would do on the outside when I'm overwhelmed with gratitude: I put my hands together in a bow. It was automatic, a small gesture of reverence. He took it in, eyes sparkling in that way he has that says, *Okay, that's enough now*, but he let it land. He seemed to understand it was something I needed to do for myself as much as for him.

Not long after that, the third member of what I started calling my Undercover Trinity showed up. He's the ultra-Brooklyn kind of guy you picture when you hear "I wanted to make a difference; I couldn't just sit on the sidelines." Cute Adidas, jeans, easy swagger. He looks like someone who should be running a community arts program, not walking tiers in a federal facility, which somehow makes him even more effective.

Because he doesn't fit the stereotype, people underestimate him. They discount what it took for him to choose this job and stick with it. As a result, he knows how to slip small acts of humanity through the cracks in the system. He's the one quietly rearranging a schedule so a woman can make a key phone call, or bending just enough on a rule to keep the dorm from boiling over. He has that rare capacity to work inside the machine without becoming the machine.

One afternoon, he had to call me out of one of the few classes they have here to tell me one of my legal documents had arrived. That kind of news is always a chest-clencher. It feels like the diagnosis just came in. You're suddenly naked, every nerve exposed, and it's hard to keep it together. But there I was in the dorm, where it's not wise to let the gravity of those moments out on display.

As if he knew I needed a beat to steady myself before I went back into the room, he just stood there with me for a second, holding the space without prying. Eventually he said, "You good?" That one second was enough for me to pull myself back in. That's how subtle every moment is in here. That's the level of care the real ones learn to track and offer. All three of them—Smith, the amusement-park officer, and the Adidas-wearing Brooklyn guy—are undercover in their own ways, carrying a deep, determined care beneath unlikely exteriors.

From the outside, it looks like every other federal jail: concrete, barbed wire, bureaucracy. From the inside, if you pay attention, it's a place where principals turn into guardians, and the people you were trained to fear turn out to be your allies.

As I keep discovering: Things are not as they appear in MDC Brooklyn.

18

A Room of One's Own

Rachel and I will meditate anywhere around the dorm, but at any moment, a gaggle of women can come crowing and cawing or a CO might come in and say they need the space. We do our best to find a quieter spot away from where the ladies happen to be. When we find a spot, we sit in our usual position, backs straight, hands resting.

TVs blare on different channels. Women shout out the windows to unseen men on other floors, or across the dorm to each other. The quiet makes us conspicuous as most manage the noise by joining it.

Sometimes, as they pass, they'll ask what we're doing.

"Meditating."

"Oh, I should try that," they say, and keep walking. Still, I feel their curiosity.

One day, as I looked for where it may be a little less populated, I noticed the craft room. We walked that way before discovering why.

There's a CO here, Miss G, who's a bit of an oddball, like me. Sensitive. I feel like I can tell by the way she listens to music. She also, along with another female officer and Santoro, buys cleaning supplies out of her own pockets. Their favorite is Fabuloso, a perfumed

91

cleaning product that comes in two flavors: "green" and "purple."

They use it to fight off the Eau de Old Meat that's baked into the dorm due to MDC deciding to go all natural when it comes to scent. Never mind that there's enough trash to qualify as a dump site, or that the aroma is so aggressive the birds outside practically fly backward. The presumption, as with most things here, is that your senses will eventually give up and flatline. For Rach and me, two women who spent decades training our sensing capacity, there isn't much hope. "Sensory assault" doesn't cover it.

But when she's overseeing the craft room, it's like there's an invisible gate around it. Women often complain she's too protective of the space. I was apprehensive. I didn't want to get into it with anyone. But what was I doing, withdrawing from a room perfectly suitable for meditation? We eased in. I could feel Miss G's care in every part of the room: the purple Fabuloso, the affirmations on the wall, the plastic flowers.

I could feel her sussing us out, catlike. No clue as to her conclusion—just that prickly sense of being watched even when a head is down. Then she smiled.

That smile felt like a small, private victory—not from reputation, not because she knew who I was. She was cautious, and in the face of that, without withdrawing and without asserting, I took my seat.

Then the miracle: She started cracking jokes. "What the heck are you guys doing? You're scaring the heck out of me!"

I laughed. "It's just meditation, I promise."

"That's what you're up to out there? You don't look relaxed."

"Well—relaxed but ready. It's not like going to sleep."

"Okay, so what do you do?"

I showed her how I sit to keep the curve of the spine so the energy flows, and how I hold my hands in the Zen position. She came over and tried it—eyes still on the room. The three of us sat there, the oddballs, while the sounds of the dorm rippled around our little bubble of quiet. One minute. Two.

She let out a long sigh and leaned back in her chair. "Okay. I'm here Monday through Friday. While I'm here, you use this room. Ten to two."

One of the better moments of my life. I'd bet my whole bank that in the craziness of prison—the personalities, the bumps, and bullies—if I keep my meditation, that will be how I make it through. You know those signs they sell at home stores—*It's humble, but it's home?* That's how I would come to feel about the craft room turned makeshift meditation room. It's the exact opposite of a formal meditation hall— and yet, in spirit, it's exactly the same. A true practice space is defined not by fancy cushions but by the steady care of the person who tends it.

Back at the bunks, we recounted the story to Luciana. Morgan overheard from her bunk and joined in the conversation. "When you first got here, none of us thought you'd make it. I'll be honest—when I saw you sitting like that, meditation? I was scared you were losing it or that you'd died or something. But you did it. You did it your way, and you made it in."

I could have danced through the dorm. That's the hope and the promise—that I don't have to change who I am to still be a part of. That this is how I make my contribution. How I relate to people. In the mix but not of it.

And, just to add to the miracles, it was baked chicken Thursday.

19

Fourth of July

I was at the computers when I heard it again—the women's frustration pointed at Janiya for "being annoying," as she belted her favorite Tina Turner, dancing her way from one end of the dorm to the other.

"You've got a big aura," I offered as she sauntered past me.

Janiya shrugged. "I'm just from the projects. That's just being me."

"Well, I like it." I smiled. And she smiled back.

That same sweetness echoed later when she showed up at my bunk with a Tupperware of prison-made banana pudding, the good kind: confetti-cookie insides, powdered milk, real bananas, a shake of cinnamon, and regular cookies from commissary. It was a gift, communication. That's how it works in here, and often through the medium of food. Food also defines the cliques: Am I sharing with you, or not?

It was the Fourth of July. Janiya was not alone in displaying her MDC culinary talents. Food piled high at every table, made from whatever the women had gathered together from their commissary supplies and what had come off the main line that day. The tilapia seemed like a bit of a gamble. I figured I'd skip and get to bed early.

Luciana: "You're not staying up to watch the fireworks???"

Me: "Where would we see them?"

Luciana: "On TV! They're my favorite."

Me (silently): I'll pass.

I was about to start my nightly regimen: flossing and brushing in the crowded bathroom, building a pillow out of my pants and top, rigging a sheet around my bunk like a tent. Miss Wu spotted me. "Enthusiasm" is too small a word. Her eyes were lit like sparklers.

"I make you sushi! You want sushi?" she said. I'd seen people beg her for it. She always waved them off: "Too much work, too much work." I knew this was an honor. I said yes.

She sprinted to her area and returned with plastic gloves and a hairnet. "I am sushi chef!"

And oh, was she. Plates don't exist in prison, so she used tray lids. Seeing her in a hairnet was like a bat signal; women drifted over with offerings—tilapia trays and a side that was technically green beans but closer to green-bean mash. Ten, maybe twelve trays. She arranged the fish into neat triangles on three lids. In a Tupperware bowl, she mixed rice with jalapeño juice to fake vinegar, then talked to the rice—looked up at me, delighted—as if telling me, *This is going to be very good.*

"No sushi roller, no problem!" She pulled out a clear garbage bag. As is the case with many things in prison, the excitement in her eyes with what she pulled out next did not compute immediately. Velveeta cheese. But, I've begun to realize that here things have their own logic. She cut it into precise shapes to match the fish—accountant-level precision. The books must balance; the cheese must mirror the fish. It was like a concentration game—find the perfect pair.

When her face clouded, which seemed to be due to there being too many shapes and not enough time, I offered to help. She flashed me a look that felt like a secret door sliding open. I'd stumbled onto the rule: Fill the need even if you don't fully understand it. While I cut,

95

she moved on to jalapeños.

Now we were ready. Rice, then fish, then cheese—all wrapped in plastic, pressed into compact bricks, each piece taking a full minute until it felt exactly right. She'd lift a finished piece, eyes asking, *Did you see that?*

At first I didn't. I saw prison fish and melty cheese pressed into rice—edible, sure, but not exactly transcendent. What I did see was the care. Michelin-star care, funneled through a hairnet.

We were an hour in. We were past my usual 8 p.m. bedtime and I still had my evening meditation ahead of me. But by then, word had spread.

"Are you making sushi, Miss Wu?" Women clutched their offering bowls and hovered. The question wasn't about sushi. It was: Can I have some of that thing you do? That thing that leaves us heady and clear at the same time?

Rach and I were the excuse to open shop. Donations formed a constellation around us. Tamara brought tuna and more rice. Amara brought the house spice. Two Latinas joined: one from Venezuela and one from Colombia who cried nonstop her first day until I handed her a turkey stick and some shampoo—the language that always translates. Now every time she sees me, she says, "*Hola*, Nicole," and I feel something in my chest unknot.

We built our circle. I contributed my terrible Spanish; they pretended it helped. Miss Wu showed us how to make "miso soup" without miso: mash the fish and green beans, add spice and bouillon, pour in hot water. I couldn't imagine it would taste like anything but fish, but that wasn't the point. In here, cooking requires imagination. These dishes are "suggestions"—and somehow, that makes them more satisfying.

Then the call rang out: recall. Back to the bunk area behind the blue line. We migrated the whole sushi bar to the empty bunk next to

Miss Wu's and turned it into a table. Twenty minutes later, we had a feast: tilapia sushi, spicy tuna sushi, regular tuna for the spice-averse, and the "miso."

"Eat! Eat!" Miss Wu commanded like an Italian nonna.

Amara, a veteran of Miss Wu's sushi nights, was already halfway through a piece and moaning like she'd remembered joy. I glanced at Rach: *Here goes*. We bit down together. The Velveeta turned the bite buttery and warm. The cooled fish was firm. The rice melted with a clean tang of jalapeño.

I remembered my Lama once telling me that when you glimpse what all this is for, the only sane response is delight. And now, here we were, seven women sitting around an empty grey bunk bed, eating cheese sushi in a place designed to starve the spirit. Miss Wu passed pieces down the row. Each woman looked chosen.

One piece remained. I asked if I could take it to Janiya. Miss Wu gave me that quick, shining look again. I understood, finally: The food was a ritual. Not holy words or incense—just a delivery system for love. It needed to go where love was needed most.

So there we were on Independence Day, a guard making sure we didn't cross a painted line on the floor, and inside the line we were celebrating a different kind of freedom—the kind that doesn't wait for permission.

20

Las Amas Organicas

E vening shift had just settled in when mail call started, the officer's voice moving down the rows with that tired end-of-day cadence everyone recognizes, the room too bright and too dull at the same time. I heard my name called. The officer held a thin envelope with Louise's handwriting on the front like a familiar face at the door. Louise is my friend Anjuli's mother. She's the kind of home cook who sends a recipe when everyone else sends a slogan, a set of instructions you can follow when your mind is loud and your hands need a job. Part of this experience of being in prison is that the diamonds in your life start throwing off more light; the good ones get brighter, and you see the cut and weight of them in ways you might have missed before.

My friend Anjuli is one of those diamonds. She makes no distinction between fighting for her life and fighting for yours; to her it is one motion. And she comes with a family who love in that same unbroken way—the kind of people who fold you in as if a place has always been set for you at their table. Her mother, Louise, the born chef, sends recipes tucked into envelopes like care packages. And her father, Ramani, writes me long, generous letters of encouragement, the kind that arrive like a steadying hand at the small of my back. I have all of this, in addition to my own mother, who keeps scrapbooks of our letters. Inside me, this love sits next to the fact that some women have no one to call, no weekend visits, no money on their books.

The recipes really started coming when Louise heard we finally had commissary. After a full week waiting for the money to clear so it would show up on our accounts, and then another week of commissary being closed for reasons no one bothered to explain, we were ready for basics: warmer clothes, Lipton tea, anything with real protein. On commissary day, some bunks look like a black-market swap meet—this one wants rice, that one wants coffee, another is hustling soup packets. The energy goes from scarcity Sunday to manna Monday in about ten minutes. One woman refused to let me pay her back for the shampoo she gave us when we arrived; she just gave me that tiny cartel nod you see in movies, and suddenly we had a shampoo pact. Tiny economies, tiny loyalties, all built on food and soap.

Rachel and I had planned our commissary list with the intensity of women prepping for a heist. Your connections on the outside can put up to $300 on your account, but you are only allowed to spend half of that per commissary order. You fill in the sheet with what you want and then hope you get it; you never know what's going to show up and what won't. We came back from our first trip carrying our loot: toiletries, snacks, sneakers, floss, a cheap digital watch for Rach so she could time our meditations, toilet paper, and of course food items—nuts, tuna, ramen, peanut butter, prison-issue chicken packets, bouillon cubes, Minute Rice, and mayo. Mayo: the backbone of prison meals. She's in everything, holding it all together, and nobody pretends otherwise.

Rach fastened the watch onto her wrist like she'd just been promoted to head monk.

Louise, who makes everything completely from scratch using ingredients from her own greenhouse and garden, understood the play immediately. We were making do with bags of meat and packaged goods, improvising like our lives depended on it. The moment she heard we had ingredients—even the prison versions—she started mailing recipes like lifelines.

Reading her chicken adobo recipe that evening, I could taste the flavors mixing together: vinegar for backbone, garlic for truth, something tender in the middle that only appears if you let time and heat do their work. "Let's make it," I told Rach, because when a lifeline shows up, you say yes.

We had no fresh chicken in sight, but we began to gather what we could: shelf-stable pouches, a jar of jalapeño brine, a few spices scrounged from neighboring bunks, Minute Rice in little cups. Rach pulled out her red commissary notebook—the same one she carried on the walking track—and flipped to a fresh page like she was about to conduct field research on an endangered bird. I teased her for being our divine scribe, but that notebook became our memory bank. While I watched the pot, she watched the room, catching the small, exact moments that might have slipped past—the joke someone cracked over the steam, the way the jalapeño vinegar hit the air, the offhand line that held a whole life. Recipes, stories the women would tell us, the bits of prison lingo they'd explain—Rachel's love would capture it word for word, true to life.

Allison noticed our efforts in the kitchen and drifted over with her quick eyes and steady hands, the kind of woman who can read a pot from across the room. She looked over the letter and said, "Marinate early, share with friends"—a recipe for life in its own right. She tasted a bit of the jalapeño vinegar, adjusted the ratio with a few shakes of garlic, and nodded like: *Now you're getting somewhere.*

We rinsed the chicken cubes with hot water from the spigot and covered them with the jalapeño vinegar. Rach crushed half a bouillon cube between her fingers, crumbling it onto the chicken. We folded in garlic and the closest thing we had to Italian herbs. The rice went into the microwave with just enough water to cover it. Rach insisted on adding a spoonful of mayo "for body," and honestly…she wasn't wrong.

Around us, the dorm kept its rhythm, a mix of bustle and patience, and I thought again how food here has a job that is bigger than calories. A woman will come back from court with her face emptied out by a judge's voice, and a warm drink appears at her bunk—mostly sugar, instant coffee, and love. Another woman is pinned by a migraine and a bowl of hot noodles shows up without ceremony. Dignity threads its way through this place in acts that look ordinary if you aren't paying attention.

While we waited for the marinade to do what marinade does, Allison told us pieces of her story, the way you hand over tools when someone asks for them. She'd raised cousins and then a nephew, ran a pop-up kitchen in Queens, missed one date she could not afford to miss, and ended up locked in here with a mind that still knows how to make food tell the truth.

Rach scribbled notes like she had been hired by Ken Burns. "I love her," she whispered, her cheeks bright with a smile.

When the rice was fluffy and the chicken had turned tender, we plated the food with what we had: rice, a ring of Miss Wu's pickled vegetables, chips for texture, and placed the chicken on top. We shared among the three of us. Rach hummed through her first spoonful like she was enjoying the tasting menu at a fine-dining restaurant. "Balanced," she said, "complex." Allison rolled her eyes, laughing with her hand over her mouth as she chewed, savoring the dish she'd helped engineer.

After that first adobo, Nevaeh nicknamed our corner *Las Amas*

Organicas, the Mothers of Real Food. Many of the women had their specialties—Dominican dishes, Soul Food, Miss Wu's sushi. Luciana could turn the basics off the main line into a meal that tasted like it came with a farm-to-table surcharge. Rach and I quickly became known for making things as healthy as humanly possible in a place with no fresh air, no sun, and ingredients fresh from the can, far removed from a garden.

We sent our "MDC knockoff" recipes back to Louise, to answer love with our own careful effort, to say "we hear you. We are here." Rach kept saying we should write a cookbook with these women, that the things they made out of mackerel, Doritos, faith, and creativity were too good to stay inside these walls. She sketched in the margins—*Eat, Pray, Commissary: The Joy of Correctional Cooking*.

When the bowls were empty and everything put away, I kept thinking that the recipes we are keeping are not just for food; they are blueprints for how to stay human here. Marinate early in what helps. Share with friends. Treat what you have as enough so it can become enough. And keep a language alive that lets you say the hard things without needing words—a language made of heat, salt, time, and the quiet relief of a bowl set in your hands when you didn't know how to ask.

Rach wrote that down too—because she knew someday we'd want to remember.

21

Chicken Adobo with Friends

There are two things to know about this dish: First, the longer you let the chicken marinate, the better; and second, prison food is always better shared with friends.

Serves: 3
Prep Time: 20-25 minutes
Marinating Time: 2-4 hours
Cook Time: 10 minutes
Ingredients

- 3 packages of Brushy Creek Premium Chunk White Chicken
- 1 jar of El Pato Jalapeño Wheels
- Spice Supreme Garlic Powder
- Spice Supreme Italian Seasoning
- 1½ Spice Supreme Bouillon Cubes, divided
- 3½ applesauce containers of Minute White Rice
- Keefe Kitchen Mayonnaise
- 1 bag of The Whole Shabang potato chips
- 1 jar of Miss Wu's Szechuan pickled vegetables
- Salt and pepper shakers

Supplies

- 2 Tupperware containers with lids
- 4 plastic sporks
- 1 empty applesauce container (to measure the rice)
- 3 bowls

1. Marinate the chicken.

You'll want the chicken to marinate for a minimum of two and up to four hours, so start your prep early. First, prepare the chicken. Open each bag, squeeze out all the liquid, then pour hot water from the spigot into the first bag until it's about two-thirds full. Let it soak for about a minute, then squeeze out all the water. Empty the bag into your Tupperware. Repeat this process with the remaining two bags of chicken. Once all the chicken cubes are in the Tupperware, pour in the full jar of vinegar from the El Pato Jalapeño Wheels (just the vinegar—not the jalapeños).

Add about a quarter-size amount each of pepper, garlic powder, and Italian seasoning, plus one crushed bouillon cube. Mix the chicken with the seasonings, stirring slowly so the pieces don't break apart. Once everything is combined, put the lid on the Tupperware and give it three good shakes while still being gentle with the chicken. Place the container somewhere safe to marinate. This can be in your locker or a spare metal bed. Marinate the chicken as long as possible.

2. Cook the rice.

About fifteen minutes before you're ready to eat, prepare the rice. Use your applesauce containers to measure 3½ containers of rice into the second Tupperware. Add 2 small dollops of mayo, ½ bouillon cube, and 2 jalapeños.

Bring the Tupperware to the hot water spigot and put in enough hot water to just cover the top of the rice. Important note: Do not fill the entire container with water, as that will make a soup; you are only putting in enough water so all of the rice is submerged. Mix everything together and pat the rice down so it's flat and fully in the water. Place the container in the microwave uncovered for three minutes. Stir the rice and cook for an additional two minutes (five minutes total). Taste and check that the rice is fluffy and cooked. If there is any remaining water, put it into the microwave again for two minutes.

Once the rice is cooked, add a bit of salt, stir, and taste. Less is always more when cooking in prison, so start with small amounts and increase as you go.

3. Build your bowls.

Divide the rice equally among the three bowls. Add Miss Wu's pickled vegetables around the edges of the bowl. Place some Shabang chips on top of the rice, and finally put the chicken on top of the chips.

Say your favorite mealtime prayer, and *bon appétit*! Make sure you have all the elements—rice, chips, veggies, and chicken—in each bite.

22

The Wheel Turns

"Scarcity is like a phantom that hypnotizes." That line keeps ringing. I can feel myself again—moving through the day from practice to people, from trying to say what I see to simply being a body in a bed, not performing for anyone. Just essence.

This morning was a turn of the wheel. Rach came to my bunk: "Amara is leaving."

Amara has always been a bridge here—the first woman to stride in with that big, booming voice and the don't-mess-with-me posture. "I ain't that kinda—nah, I'm Muslim," she'd say, then grin and announce to the room, "Y'all my favorite white girls." I'd tease back, "Drop the 'white girls' part and admit it—we're just your favorites." She worried I'd think she was being racist, which was funny. "No, no, I'm joking," I told her. She squinted at me, then laughed. "Ahhh, you alright, Housewife."

No one here ever really knows what's next for them when they leave. We don't know if she's going to a longer-term facility (probably) or home (less likely). Rach, Mari, and I helped her pack. I realized we'd somehow become the unofficial morning crew for transitions. We're the ones awake early.

It reminds me of what I heard about farm life: If you keep animals, you learn the circle of life up close. That's how it is here. People move, disappear, reappear. The lines marking the social divisions of the dorm get drawn and then redrawn every day. We thought Alyssa was out; then she was back. Everything shifts. Nothing is certain.

I was reading a book on meditation, it said there's "no single cause" for anything. That line lit a fuse in me. The world loves simple stories: one cause, one culprit. But suffering is a system—a web that's got all of us by the scruff of the neck. We're each tugging on our own knot, too consumed to notice the whole net.

There's this raw, lucid awareness underneath all our roles and reputations. They call it "one taste"—meaning everything belongs to the same open field of experience. It's not "beyond ethics" like ethics don't matter; it's beyond the shame-and-punishment reflex that keeps us from seeing each other. That's how I can sit in here and meet the woman under the conviction, the person beneath the crew she runs with.

Sometimes I hear someone's charges and, yes, I flinch. I don't choose to care for them in spite of the charges or the risk they could turn on me. I care *with* all of it in view. Neither naïve nor jaded. Who is this woman to me right now, in this breath?

So I work the aperture: When someone feels slippery, I give space; when they feel real, I move closer. Offer warmth; don't get pulled into the tornado. Because the tornado? It will not set you down gently.

A few days later, the air in the dorm went wavy, like heat over asphalt. Some new women had arrived. Miriam, Josie, and Dakina. "That's her," Luciana hissed. "Dakina's back." I realized she was the woman with that ungovernable hunger for flight that Luciana had done an imitation of a few weeks before, arms outstretched, shaking and howling.

Dakina was all angles and electricity: hair sprung like a crown, eyes bright as polished bone, body moving sideways like a wary wolf. Her first sound was a bellow that rolled through the bunks. Officers steered her to Row Ten—Royal's row, the farthest corner. I've always envied that row. It's quiet, almost monastic. Royal sleeps by day and reads by night. If not for my bunkmates, I'd ask to switch.

That night there was a new rhythm in the dorm: *thud-thud-thud*, as if someone tossed sneakers in a dryer. We peeked down the aisle to see Dakina sprinting on her top bunk—knees high, arms pumping— running in place, full tilt on the metal bed. Preparing for flight.

23

Pink Handcuffs

Here's my quandary: I am, in so many ways, happy where I am. That's the honest truth. And yet a voice keeps asking—am I doing harm by not fighting harder? What message does my being in prison send to the world?

I once told a friend, "I could be happy anywhere. Some people did more justice work from prison than outside." He answered, gently but firmly, "Those were men. Women—especially sexual women—are already presumed guilty." His point wasn't subtle: The culture has so little imagination for an unapologetically sexual woman's innocence that anything I say might bounce off armor.

I'm not sure he's entirely right. There is a powerful cohort of women who see what's happening. They sense that the next turn of feminism is not more bubble wrap; it's cutting the bubble wrap off. It's seeing "protected status" for what it often is—pink handcuffs. It's unmasking the soft bias of low expectations: You're fragile. You're special. Sit still. We'll handle this.

The price of that protection is your power.

This is where we've been stuck since Gloria Steinem: revving the engine of fragility in a mud ditch. But I think we're in the death throes of the collective female ego—the part that believes our safety depends on smallness. When that story unravels, the knot comes loose and there we are underneath it: the ones who hold the power. If the convulsions feel violent, it's because a system is dying hard.

The entrenched, establishment version of feminism—the one that sometimes feels like misogyny in a pantsuit—has long profited from our "original weakness." If we discovered the ruse, the economy of our brokenness would shudder: fewer women medicated into numbness, fewer drinking with the other "broken girls," fewer buying empowerment like a handbag, fewer feeding the self-help-and-trauma industrial complex. Imagine the upheaval if women collectively remembered: We are not problems to be managed; we are forces to be reckoned with.

Why don't we just walk? Stockholm syndrome helps explain it. The pink-handcuff bargain offers housing, food, a script. Relinquish your rights, take your pills (you must be broken), live at an approved temperature (not too hot, not too cold), and stay cute and compliant. Get called a fox, a pussy, catty, a cougar, a bitch—pet or predator depending on the lighting—and learn to rub up against the hand that feeds you. Step out of line and you're the "bad animal." Back in the cage. The crowd came for a zoo show, not a jailbreak.

Here's the cruel brilliance of the design, something the Stanford Prison Experiment and prison itself both taught me: Make power scarce and deputize a few women to police the rest. Some will become colder and more punitive than any man. The man at the top stays hands-off while the women of the "inferior class" fight each other for a thimbleful of status. We circle the wagons and aim inward. Welcome to the realm of the jealous gods.

I heard that a few female "empowerment" teachers were gleeful about my incarceration. Textbook. That's the lab-made virus: Keep women separate at any cost by insisting there's only one position available—one grant, one seat at the table, one "good girl." Infect us with paranoid status-protection so we forget our interdependence. Because if we ever remembered that what happens to you *happens to me*, the locks would rust and fall.

Until we see that, we stay chained together—each tugging the other's fetter.

There is, to me, one way off the merry-go-round of victim/savior/ perpetrator: Be *for*. Be for women. Be for the truth. Be for the next brave thing. Prison is a magnified version of the outer world, an inner sanctum where you see it all up close. I marvel at the amount of belly laughter—middle-of-the-night, uncontained, body-shaking laughter. I marvel at the way food gets prepared and shared like communion. When a new woman arrives, sobbing and unable to get out of bed, someone always shakes her shoulder and says, "Come sit with us." I've been in spiritual communities that couldn't improvise love like that. Here, it can save your life.

And—because we're still human—you also see the pile-on. The brown-nosing. The background hum of character assassination. Tall poppy syndrome is alive and well. In here, "having more" might mean she scored extra creamers or cleans the visiting room and gets time out of the dorm. She must be "right-sized" when she returns. Sympathetic joy is still in short supply, and jealousy tears us apart faster than any lock and key.

The most painful part? It is often the female guards who are the harshest. Not all—some are deeply compassionate—but too many wield cruelty like a passport, desperate to separate themselves from the stigma of the "wild, dangerous woman" they're policing. It's as if they have to prove, over and over, "I'm not *her*."

And yet—even here—there is a paradoxical freedom. For all the confinement, we are not constantly asked to button our girdles and make our faces acceptable. The wild shows through our cracks.

Sometimes I want to say to the women who are cruelest, "You might be excellent at your role, but there is a violation deeper than any rule—don't forget you are a woman." I don't say it. I witness instead. I practice being sunlight so the black mold of feminine self-loathing doesn't spread in the dark. Witnessing isn't passive; it's a disinfectant.

So this is where I land in my quandary: I can be happy here, and I can hold a line. I can honor the joy—yes, *joy*—that keeps breaking through, and I can refuse the story that women are fragile creatures who need to be herded and hushed. I can be for the women in this dorm, for the women who think they hate me, for the women who will never meet me, for the women who will be punished for daring to laugh too loud.

If I'm sending any message by being here, let it be this: The pink handcuffs are not protection; they are props. Take them off, and your hands are free. Free to cook for each other. Free to tell the truth. Free to hold the line when scarcity hisses in your ear. Free to throw your head back and laugh like the whole dorm is your cathedral.

Free to remember what we forgot: We are not waiting to be saved. We are practicing being sovereign—together.

24

Generosity

I was in Mongolia when I learned I had been indicted. The call came at 2:30 in the morning. The tour scrambled plans to get me back to the city so I could catch a flight back to New York. I spent the night vomiting, then someone arranged a *mo*, a divination reading with a Tibetan oracle. Strings were pulled—this was not something taken lightly. Reading the signs, the oracle declared, "It will be difficult but you will be born into supreme happiness." In the altitude I have since been launched into, that sentence has been the only thing to which I could hold.

The bad news is you are falling through the sky; the good news is there is no ground. The indictment came two and a half years ago. I spent the time since preparing for impact, surprised to find there was none. Only now am I learning to ride the current without fighting, to let the air carry me.

I asked my Lama to be straight with me. "Please tell me the oracle doesn't just mean spiritual peace. Tell me it includes what happens in the physical world." He laughed. I took it as a yes. I am writing this from prison, so apparently not. And yet.

My Zen friend Ed always shares poems. I have found myself guided through life by one of his favorites, William Stafford's "The Way It Is." As it says, "There is a thread you follow…" I followed it here. Now it is the season of the "marvelous error," the kind that makes a woman who rarely cries lie in bed with tears clinging at the corners of her eyes. The kind of tears you cry on the peak of LSD when the curtain of the ordinary, even the curtain of the extraordinary-ordinary, is pulled back. In one golden shock, love stands in front of you and nothing is the same. The clock cannot be turned back.

Of course you try to tell people. You try to sing the gospel of what split your life open, the truth that the faded, get-through-it version of living is not all there is.

My meditation lately has been like that. If it were sex, I would smoke a cigarette after. Presence without absence. The membrane thins and I fall through into the next astonishment. The only thing that slows me is the urge to pause and look around. Effulgence is a big word, but it fits. There is no grasping, only awe.

My favorite place right now is my little tented bunk—sheets clipped up to block the light, a thin foam pad on metal, a sweatpants pillow. Cozy, warm, sheltered. My mind fills the space because there isn't much space to fill. I love it more than my very comfortable bed at home with the linen duvet and soft flannel sheets. Here, I have a weightless feeling—my yoke loose, my burden light.

The visions come in so powerfully. I keep visiting a basement. Last night I felt as if something were turning on inside of me. A familiar heat. Light pouring in. I felt protected, like someone was standing guard so I could do the quiet, underground work I'm here to do: set a clear intention, then let the current move through it into the power of the women around me.

Then came a place I have not touched before, neither sleep nor meditation nor lucid dream; realer than real. I would call it distance-viewing. I was sky, watching myself on red earth. The Dalai Lama, the head of Tibetan Buddhism, pressed his forehead to mine. A current like a rainbow, not pastel but jewel-deep, poured into my mind. My whole being drank. He pulled back with laughing eyes that seemed to say, "There, now is that not fun?" Not "You are okay," not "This will be okay." Something far beyond comfort. Play.

Like a little girl being tossed and caught by her father, I said, "Do it again." He did, again and again, until doubt had no room left. When he pulled away, I saw an indentation at his brow that matched mine. I understood it to mean this is available whenever I am available.

Things are shaking loose from concepts. I was washing my hands and there was Janiya beside me at the sink. Suddenly the face of my guide from an acid trip thirty years ago washed over hers. In a flash I understood it in what felt like spherical time, a sense that events are stacked rather than lined up. The pull to care for her now was part of the pull to learn then. Time and space dropped their cubicle walls. I also saw why people need preparation or they can lose their minds. The universe is generous. It will show you everything. Everything, all at once, can drown you. This is why you work through the greed impulse that always wants more: more visions, more powers, more proof. Yes, it is fun at another magnitude, but get tossed in the air enough times and you will vomit, no matter how much you laugh.

Then came another kind of beauty. Mari loaned us shorts and tea when we first arrived and had nothing. She is the de facto chef, presiding at a central table where a cohort gathers. She remixes whatever we are served into something edible. Spiced chicken gets washed and re-seasoned. Hard potatoes become mashed. Questionable coleslaw gets rinsed and turned into tuna cakes. She is not specifically tender to us, more a sideways curiosity. Mari is famous for cappuccinos. When someone returns from court without bail, or when Royal's back is aching and she cannot get out of bed, the cappuccino appears. The fact that it is basically sugar, instant coffee, and powdered creamer is beside the point. It has sweetness, energy, and something that passes for milk. I have watched women make the pilgrimage to her bunk and leave revived, alive.

Rachel and I owed her for the tea. We also wanted to thank her for the way she takes care of this place. We brought her a trio: coffee, cappuccino mix, and creamer. "No, you guys, I cannot," she said, which is exactly how the generous act when you try to repay them. Prison economics matter, so I named everyone who had helped us and said this was for the table, not for her alone.

"You look out for all of us," the women said from their bunks. Her melting melted us. Giving really is addictive. What had been cool turned warm.

The night I had the Dalai Lama dream, I woke around three in the morning to pee. On the way back I saw an Indian woman sitting on her bed with tea. She was about my age with long, thick black hair, onyx eyes, a subtle head tilt. She looked like an apparition, terrified on her first night inside. Luciana sat with her, offering the same gentle reassurance she had gifted me when Rachel and I had first arrived to MDC.

When I woke again two hours later, I took over for Luci, letting her slip away to her bunk for some well-earned sleep. I offered the woman a Nutri-Grain bar I had saved from a minister's visit the previous Sunday. "No, that is your food," she tried to refuse. I handed it to her anyway and watched the kind of gratitude you only see in places like this, where nothing is wasted. She spoke of her children and her fear. She was in her fifties, detained, and worried she would not get her heart medication. She repeated that she had to tell her daughter she was safe.

"*Om tara tuttare ture soha*," I recited without thinking, a Buddhist mantra for compassion I've practiced for years. Her eyes lit.

"You are Buddhist," she said. I told her I practice deeply. "*Namaste*," she said, hands together to say the traditional Indian welcome. "I taught my grandson *namaste*. The divine bowing to each other," as relief washed over her face; something familiar in a foreign room.

But panic crept back into her expression. "Please, I must tell my daughter I am okay." We promised she could email at six when the computers opened, and encouraged her to rest so she would be steady for her daughter.

At 6:04, she was beside me, pale and shaking. "I am dizzy. I did not get my heart medication." She started toward Luciana, who had been on night shift. I asked her to let Luciana sleep while I took her name and Bureau of Prisons number to the officer.

There is a ritual here. You stand by the office door until you catch a guard's eye. You say "excuse me" and wait for any sign that you can proceed. Some guards hold you there, a dominance dance. This one met me with open eyes. "The new woman is dizzy and says she did not get her heart meds." Genuine concern crossed the guard's face. She picked up the phone. For a moment there were no roles, just two women caring about a third. I left before the spell could break.

An hour later, they called the woman's name. She froze. I moved toward the hallway and said, "It is just the office. I can see the door from here."

Her eyes were saucers. "Please tell my daughter."

"I will," I said. The unknown was dragging old terrors into the room. I promised what I could promise, which is that she would talk with staff and they would get her the medication, maybe not immediately, but they would. She met my eyes and decided to trust.

After she walked away with the guard, I began praying again. I picked up borrowed rosary beads, fifty-four beads that I count twice to 108, the traditional number in Tibetan Buddhism, repeating the compassion mantra silently. In plain words: May a fierce, mothering kindness keep us safe, strong, and clear.

25

Kay-Kay

I t was a big day socializing with Miss Wu. She made tea sandwiches, three kinds. In a photo, they would look impossibly elegant. Inside, though, one was Spam, the second was commissary sausage, and the third was tuna.

It was lovely. To balance all that talking, Rachel and I did three back-to-back 45-minute meditations. Beautiful. Replenishing. Warm golden light, warmer than the showers, quietly filling tight places. I could have stayed there all night, but dinner was called. It was hotdogs and tater tots, so I skipped it on purpose, a small act of discipline that felt good.

I told Rachel what I see in the women's ecosystem. It can be an endless carousel of comparison, the old "jealous gods" game where everyone leaves little calling cards to top the next woman. There is always someone more *something* than you. Even your best asset gets stacked against someone else's. If you are short, you may crave height. If you are soft, you may crave edge.

Here is the antidote, I told her. Do what we do here. Keep a steady practice. Be warm with everyone. Help where you can. Stay out of the drama. Drama trades at a premium here; if you do not trade in it, nothing hooks you. Things pass through your field without pulling you into the undertow, and your chances of landing in solitary drop.

Men have it different. They cannot disengage as easily when the storm starts. In those exchanges, their role is small. Too often they are like fire hydrants, left with messages other women want seen:

"I am prettier."

"I am lustier."

"I am softer."

"I am more wife material."

And the carousel keeps turning.

Later we sat with Kay-Kay, who speaks no English and works in the laundry. Some women slit their sweatshirts up the middle to make cardigans. Kay-Kay wears her brown one proudly, oblivious or indifferent to the big white letters across the back that say "Detainee."

Every so often someone yells, "Kay-Kayyyyyy," and it means one of two things: Either she did not show up for recall and is strolling the common area, or a cockroach needs to be handled with her shower shoe. Wherever she is, she pivots, tracks, and prepares to strike.

Miss Wu must have told her we were good so Kay-Kay opened to us. Looking at me, questioningly, she crossed her arms and squeezed her shoulders as if hugging herself like she was cold. Sensing my lack of understanding, she ran out and returned with a thermal shirt for me. I thanked her but, deciding that wasn't enough, she ran out again, returning with a jacket. Then, a smile across her face, she looked at me and my new layers, satisfied with her generosity.

I do not know her whole story. Here is what I know. She was on house arrest for seven years with an ankle monitor. She got a call that a relative was dying. She kept calling her probation officer and got no response. So she finally cut off the monitor and went to her relative. Kay-Kay arrived too late. Her relative had died. And afterward, she was brought here.

"She blames herself. Depression," someone explained, miming the motion of eating. "For depression they gave medicine that makes you blow up." The weight gain is obvious and cruel.

And still, everything in her gives. She knits like a woman on a mission. Her hats and slippers are everywhere. She especially loves to keep people warm. Rachel and I are now among the ones receiving the kind of care that, in a strange way, is what brought her here in the first place.

26

Gratitude

I went to sleep with my mind feeling sluggish, like all the hues were getting a brown wash. Dakina had spent the night climbing on top of her bunk, even with several of the women continuing to coax her down. Loud, rhythmic hoots emitted from her, the dorm echoing with the sound of her howls.

Yet somehow, when I woke up, I felt lighter. Calmer. An emotional rain from the day before seemed to have cleared the air and left a rainbow on the sidewalk. I was grateful not to be painting a rainbow over mud. I found out later when I checked my email that my friend Kate had worked on my energies long-distance. Do I know how that works? Not really. Is it a message from the under-layer of consciousness, the hum beneath everything? Maybe. Whatever it is, I'll take it.

I have my usual morning routine: the preset hot-and-cold mug waiting by my bunk; a scoop and a half of instant coffee; two scoops of nondairy creamer; one packet of sugar substitute. I joke to Rachel it's like waking up to candy. Prison is hardcore; it turns tea snobs into coffee lovers.

I gather my bathroom things including enough toilet paper to dry my hands with, then make the one-stop trip across the dorm to the sink. In the middle of the night, it's no small thing to pass the night crew—the women who sit bunk-side of the blue line, crocheting or watching TV till dawn, then sleeping all day. They tease us that they're the college night owls and Rach and I are the grandmas, bumping into each other at 4 a.m., them brushing before bed, us brushing to start the day.

It has the feel of camping in the middle of winter. Though it's summer outside, the A/C is set to full power for reasons I can't fathom. I practice tummo daily, a breathing technique that warms your body from the inside. In the cold of Tibet, cave-dwelling meditators developed the practice to speed transformation; as a by-product, it generates inner heat. I'd seen videos of monks soaking their shawls before sitting outside in the cold. Steam poured off their shoulders until the shawls dried. After weeks of sleeping in two pairs of socks, crocheted slippers, and a sweatshirt, I slept barefoot last night. It seems I am making progress.

As part of my practice this morning, I did my prison version of a Tenth Step—a daily moral inventory from Alcoholics Anonymous. I wrote down the tiny biting fears I avoid, and then my desires.

When I'm upset "because of someone," a thin membrane of separation forms. There's an urge to attack and pick apart their motives so I can feel better. It never works. I've seen that the only way out is through: aim attention at the seed of the upset, right where it starts, until it dissolves. The looping thoughts create confusion, which merely hides the truth. Relief only comes when I go all the way back to the origin.

This happened recently in an attorney meeting. I was holding my breath without realizing it and ended up flattened afterward. Bracing builds a shell, and then I'm left trying to soothe the shell. Or I can skip the shell entirely: soften before, during, and after. Clamping down cuts me off from wisdom and lets ego run the show. Contraction causes wreckage.

I want to live in fluid, dancing flight. I want to be clear of confusion. I want to understand others wordlessly, and be understood.

I've been a member of Alcoholics Anonymous for years. Step One says: "We admitted we were powerless over alcohol and that our lives had become unmanageable." My ego finally conceded. In a single snap of clarity I saw it: Every spike of upset, anger, or discomfort comes from trying to steer the infinite instead of letting it carry me. I pictured the wink of my Lama, a slight whistle in his breath, riding the wind.

All the talk people do about "manifestation," vision boards, trying to force a dream without wisdom—it's just trying to control and drive reality from up on high. Years ago I made the commitment to keep going until I was free. Scribbling through the writing exercise this morning, I understood the missing half: Trust how freedom unfolds. Let things unknit themselves. I was still trying to *do* it, instead of collaborating with that which already knows the way.

Einstein said intuition is the gift and the rational mind is the faithful servant. I had been ordering the servant of my mind to build the road I preferred, instead of listening for the road that wanted to appear for my liberation.

The ego is powerless over the infinite.

When I finish my practice, I feel like the pixels have been sharpened. Colors click into focus. As I walk over to the computers to check my email, I pass Jingyi. She recently finished her "impossible puzzle"—three thousand Marvel posters mashed into one image—and started a new one called the Diamond Puzzle. It's shaped like a diamond, each piece a tiny shard that looks part crystal, part mirror, part gemstone, catching different light at different angles.

I have never spoken to Jingyi. She's the quiet definition of beauty:

a round, strong face; perfectly set eyes; hair down to her waist; composed in silence. Up until then, our only exchange had been the extra coffee or sugar packets she would occasionally drop on our table with no words; just a quick glance, a small act of kinship.

"That's my favorite color," I say, passing her and the glittering puzzle.

"It's transparent," she replies without looking up, though there's a question tucked in the words.

"Yes, but with light running through it." I shift, and the light cast on the table slides from orange-red to green. She takes a piece in her hand, moving it to create the same effect.

"Ah, from clear light to color," she affirms, adjusting the angle of the piece. "Magic."

27

Wanting Little

I had always imagined prison as an austere experience: separated from your worldly possessions, placed in a concrete cell with little more than a uniform, a towel, and a book. I was surprised to discover how easy it is to accumulate as much clutter here as someone might on the outside.

Stuff creeps in here if you let it. People leave and offer you T-shirts; others want to offload whatever they've collected. The contrast between stark and crowded can make you want to hoard food, clothes, anything to recreate the outside. It takes discipline to say no. It's hard being a people-pleaser in prison—I don't want to hurt anyone's feelings by turning down their gifts, but I don't want more. I have to sit inside my actual desire, not measure myself against someone's cuter shirt or cushier bed. I'm in prison. Who cares?

The truth is I'm happiest living like a nun in a monastery. That's my essence. When I stray from it, I'm miserable. Shopping is miserable. Face lotions are miserable. Excess space is miserable. The more I add, the duller I feel—like I've put layers of bubble wrap between me and the world. I used to bribe myself with a "new" dress or product to cut through the discomfort of being alive. I kept adding instead of subtracting. Joke's on me: The Kiwi VO5 shampoo in here makes my hair shinier than the fancy brand; vitamin E and, yes, Preparation H, moisturize better than the potions I bought at Nordstrom. I like having just one uniform. Some women rebel and sneak little embellishments. Me? Give me my brown T-shirt. If it's cold, I'll wear the thermal under it so the guards can still see the uniform like they want.

I used to think I was failing at being human because I craved simplicity. Shouldn't I want curated and exquisite? I remember visiting a very expensive house once and feeling overwhelmed just stepping into the foyer. I couldn't keep track of the rooms. I didn't want to. I do best when I let life move me instead of trying to force it to match a vision board. Steering the river is a Western romance. We love the story that willpower plus strategy equals destiny. It works—until it doesn't. Then we double down rather than admit it doesn't work.

For me, the saner rhythm is to get in the water and learn how it moves. I can set a direction, sure, but I'm more sail than rudder. Every time I've tried to muscle life into place, I lose touch with the quiet part of me that knows the next right thing. That's the piece I'm practicing now: Listen, align, and let the current help.

Simplicity keeps me aligned. In more extroverted times in my life, I would dream of escaping to a small cabin in the woods with a beat-up coffee pot on the fire. Even that might be too ornate. Creativity comes best there: a clean, bare space where the mind can be bare, too. When it gets too fancy, too comfortable, the signal gets fuzzy. From simplicity, I have more to offer.

I once read in a book that today's psychology often diagnoses the urge to help others as a kind of pathology—dangerous, self-erasing, likely to end in burnout. I felt the sting of recognition. The path I choose to live is so often painted as dangerous or as some kind of mental illness by those looking from the outside. But I don't experience it that way. For me, the impulse to care is not self-destruction; it's oxygen. I just have to keep the boundary firm: My job is to offer warmth, not to bleed out.

There's a collective reset we're being asked to make as a whole society. We can't keep gripping beliefs that don't match reality and call that strength. Surrender—real, adult surrender—is admitting what's working and what isn't. It takes humility, presence, and a willingness to be changed by what's true. In recovery circles, they call it turning your will over to a higher power. I'd say it more plainly— stop pretending you're in charge of the weather and learn how to sail.

So I keep choosing less. Less stuff, less noise, fewer decisions, one uniform. The paradox is that less gives me more: more contact with the air on my skin, with the feeling of the room, with the woman crying softly in the elevator. More gratitude for simple things. More humor. More room for the dream to crack open and flood the basement with daylight.

Wanting little is not deprivation for me; it's devotion. It's how I remember what matters and hear the quiet instructions underneath the static. It's how I stay honest. It's how I keep my burden light.

28

After Prison

Three women left this morning—two to other facilities, one to court. I was on the morning shift: prayers, hugs, goodbyes. Waves of time and experience roll through this place, and they always will.

Luciana knows a guy who did a year in prison for something related to Bitcoin—one of those Rogan-listening, ice-bath-taking types—and now he's "preparing her" for life after release.

"Luci, you don't understand," he told her. "People will look at you and they won't believe you were in prison. They'll say, *You? You were in prison?*' And they'll mean it as disbelief. But you'll mean something completely different when you say, *Yeah, I was.'"*

She nodded like someone who already knew. "It's a whole world here," she said. "People don't want to understand that."

She keeps describing this image of herself sitting onstage in a red power suit, lights around her, talking business to a full audience.

"They're impressed by what I know," she said. "And then I tell them I was in prison, and they're shocked—and the stigma disappears. I want to remove the stigma."

She was sitting on the makeshift bench in front of the empty bunk we call our "counter," stirring a bowl of mackerel rice. When she lifted it toward me, I hesitated. Mackerel scares me. Mackerel from a *bag* really scares me. I told her as much.

"Not my mackerel!" she said, proud. "I know exactly how to make it so it's not too strong." She half shook her head at my lack of faith in her prison-cooking genius.

"That's not enough," I said quietly.

"Huh?"

"Ending the stigma. It's not that you want too much—it's that you don't want enough."

She looked confused but kept talking. Luciana is quick—she moves, thinks, and speaks fast.

"It's a whole world here," she said again. "People don't get it. There are things I've learned here I never could've learned outside. Having a job in here, learning to work with all the personalities. If I can do it here…"

"You can do it anywhere," I said. "It's like high-altitude training. Sea level will be nothing by comparison."

"Yeah," she said, stirring her rice. "I can make do with nothing. I used to think I needed so much to be happy. I know how to be with myself now. I know how to be alone."

"That's what I mean," I agreed. "You know things most of the world will never know. You have jewels—real wealth. Lead with that. It's not enough to erase stigma; you have to redefine what strength looks like. Think about it: Psychedelics went from being criminalized to being used in trauma therapy. The same people who once outlawed them are now paying to study them. That's what we have here. We've mined something deep. We've seen the underworld and found the light in it."

That caught her off guard—rare for Luciana. Her eyes widened; she wagged her finger. "Ohhh," she breathed. "I *like* that."

I keep thinking: If the people who end up in prison had spent time on silent retreat, they'd recognize the same landscape. Both are stripped-down worlds where the usual distractions fall away. You see everything—raw and unfiltered. The bad, the ugly, the self-protective, the cruel. But also kindness, in doses that stun you.

Someone notices your mayonnaise jar is empty—a real staple in here—and offers a squirt of theirs. Someone comes back from court, wrists still marked from shackles, eyes hollow from bad news, and the women gather around her bunk with oatmeal cookies and soft voices: *Keep your head up.*

In here, we learn to see causes, conditions, and complexity. We learn how to love the people the outside world finds unlovable. It's not always pretty. We gripe, we bite. But at the end of the day, no other place—except maybe a hospice ward—shows humans this naked. Hearts without armor. What an honor to witness that.

You can lie in prison. I've seen women lie about almost anything. But you also can't lie in prison. It's too extreme. It's like being in an arranged marriage with yourself—you can't escape the person you're with. You either can or can't get out of bed. You either can or can't stop crying. There's no pretending.

Then one day, something shifts. You see it happen. Alma, who spent weeks with tears streaming down her face, still managed to braid her hair each morning and whisper, "*Hola*, Nicole," like it weighed fifty pounds. Now she's an orderly—cleaning, working, moving with purpose again. She offers a lighter, "*Buenos días*, Nicole," without me having to break into her cloud.

Time here is different—optional in a way it isn't outside. Without windows or phones, you lose track. You can kill time, fill time, or make time. Rach wears a watch so we can time our meditations; otherwise, an hour and ten minutes both feel the same.

I like it. I like the simplicity. Be behind the blue line for recall at

3:30 and 9:15 p.m. Be by your bed at 4:00 and 9:30 p.m. for count. There's even something like a prison siesta in between. Enforced rest. I like that too. The rest of the day floats, unanchored by clocks. For someone like me, that feels like a taste of the eternal present.

That's the secret of prison, really—the hidden practice beneath it all. You come here to meet yourself. The irritations aren't obstacles; they're the curriculum. There's no breaking out because the real prison isn't these walls—it's the self. In the end, you become the key to your own gate.

29

Men Are the Narcotic of Women

There are moments when it all feels ridiculous—when I can see straight through the overlay, this eternal game of hide-and-seek we call life. The naked mind, dressed up in costumes, acting out its own little play. The purpose of it all? Maybe just delight. Can you find delight in the kaleidoscope, no matter how it turns? That seems to be the game—and apparently there are levels to it.

I think of Kanye saying he signed up for the "level-ten video game." Love you, Ye, but I'm not sure that's it. Maybe there are levels within levels—the way some spiritual traditions describe paths of discipline, compassion, and finally the audacious stage where you stop pretending to be anything less than divine and just live the truth out loud. Maybe Kanye's playing level ten of the everyday world. The real game starts when life tosses you somewhere unexpected—and you have to find yourself there.

Imagine this:

"Alright, you wanted to wake up. You wanted to serve humanity. The people in the high seats said you really had it in you. Great. Now add this: You're sent to prison, called a fraud, and dropped into a dorm with thirty-seven women who think meditation is an Illuminati ritual. Go!"

"Um..."

"Too slow. You look confused. In here, confusion looks like weakness. And weak is not how you want to look. Have fun!"

So you do. You learn to have fun fast. You make sweet-and-sour noodles out of vitamin-C packets, sugar-free honey, and ramen. You finally meditate the way they told you to for thirty years—like your hair's on fire. You turn the sadism of certain correctional officers into part of your obstacle course. You reframe it all as a cosmic game: how to stay human in the most inhuman conditions; how to remember you still have wings when every rule in the place is designed to tie you to the ground.

And you tell yourself jokes pretty much all day long. Like when they reward the girls with candy for keeping the dorm neat. And you just wish you could have some vegetables. Or when you think you've got it down, quietly meditating in your bunk but the rug gets pulled out from under you and you realize your enlightened activity is really disengagement because you were just using it to avoid the fact that there is someone in here with serious mental disabilities who jumps on her top bunk and eats plastic and that there are no adults in the institution who have any idea what to do other than let a bunch of convicted felons look after her.

So I make up my own sayings. Like, *"May your hopes-and-dreams rug be pulled out from under you."* Because maybe the real miracle isn't in peace and quiet—it's when your idyllic vacation turns into your car landing in a ditch and a bear stealing your food and you're not quite sure how you are going to survive this but the townspeople come to help. That's where the story gets good.

And then I start to notice the theme running through every woman's story here. The same one I saw before entering this karmic boot camp of prison: men. If religion is the opium of the masses, then men are the narcotic of women.

Every woman here—except maybe two—has a man at the center of her story. Almost every one of them says to the judge, "He made me do it." It's baked into the script, whether the prison is internal or external.

They still organize their lives around men—real, imagined, or long gone. Men occupy the floors above us. Women will stand at the "gate" to the outside we are not allowed out to and yell to the men waiting at the windows above. They can hear but not see each other. Some of the women lose themselves to the "gate," waiting for their man to yell back. They risk their freedom to do it. These women "fall in love" with men who are also incarcerated, fighting over disembodied voices through metal bars. One woman is obsessed with a man everyone swears is ugly, but she calls him beautiful—saying his name like a spell. She lives for the gate. If her best friend in here tries to feed her dinner and it delays her gate time, she drops her friend without blinking. It's like watching addiction in real time.

I want to shake them and ask, *If you never get out, what will your life have amounted to?* But I don't. I don't go near the gate. I've learned better than to get between a woman and her high.

They ride a merry-go-round: some horses go up, some go down, some never move. Up is when they're "the best"—the prettiest pony, the one who got called *special*. Down is when they're forgotten. We just lost one of my favorite women to the gate. She'd never been. Went out to crochet. Heard a whistle. Now she's gone—hooked.

It hasn't dawned on them that the ride's rigged. The up isn't really up, the down isn't really down, and the horses that don't move—the marriages, the "stable" ones—aren't stable either. They're hypnotized by the pendulum of male approval, not noticing the wild horses running free just a few feet away.

They think rebellion means risking it all for a man. But true defiance—the kind that changes you—is choosing yourself even at the risk of "not belonging." It's when you stop organizing your life around a man.

Luciana keeps talking about how, when she gets out, she'll show them, prove them wrong, make it to "the top." I tell her there is no top. The "top" is an illusion built on comparison. People tell her she's "better than this place." I tell her there is no place—only the best *you*, wherever you stand. Being loving is the only wealth.

She panics about her looks, about if she'll "get ahead" fast enough. Because she's heading back into the world of transaction, where currency is measured in desirability. She's preparing to sell herself—if she wants to get ahead in that game, she'd better have an alluring product.

The real game, where the real treasure can be found, is the other side of success. In the everyday world, whether on the inside or the outside, people cheat and hustle for "the best": the bag, the rich boyfriend, the happy-looking family, the résumé polished with just enough virtue signaling to seem noble. You check everything off the list—the job, the man, the baby—and in exchange, you receive the praise, the validation. And while you might have the validation and you might have the money, you live in a world of limited resources, where no one generates anything of true value—they just hoard it. Creativity is lacking. You starve yourself for the right body, pretend not to compete, and secretly glow when another woman loses. You live by the law of scarcity: There's only so much "best" to go around. Get yours before it's gone.

But on the other side, you unlock a different kind of power—the power to *bestow* value. You master your mind, become resourceful and fast on your feet, and detach from any labels, whether designer or cultural. You stop chasing worth and start radiating it. You take what you have—your scraps, your wisdom, your mackerel rice—and turn it into gold by the force of your perception. You don't make things valuable; you *see* their value. You live from the deep, not the surface.

Then you wake up in the morning and give thanks. Real, bone-deep appreciation. You thank whatever gods or coincidences you believe in for your bowl of bran cereal with sweetener, your two hours of quiet to meditate and do breathing exercises, and the faint sense of being in love with everything you see.

And slowly, the other women start to notice. They start choosing nutrition over the sweets. They start copying your peace instead of your lipstick. They try to steal a glance at how you do it. Not all of them, of course, but that's not the point.

The point is to fall in love with what you already have. That's the real rebellion. That's the game. You free yourself first—and somehow, that frees everyone around you.

30

We Good

I have to make a trip to the courthouse to meet with probation about my pre-sentence report. I am taken from the dorm down to holding, along with Miriam. Seems she was headed to court as well. We will have a long day together, 6 a.m. to at least 6 p.m. I've heard the day would hold multiple strip searches, shackles, a bumpy bus ride, other unknowns. A meeting that could shape my sentence. There's no faking at that intensity.

When Miriam first arrived here, I hadn't been sure about her. She's tall like me, but built like a protector. She brought big-block energy to a row already loud enough. Territory staked; order asserted. I held onto my vote.

Then I overheard her telling a notorious pot-stirrer, calm and flint-hard: "Not on my watch. Are we clear?" The woman backed down. No escalation, no show, just clean leadership.

I'd heard Miriam loved banana sandwiches so much she could live on them. One afternoon in the dorm, I passed her two without a word. The look on her face was a warrior caught off guard by kindness. Okay, I thought. Noted.

We sit in that unfamiliar holding cell, me eating my bran flakes, her eating her breakfast cake. "Ever think we're here for something more than the obvious?" I ask Miriam. I'm not known for my small talk.

She doesn't miss a beat. "I'll tell you what I know. The Lord put me here for a reason." Her tone says: Make it worth my time or stop talking.

"I hear you," I say. "I think you could bring a lot of benefit to these women."

She stares at the wall, then: "Look. I love people but I don't like people. I'm gonna do my time and go home. I got work."

"Got it," I say. "I just notice you cut division when you see it. That changes a place."

A small smile gets away from her.

Filing onto the bus, she stands behind me on the steps so I won't topple if I happen to trip over the shackles that bind my ankles together. Once the two of us are seated in place, they load in the men. Her husband is one of them. She hadn't known he'd be coming, hadn't seen him since their arrest. He sits behind us, his eyes filled with tears, knocking his forehead against the window that divides the men and the women. "I'm sorry, I'm sorry," he mouths.

"We good," she says, voice like gravel and oak. "You hear me? We GOOD. We gonna get through this."

Right then, I know everything I need to know about the two of them. You can tell a person by who they stand next to, who they walk into the storm with. He isn't a coward and she isn't some wilted flower pretending she didn't know better. They have that look you only see on people who've survived something together and come out with a code. Not the kind you say out loud, the kind you live.

Inside here, most folks never touch it. Pressure hits and they scatter, or they fold, or they start telling stories. But the ones who follow the code? We spot each other quick. We don't always look the same, or sound the same, or move the same, but there's this quiet click—oh, you're built from that fire too. We recognize each other by feel.

The others? We see them just as clearly. You can be polite, even kind, but you don't mistake them for your people. They haven't been forged. The real ones, those who've walked through something and stayed true, carry a stillness. They are always granted peace.

31

Bridging the Gap

It was a hard day. Maybe it was because I went deeper in my meditation and that stirred stuff up. Maybe the trip to court earlier in the week. Maybe because I felt less connected to loved ones on the outside this week, or because "Party Row" behind us folks in "Religion Row" really was having a party. Or maybe it was just me—caught somewhere between effort and exhaustion, trying to convince myself I could coast on the trust fund of all my past practice instead of earning it again today.

Whatever the reason, frustration moved in. The kind that simmers under the surface, then bubbles up, daring you to say something you'll regret. I've learned that when anger doesn't have a place to go, it turns toxic. It corrodes the very thing it wants to defend.

For years, I've watched the world do that—lash out instead of understanding. Just like I told Luciana, it took decades for people to see psychedelics as medicine, not madness. The same pattern is playing out again, just with a new target. The war isn't on drugs this time; it's on sex. The minute the word 'sex' is spoken, reason flies out the window.

It's a strange thing to dedicate your life to something people fear.

To know you're holding medicine, and still be called poison. There's a philosopher who claimed culture always follows the same cycle: first ridicule, then attack, before finally reaching acceptance. Every truth goes through all three. I've made it to the phase of coming under attack. Oddly, that's progress.

The work now is to stay steady—to keep building understanding instead of outrage. You can't scream your way to clarity. You have to teach the giant to see.

There are moments when all I want is to rest on my laurels. To say, *I've done enough.* To stop being the one who keeps trying to explain the unexplainable. But I can't. Not because I'm noble, but because I've seen what happens when you stop. The energy you don't use turns inward—it mutates into resentment or despair.

I sit here with a treasure chest of practices and hesitate to offer them, afraid of being misunderstood or, worse, depended on. The irony isn't lost on me: I was accused of making people reliant on me, when dependency is the one thing I can't stand.

Still, I know what it feels like to resist. I've been that woman—the one who was given every tool, every teaching, and still wanted a shortcut. The one who'd rather talk about transformation than do the work. And I remember the people who were patient with me through all that. It's my turn now.

I believe meditation is the master key out of every prison. It can free a person from gossip, addiction, loneliness, the endless loop of their own mind. I dream of offering it to every woman in here. I see how it could change things. The women seem curious. Some even say they want to learn.

But then comes the application—the hardest part.

A yoga teacher I once studied with told me, "There's nothing more painful than bringing an ideal down to earth." He was right. It's beautiful in theory. But the moment you try to ground it, it gets messy.

You dream of giving people the keys to the kingdom and forget that getting the key in the door takes grumpy, confused, impatient work.

And I've been no better. I've had all the keys—yoga, breath, mantra—and still wanted the easy way. Now that I'm back inside the discipline, it's humbling. I remind myself about the monks in the Himalayas meditating in the snow, and here I am complaining about my cold hands in a Brooklyn dorm.

Comfort, I've realized, is the most seductive drug there is. It's the quiet addiction no one talks about. It keeps you just numb enough to stop growing.

I catch myself bargaining—telling myself I can skip a page of practice, let my mind wander, cut a corner, and it'll be fine. But it never is. The fire doesn't light halfway. It's all or nothing.

And that's what makes me mad. The laws of growth are as unforgiving as the laws of physics. You can't cheat them. You eat the pizza, you feel bad. You eat the greens, you feel good. The universe is that blunt.

The dream always starts bright. Then reality crashes in: the gossip, the cold, the noise, the inertia. I read about enlightenment while women play bingo for candy. The space between the possible and the real feels like a canyon. There's an old saying: *When the solution becomes the problem.* I can think I know a better way but it only helps if others see it. To bring heaven to Earth, there's a gap to bridge.

32

What to Do with Pain

I woke up to my best Thursday yet. I'm learning the waves here—how to ride them, how to not be dragged under. The week moves like tides. Wednesday is high tide. By Tuesday night, I can feel the pull, and on Wednesday morning I wake with tears at the back of my eyes. Everyone's bracing: seeing family, not seeing family, being seen like this. In the elevator after visiting hours, women stare forward, trying not to wipe their cheeks. The meanest woman in the dorm is often the softest woman in that elevator. You've just watched her at the blue table, family circled around her with the same question in their eyes: *How did this happen?* You see the faces of those who crossed a border for hope and met the particular hopelessness America reserves for immigrants.

The hardest part is the karmic stream—no neat causes, no tidy fixes. I want to point at easy villains, but that's ignorance.

If pain had a body, it would be Dakina's. If confusion wanted a case study, it would be her life. She seems profoundly autistic, maybe has Tourette's or some profound trauma in her past. Occasionally her howls take on words: "Make it end. Make him stop hurting me." Her head trembles like late-stage Parkinson's. She smears feces on the dorm walls. She screams from the shower. And she's here among women drowning in their own pain, some of them yelling for her to shut up, some mocking anyone who tries to be kind. It's unimaginable until you see it.

Claire—the youngest—survives by cutting off feeling. She's the coldest about Dakina. "She shouldn't even exist," she says. Useless. That's what pain says to pain. The officers and inmates stand helpless before Dakina, and in them I see our larger bewilderment: We don't know how to be with suffering.

Then there's Miriam, by the phones, scolding someone: "That woman has profound mental challenges. You're not making fun of her on my watch." Miriam has been to hell, met her own challenges there, and knows the way through.

I keep saying it: Dakina is our collective pain. Those are the cries we don't cry, the screams we swallow. The only medicine is warmth. Warmth toward Dakina is warmth toward ourselves. I don't want to hear the jokes. Claire rolls her eyes. I'm still "Grandma": in bed at 8 p.m., rising when Claire is just going down. We pass each other with toothbrushes, same ritual, opposite reasons.

I told Claire, gently, that she'd lost weight. She was already 107 pounds, and had gone down to 100 after she stopped hanging out with Luciana who often cooked for her. She's afraid of the main line— "hormones in the food," she says. I told her, "We cook every day. You don't have to talk to us, but you do have to eat. Politics or no politics."

She mumbled, "I miss Luciana," and an hour later sidled back to our row. I teased her like a daughter returning from a bad semester: messy, but home. I gave them space.

"Night-owl time for me," I joked. "Eight fifteen—too late for me. Do what you need; I'm going to sleep."

I fell asleep to Luciana's voice: "Okay, go get some cheese." She'd agreed to make Claire's favorite—Shabang Nachos, a Claire invention:

vinegar, BBQ, Spicy Doritos. A culinary crime scene, yes, but the sweetness of it with Claire bringing the cheese, tacitly admitting she needed care. She couldn't offer it yet—to herself or anyone—but she could receive it. Tonight, that was enough.

33

For the Woman in the Bunk Next to Me, Part Two

She says, all coy, there's something about me—something she can't name. Maybe you'd call it sex appeal. How I move through the dorm, how I sit at meals, how I listen. "It's like you aren't waiting on anyone," she says. "They're waiting on you." I laugh because I thought I was undercover: federal-issue granny panties, East L.A. khakis, no hair product, no makeup. And still the light shines through.

Part of her question, I suspect, is how a woman nearly twice her age could carry something she learned to associate with the young and the pretty. I know I'm beautiful, but I don't put my beauty in the storefront. I've seen what happens when people walk in dazzled and find there's nothing behind it. I keep my valuables in the back room, the one you have to get buzzed into.

Years ago I made a choice. I had watched the flicker of surface beauty—the bulbs dim, the bulbs get replaced—and decided I wanted something that didn't burn out. Then I met women who felt like that to me: steady as a river. When I asked how, they taught me to plug into a quieter power already inside me. They called it "orgasm," but not the fireworks kind—more like a saturating warmth. They drenched me in it until I could feel the source for myself. Beauty as a by-product of bliss, not the other way around. Not dressing up, but unblocking what's already shining. That's what real sex appeal is: Surrender to the radiance that wants to move through you.

You know the woman who descends the stairs and turns every head, women and men. The minds turn, too. For some, there's simple appreciation: Look at her. For others, reflex: judge, diminish, own, outshine. Our response to another woman's light tells the truth about our own. And here's the heartbreak—our culture is taught there are only three options when faced with radiance: Consume it, control it, or destroy it. "Fuck, kill, or marry." All three snuff the very light we're starving for.

You can list the high-risk jobs—power lines, rooftops, mines—but I laugh because I believe a woman's work of illumination is just as dangerous. If she won't dim on command, the world will try character assassination. If that doesn't work, it will demand she police herself until she forgets her appetite. If *that* fails, there are always shackles. How many women end up in places like MDC because she didn't die on cue? Here they make us play dead under fluorescent lights. I want to tell the guards they'd have more fun letting us live, but humor is the dialect of the sexual and this place doesn't speak it.

She tells me the stories every woman wishes to tell—the lover who finished when your mouths met and blamed you while never thinking to satisfy you; the trainer you finally slept with because you were tired of humping pillows; the games you play to keep some semblance of control. I hear the bravado and the ache. And I want to say, with love: That's the "best of" a bad playlist. We keep being placed under a ceiling so low we have to stoop to fit, and then we're told to call it empowerment. Control is not rapture. Transaction is not nourishment. Revenge is not intimacy.

There is more. Infinitely more. Not just gasps and spikes and the chase for peak moments, but an underlying country—call it a hidden realm where the weather is always ecstatic, and our bodies are made to take flight into it. The promised land is not a metaphor; it has a zip code inside your skin. Milk and honey are not souvenirs; they're how your rivers run when no one dams them. But they have been dammed—rerouted to power someone else's project: production, property, reputation. We end up thirsty in a house built over a spring.

So we gnaw the box and read the label—*GREAT SEX*—and tell ourselves we've eaten. We haven't. We've forgotten the low groan, the mindless shudder, the devotion that rises when you are truly fed. We settle for head games because our bodies don't feel safe enough to let go. We think we can perform our way into ecstasy and control our way into abandon, which is like swapping shackles and calling it freedom.

"Who?" she asks. "Who could take me there?" It's a fair question. Who can stand in the heat of your force and not flinch? Who can say, "More," without their own fear pulling you back? Who can unbridle even your fears and mean it when they say, "Run free. I'm not going anywhere"?

Here's where I start the initiation—gently, because this is tender ground. It's not about sex at first; it's about power. Not power-over, not power-as-status, but the responsible electricity of being fully alive. When you turn up your arousal, you move people. That comes with responsibility. You don't hype it; you steward it. Your job isn't to perform. Your job is to relax and receive so completely that your wealth spills over. The world doesn't need more performance. The world needs women whose presence wakes everything up.

Men have their path—earning, proving, offering. That makes sense for them. They're working their way *to* something. But we are the destination. We keep forgetting and clocking in to their job, scrubbing floors in our queen's robes, trying to earn access to what is already ours. We chase after men down the same road they're traveling to reach us, and then wonder why the gardens we left untended at home are dry.

There is one instruction, so simple we skip it: Relax. Really relax. Loosen the clench you've been holding since you were told, directly or between lines, that your desire is dangerous, silly, too much. What you fear will escape if you let go is precisely what the world needs you to spill. That inner wealth—rapture, tenderness, appetite, generosity— has never been touched by anyone's hands. It does not need to be earned. It does not need to be explained. It wants out.

This is not a summons to recklessness. It's an invitation to sovereignty. Your radiance is not for sale, not for ransom, not for proof. It's for lighting rooms where shame has kept women small; for flooding the fields that have gone fallow; for nourishing those who have forgotten they, too, are made of honey. When you free what lives within you, you don't just free yourself. You loosen the locks on the whole world.

34

Dropping Keys

I heard a clunk in the night. Then a rush of movement—women springing from their bunks, not with fear but excitement.

"Someone's going home!"

I slipped on my shower shoes, grabbed Rach, and followed the stampede toward the noise. A guard stood in the middle of the dorm, surrounded by women like kids circling an ice cream truck. She had dropped her keys.

In prison, that's a sign. If a guard drops their keys, it's our version of *every time a bell rings, an angel gets their wings.* When the keys drop, a jailbird flies.

The keys they carry are a funny thing. I think of them like the bell you put on a cat so birds hear it coming—an odd mercy for everyone involved. I'll be in the gym and hear the *clinkity-clinkity-clink* of them approaching. It's strange how sounds can flip meanings: What once symbolized dominance now feels like safety.

Somewhere along the way, I've started caring about these guards. The line between *us* and *them* has blurred into something more like *US.*

Still, it seems like a cruel punishment to make them wear those heavy chains. If I ran this place, I'd give them fingerprint locks; they seem less burdensome and more secure. I once read that insecure people jingle coins in their pockets to signal wealth. Maybe the guards' keys are their version of that—a nervous rattle that says, *This job is scary. I have to wear a security vest and carry pepper spray.* In some way it goes against the human grain.

Anyway, someone's going home. And that's good news.

Karma isn't linear. It's not simple cause and effect—it's a web. Sometimes the thing that lands you in the hardest place is just the seed of an old pattern ripening.

There are also *collective* karmas—trends in time that sweep us along. I was a woman teaching sexuality in a puritanical culture. Intent doesn't shield you from consequences but it protects your *mind* from being destroyed by them.

This morning, I saw another layer in it. Maybe it's not just cultural karma. Maybe it's also my personal karma.

I came into this world reluctantly—two weeks late, forty-eight hours of labor before they finally pulled me out. I've always had a streak of resistance, like I wasn't entirely sold on being human. There's a kind of suffering that comes from not wanting to exist at all. I think I've known that flavor since birth.

So of course my fate would involve confinement of the most extreme version. If you spend your life wanting to escape the human experience, life eventually says, *Fine, try to escape this.*

And strangely, that realization feels good. Like starting a diet after years of denial. You haven't lost the weight yet, but you're finally doing something honest about it.

I'm still not thrilled to be here on Earth, but at least now there's no illusion to hide behind. No more bribing myself to stay with "special" food, "beautiful" clothes, or "rich" moments of distraction. I'm here, bare and uninsulated—and it's not bad.

Rach confessed to me the other day that it's a relief to stop pretending. She loves not wearing makeup, not dyeing her hair, not competing. "I even like my grey," she said.

In here, no one's trying to out-beauty anyone else. There's comfort in that. Most women have gained weight; some have half-grown-out dye jobs or missing teeth. But the comparison game—the real prison women live in—has been suspended.

Well, except on Wednesdays. That's when the beauty parlor comes alive. Everyone's prepping for visiting hours. The old hair dryer gets dragged out. Women braid and twist and cornrow each other's hair. It's chaos and ritual all at once—an echo of freedom.

I tried dressing up the first few weeks, but it's too much work. My fancy pants are tight around the ankles and take forever to peel off. Which is fine on the outside when you're taking them off at the end of the day in the privacy of your own bedroom. But, when you're taking them off for your strip search while the rest of the women are waiting to all go back upstairs, it's not great. Now I wear the soft pants Luciana gave me. Nice, simple, easy on and off. Freedom, defined differently.

When I was little, I used to crawl under decks and hide in closets—dark, enclosed places. My dad said I talked to God there. He used to joke that I was giving God a piece of my mind. Some things don't change.

Now I find that quiet place inside myself while someone's yelling on the phone and there's a crew playing a loud card game, and three TVs blare true-crime shows that everyone insists on watching. I call it *criminal porn*—people obsessed with watching the very thing we're living.

Behind me, women chatter half in English, half in Spanish about mandatory sentences.

And I do what I've always done. I go down the trapdoor inside myself, to the only safe, silent place there is.

They say prison exists to protect the world from us. But for women, it feels more like the opposite—like it's protecting *us* from the world.

Sometimes it even feels like a strange kind of play, this life inside the cage. Like the universe made a stage out of concrete walls, just to see if we could still find the joy in being alive.

35

Stay in the Discomfort

I n the early stages of addiction recovery, there's a moment when you first decide to get sober. Then, further down that path, you decide to really *live* recovery. And then, if you keep going, there's a point you decide you'll never let yourself slide into complacency again.

That's what I'm confronting now, in a new form of practice: the feeling of being on fire, not because life is hard, but because I don't want my practice to depend on hardship. If my drive only comes from difficulty, what happens when things ease up? I'll drift, grow lazy, lose the very clarity I've fought to gain.

When I got sober, I had a great program. I went to meetings every day, worked the Steps, stayed connected. I want that same devotion now—not just enough practice to get by, but enough to keep opening all the doors that life offers. That's what I love about the way they taught at the Zen Center I used to go to: It's not a one-and-done experience. It's lifelong. You keep learning how to live.

At the same time, I can feel the grooves of all the years I've already practiced. I don't want to discount that. My mind rarely veers far now, rarely takes an off-ramp. I'm grateful for that steadiness.

You know those times when doubt or anxiety sweep in like bad weather? I used to have no shelter for that. I'd just stand there in the storm, naked, waiting it out, unsure when it would end. This morning, a few of those old clouds rolled in. The kind that feel like emotional sewage backing up. But this time, I didn't fix, compare, or resist. I just let it be there. And now, what's left is a simple urge to cry—not for a reason, just as release.

A woman here told me she can't cry inside because the others would think she's weak. "They'd love it," she said, "to see me lose it." I told her I saw it differently—that we'd all be glad to hold her, the way she's held us. She shed a few tears.

It made me think of something I once read and later taught: Women can't enter their involuntary—the state where the body's natural responses take over, beyond control or performance—unless they feel safe. Laughing or tears or orgasm—they're all a kind of emotional exhale, a surrender of the nervous system. Crying is just another form of letting go.

So the real question is: How do you release in a place designed to keep you pent up?

This place is full of provocations—noise, cold, chaos, deprivation. In this video game, these are the obstacles. How do I find peace *here*, when all the usual tools for health are stripped away?

This morning, I told Rach one of my mental tricks for when things look bleak. When I wake up and remember where I am, when I feel the weight of contending with the cold, the food that messes up digestion, the howls of Dakina in the night, the constant noise of the TVs and fan and women talking, the lack of sunlight, when I think, *What do I do here?*, I remind myself of the cave yogis. Those ancient meditators lived in freezing mountains with even less than I have, and yet they were said to be the happiest people in the world. The only time I suffer here is when I compare myself to "the outside"—to comfort, to freedom, to normal life.

When I remember the cave yogis, I realize: This is the same practice. Withdrawal from comfort. Withdrawal from distraction. It's not *because* I'm in prison—it's what I've been trying to do all along.

Nothing I lack here could bring me closer to peace. The work is simply to meet these conditions as they are. Even if Janiya is blow-drying her hair two feet from me while I meditate for forty minutes, that's the practice. It's not the obstacle; it's the arena.

I talk to Luciana, all full of purpose and plans as she's getting ready to be released. "I have a big calling," she says. "Something important to do in the world."

Miss Wu says the same—that she's meant to be a spiritual leader.

I told Luciana I'm happy to be lifting this place up in small ways. She looked at me, wide-eyed. "But you know so much. You can do so much. The world will see."

She had a whole vision for how I could rebuild my reputation, reclaim my platform, prove my worth. But the truth is, I don't need to prove anything anymore. I'm free from the illusion that "big" is better than "this."

Yes, I've practiced for decades. I know what I know. But that's exactly why I don't need anyone else to recognize it. That kind of knowing frees you from the madness of needing validation—from doing the acrobatics people do to be seen as legitimate.

Now, I can just do what's in front of me. Some days that means expanding on my vision of prison as a monastery. Other days it means scrubbing yoga mats.

The sobriety I've kept isn't just about abstaining from substances. It's also about abstaining from *spiritual materialism*—from the compulsion to put on the show of enlightened superiority.

That freedom releases me from both fame and infamy.

There's a quiet relaxation in my soul lately, like I've finally landed in a plane of calm intention. I think of the older teachers I admired, the ones who had stopped striving. They'd seen everything and so had nothing to chase, nothing to prove. But when something needed to be done, they moved with precision and grace. That's the place I'm finding. The absence of striving, but also the absence of resistance to being used by life.

Sometimes life still looks impossibly messy. I get overwhelmed. *'I can't possibly handle all this,'* I think, as I visualize images of deities with a thousand arms because there's too much to do with only two.

And it's true. I can't. But I can do the one simple thing in front of me. Sometimes that's lying flat on my bunk, doing a breathing meditation to clear out the static.

This morning, I had what I can only describe as a collision with clarity—the kind of quiet inner light that makes everything still. For a moment, I felt like a child being gathered home.

Maybe that's all this practice really asks: Stay.

Stay in the discomfort. Stay when you want to run. Stay in the pose, in the cold, in the noise.

Stay—and let it open.

36

The Pull Toward Flight

Since my arrival at MDC, I'd been rebuilding my yoga practice. The weight of the last two years, with the looming trial, then trial itself, had made it hard for me to reach what I knew was reachable in the practice. But yoga and I go way back. It's an old love I enjoyed meeting again each morning.

Rach and I built up to the 90-minute Rodney Yee class we found on a video here. Then Mari started offering her impromptu classes— one of those hidden talents that show up in a place like this, women pulling pieces of their old lives into the present. She'd run us through a harder flow, and it felt good.

The day after a particularly intense class of Mari's, I needed something gentler and pulled up the Rodney Yee "strength" video— slow, deliberate, no chasing anything. Breath and blood moved where they were supposed to move. Something in me untangled. Something old came back online.

I lay on the thin mat afterward, the concrete cold against my spine, and whispered "thank you."

That's what I love about practice—it produces itself. The more I show up, the more it shows up for me.

In this place, there's a familiar pull. The pull toward climax. Toward certainty, resolution, completion. It's powerful—the kind of energy that can make you mistake the momentum for the meaning. The habit is to ground it, to force it somewhere, into some fixed form. But there's another way: to stay with it. To stay awake as the senses sharpen—the brightness, the quickening, the pull toward *now*. I find that if I can hold steady in that intensity, there's a window where I can let go of the outcome entirely. I can set down the finish-line fantasy and feel myself suspended, weightless, in intimacy with everything.

It's like the pause between inhale and exhale. A living precision. A balance where I am both alive and aloft.

Some mornings I watch Dakina chasing that same lift in her own way. She'll run full speed on the top bunk—knees high, arms pumping—trying to get enough momentum to break gravity. It's the same impulse that sent her sneaking onto runways, convinced that if she could just get airborne, everything inside her would quiet. People call her "crazy" and don't know what to do with her. But I recognize the longing. The pull toward flight isn't madness. It's the body remembering freedom.

I've touched that place before—in sex, in writing, in meditation. It's the same field under different names. Awareness is the practice; the body is the entry point. I've learned to stay in the space between impulse and release. To let energy rise without trying to control it.

Lately I've been reading Robert Thurman. His writing on compassion feels refreshingly human. He says that when you finally stop suffering, your first impulse is to look around and want everyone else to feel that same freedom.

So much writing about compassion makes it sound unreachable, like it's reserved for saints. But I feel drenched in it here. I want to start a yin yoga class for the women who stay curled in their bunks all day so their bodies can unfurl. I want to keep walking with the women around the gym each day. I want to teach self-reflection to the women who shrug and say, "It is what it is," because they can't imagine another way, as their families are torn apart, their children raised by people who don't speak the same language, women whose families refuse to speak to them or whose sentencing is set to take them far from anyone they love.

Being here has stripped away everything unnecessary. It's shown me how many of these women simply never learned how to live—how to move their bodies, breathe through pain, or name what they feel. There was almost no way they *wouldn't* end up here. And yet, in some strange way, it feels like grace that they did. Maybe life loved them enough to give them a chance to finally find the jewels buried under all that wreckage.

I just pray that somehow, the tools of practice—breath, movement, meditation, self-awareness—can find their way into every prison.

Sometimes I worry I'm boring, like all I ever think about is practice—my own and how to share it. I don't get pulled into the curious social dramas of the dorm. But I'm not numb; I'm alive in the doing. I loved drawing Mari's quiet brilliance. Initially, she'd been too shy to teach yoga classes here. When she finally taught a class inside, a woman who hates her body attended and did her first headstand.

If you sit with someone's complaints long enough, she'll discover she has the nobility to find a solution. I take what shows neglect—the yoga mats that reek, the mirrors falling off the walls—and I do what is needed. Clean the mats. Fix the mirrors. Raise the energy one inch at a time.

But I noticed, I started leaving my own desires out of my prayers. Heard some quiet martyr in me whispering, *Why bother? You're not going to help me anyway.* Why do we do that?

I'm changing that. I'm letting myself want things again. I want to master the yoga flow, to stop dropping my right shoulder and struggling to lower myself down. I want my inner fire to feel natural, not strained. I want to silence the inner critic. I want to see justice in ways I can't yet imagine. And most of all, I want to live the simple life of practice—the hours, the structure, the devotion. Because I've loved this rhythm before. I loved it on the outside and I love it here, too. Freedom is anywhere you're willing to stay in the pose long enough to feel something in you quietly lift off.

37

Diamond Pride

At 7:45 p.m., I could barely keep my eyes open after a big day of yoga and many miles of laps around the track. I'd asked Rach to remind me to take my progesterone, but instead she quietly got up, fetched my medicine and a cup of water, and handed them to me with a gentleness that feels ancient—the kind of caretaking women have always known. She tucked me in like a sister.

I woke at 5:00 a.m. to the dorm at its most quiet, the in-between time after the night owls have gone to bed and the early risers haven't begun to stir. I don't mind that the women are loud most of the night—because when they finally sleep in, I am gifted with these strange pockets of quiet. I can watch the sunrise reflecting off the wall, a pale gold smudge. I sat on my bunk and looked out the narrow slat beside Luciana's bed—our "window," ten inches wide, covered in metal mesh. Through it I could see the city lights fading as the sun began to rise.

I let my gaze go soft and unstructured. Structure is usually my gift, perhaps from having sat on so many meditation retreats. The Zen practitioner in me sets simple timers so my mind can roam inside a safe fence. The meditation starts and then ends. Some call that discipline but I find that word too harsh. I think of it as friendly guidance. My mind is a workhorse—strong, eager, and prone to charging into the nearest mud pit. Having one clear intention keeps it steady and on my side. Still, sometimes you have to let the mind wander and graze—let it remember its own wildness. Like the Zen gardener Wendy Johnson says, even the most manicured garden should leave ten percent wild, to remember its nature. That's what this morning felt like.

Earlier in the week, I had received a letter from my dear friend Ed, the Zen priest. It was one of those rare communications that reaches straight through time and touches the core of who you are. He wrote that I was here "to purify my love," that I've always been uncontrived and quick to send people back to their own internal laboratories to find truth inside themselves.

His letter wasn't dramatic or flattering. It was precise and human. Ed and I both took the same vow long ago: to keep loving, no matter what. It's not the vow of a saint who tries to scrub out her flaws. It's a vow to stay human while loving through it.

Ed embodies that. He cries, he rages, he feels everything, without pretense. He's a reminder that awakening isn't about escaping humanity—it's about including it. You don't transcend your humanness; you live it awake.

That's why Ed unsettles people. He makes you face the truth that you can't bleach out your darkness to become pure light. You can't divide yourself into "good" and "bad" and expect to be whole. Spiritual life isn't about perfection; it's about living and holding the grace and the grit without pretending you're finished. That's where the real freedom starts.

As I sat at the window thinking of him, I wondered what had knocked me out so completely last night. Maybe exhaustion. Or maybe something stranger.

Years ago I had a teacher who spoke about "walk-ins"—the idea that sometimes a soul gets swapped out, like a mechanic replacing a carburetor. You wake up feeling the same but somehow lighter, as if a new spirit took over the job. I laughed, imagining my old spirit saying, "I love you, but I'm out," while some brave new one stepped in: "Now that looks like an adventure."

By 6 a.m., I still hadn't done any of my practices, just my unstructured window-gazing. I found myself wishing I could have tea with Ed, eat his persimmons, tease him that we're best friends. I wanted him to know what his letter stirred in me—how it reminded me to love more cleanly, without defense.

I started pulling down the sheet of the privacy tent I'd draped over my bunk, putting on the sweatshirt I use as a pillow, and tucking my blankets military-style so I'd pass inspection. Then something stopped me, like a hand on my shoulder. I looked up at the room, half lit because it was still early (but in prison that's still about as bright as an operating room) and felt a wave of clarity.

Someone had suggested I talk to the chaplain about what I envisioned for this place. Prison as an institution reduces humans down to labels and populations, a sorting and holding system for sacks of meat it has been charged to store. I keep imagining what this place could be if we first considered it from life's perspective: women walking with herbal tea "mocktails," writing at tables covered with questions for self-reflection. I imagine it feeling less like a warehouse and more like a place for discovery, for women waking up to themselves and discovering that the bliss they were always looking for is right there.

The thought scared me a little. In here, it's safer to stay small. Keep your head down. Don't stand out. But to speak with the chaplain would mean stepping forward, risking visibility.

I'd been reading a Robert Thurman book and his definition of *vajra pride* resonated with me. I understood it as a quiet, unshakable self-respect. Not the kind of pride which can lead to arrogance, but a diamond pride where you know who you are underneath everything. It's knowing you are built for goodness and are responsible for goodness. It doesn't allow for feeling ashamed or hiding, for indulging in feelings of inferiority or superiority. It's pride that lets you receive feedback from others, and have compassion for others. With it, when you make a mistake you course-correct without collapsing. The only sin is forgetting your vajra pride.

When we first arrived, Rach and I couldn't find a place to meditate. Everything here is territorial—claimed by this group or that. The only spot available was the puzzle room, and I'd thought, *We can't just sit there cross-legged like statues; people will think we're casting spells.*

But one night before bed, a quiet voice inside declared, *Stop hiding.* You came here to be of benefit to others. Take your seat.

Then the next day we had that whole interaction with the guard who ended up offering up the craft room to meditate in. That moment cracked something open. We talked. We laughed. She told us about her hopes for the women here and how much she gives of herself. She switched from being an "authority figure" to a beautiful human who explained what she wants for the women. I learned that so much of what she offers comes from her own reserves.

The flash that gave me the courage to walk into that room in the morning to meditate, that's my understanding of vajra pride, that diamond confidence. It's the strength that lifts your spine when life tries to bow it, resulting sometimes in moments of humanity between people from two seemingly opposing groups.

So there I was this morning, standing by my bunk, feeling that same surge rise again. My back straightened. My eyes lifted. It wasn't just pride—it was presence. As if my backbone had turned to diamond, steady and bright.

38

Miriam

At 6 in the morning, we are allowed to venture beyond the blue line that separates the bunk area from the rest of the dorm, including the six computers. We can use them from 6 a.m. to 9 p.m., one hour at a time, then return an hour later for another slot. Dressed in my uniform, I headed over to the computers early and read through the overnight messages. News from friends on the outside. One was from my mom. By the time I got through them all, my hour at the computer was up. Main line was being called, time for breakfast.

I walked over for bran flakes. Miriam joined with her cake. The dorm was waking up, TV volumes increasing, some women waking up while the daytime sleepers had just begun their slumber.

"My mom wrote," I said to Miriam. "She numbers all our emails. Today was number eighteen. She's kept scrapbooks my whole life. Photos, letters, newspaper articles. While I'm in here, the scrapbooks are our correspondence."

Miriam smiled gently. "What will you write her?"

"Everything. I tell her everything. My mother and I have always been close, but this—these years of investigation, indictment, trial, landing here—this was the kind of pressure that shows you what a person is really made of. I worried about her more than I worried about myself. How was I supposed to watch over her from in here? How was she supposed to carry all this? But she has. She's shown up in a way I didn't even know to hope for. Whatever fear she has, it doesn't stop her. We talk every week, and write even more often, and somehow we're closer now than we were before—which says something, because we were already tight."

"Oh yeah, like what?" Miriam asked, genuinely curious about our relationship.

"She was a single mom. I was her only child. She took care of me, my grandma, my uncle. We all lived together. I was a writer even back in high school. I'd wake my mom up in the middle of the night to read her my poems. She'd always listen, even though she had work in the morning. Anyway, I see now she's tougher than I ever gave her credit for."

Miriam pushed her cake around the tray for a moment, thinking. Then she nodded slowly, like she'd decided something.

"I get that. My mom—she gave me freedom." She tapped the table with her fingertip, a tiny drumbeat of emphasis. "Structure, too— she'd pull my ear when I needed it—but mostly freedom. I could be who I wanted. She didn't try to make me smaller or bigger. Just...let me be."

She exhaled, settling into herself, into the story.

"I was twenty when I had my first son," she said. "Just me and my baby. I wasn't with his father and didn't wanna be. I said, 'I'm doing what I wanna do, and if he wants to be in the boy's life, fine.' And you know—my mom didn't shame me for that. She held the line but didn't hold me down."

She took a bite of cake, chewed, swallowed, and continued.

"Then I met my first husband. And, Nicole..." She gave a soft laugh.

167

"I basically adopted a grown man."

I laughed along, understanding exactly what she meant.

"He couldn't read. Couldn't write. His mother—she loved him, but she kept him broken. Her kids were checks. That's all they knew. And I came right in and said, 'Okay, baby, I'll teach you to walk again.' I became his provider, his mother, his everything. And I thought that was strength."

She shook her head. "We got married in ninety-seven. There was pressure—my grandmother was sick, everyone talking about how the boys needed a father. I thought I was doing the right thing. And for a while, maybe I was."

Miriam folded her arms, not defensively but like she needed to hold the weight of the memory.

"But he stopped appreciating me," she said. "Stopped seeing what I did to hold us all together. And my middle son...he stood up for me. That boy put himself between us and said, 'No.' And I thought—if I stay, they're gonna hate him. And maybe they'll hate me too."

The tenor shifted, the way life often does along with the story we tell to make sense of it.

"I had stopped being Miriam," she said quietly. "I became Mom, Provider, Fixer. Everything except myself. And I needed to show my boys what strength actually looks like. So I left. After seventeen years. Picked myself up and walked."

She looked at her own hands like they were something new.

"And then...this man," she said, half smiling. "My husband now. Nicole, I swear to you, I did not want that man at first." She shook her head, amused at her own past stubbornness. "He will proudly tell anyone who asks."

"What made you marry him?" I asked.

"He came in gentle, not weak. He gave me space to breathe. We were both newborn in our own ways. We helped each other grow up, hide

168

when we needed to, face the world when we could." Miriam looked up, softness in her face. "He loved me without needing me to be his mother. He didn't need fixing. Didn't need raising. He just—wanted me. As I am."

She set down her fork, done with her cake, done holding back.

"He tells me all the time, 'There's nothing you can't do.' And the thing is…he believes it. And when someone believes in you like that, you start remembering who you were before the world leaned on you."

She gave a small, warm smile.

"That's what I'd write my mom," she said. "Not all the details. Just that I found someone who lets me be myself again. Who doesn't shrink me or stretch me. Someone who knows I'm a fully dressed table."

I laughed softly. "A fully dressed table?"

"Yes," she said, proud of it. "I got everything I need. Anyone walking in now better be an enhancement, not a repair job."

Miriam stood, picked up her tray.

I headed back to the computer to reply to my mom.

The morning had begun, and somehow, we were both a little more ourselves inside it.

39

The Benefit of No Comfort

MDC Brooklyn is a detention center, a rest stop before or after sentencing, people on their way in or on their way out. Think Times Square subway: everyone headed somewhere else. Some women are almost out and you can feel their lift. Others arrive stunned—no cup, no toothbrush, no sweatshirt in the freezing air—waiting to be "picked up" by guides who will show them how to survive the first hours. Faces run the spectrum: open sobbing you can't stop, or the ones who get strong fast and get in the game.

Life here is a radical practice in non-attachment, married with deep intimacy. We are all in the desert together—each woman wrestling with her attorney, her family, herself. Suffering, here, is the great equalizer.

Community helps, and so does any training that teaches you how to be alone with yourself. Retreats. Recovery rooms. Communal living. Prison is the extreme version of all of it. It makes the insanity of clinging and pushing away painfully clear, then dissolves both fast— because the consequences for grasping or fighting are amplified. I've lost count of how many identities have fallen off. Each one gone is a relief. Around here it's simple: Let go or get dragged.

The physical world is stripped to the studs. Three TVs face the bunks, and the commercials look absurd against the real lives on either side of me—the shampoo sparkle effect playing while I talk through a bunk to Carla about sentencing and whether she'll ever get another shot on the outside. Thirty-five years old with a whole lifetime lived in lockdown. The news anchors look contoured and airbrushed. The drama on-screen is a thin swap for the aliveness that shows up when you drop pretense.

There's no insulation—no pillows or quiet or cozy. You sneak small delights where you can. On the rec deck, a cement slab behind heavy metal mesh, you can sometimes catch sunlight. If you go at the perfect time—around two—you can lie on a mat with your head against the gate and the sun will touch your face for half an hour. The mats have bird droppings even after we wipe them down, ants march in formation, women are screaming, and the heavy door booms louder than thunder, but that slice of sun feeds something starved.

The water runs into the sink ice-cold and brown from the rusty pipes. It makes my skin itch. I fantasize about toast with butter (there's no butter in prison), two eggs over medium, blueberries, and smoked salmon. I always loved nature, but you don't understand the holiness of a tree until you're barred from going outside at all. One slat of sun, that microdose of vitamin D, can make you weep.

The women themselves—this is where the warmth is. I wish you could see them. They don't miss a thing. Their faces shift with the need of the moment. Trust clicks and a whole new face appears. It's not only the constant hum of "threat" that hones awareness. I think many ended up here because their awareness outpaced what the outside world could use. In a way, maybe they were bored.

Prison compresses time. More happens in three minutes than in a week outside. Nothing is predictable. It depends on a guard's mood or something that happened on the men's side or an unknown factor you'll never learn. What time is breakfast? No one knows. Will there be a woman running like an airplane next to her bed all night while people shout, "Shut up"? Probably. Will she then sweetly call, "Goodnight," to the few who were kind, making everyone else a little jealous? Yes. There's no guidebook for this level of surreality. Mostly you just learn the terrain by walking it.

You can't game it. I don't mean gaming the institution; I mean you cannot hang your awareness on a hook and coast. Every second asks for a turn-on-a-dime mind. Coping isn't enough. You learn to navigate the hidden forest with bare attention—beyond happy or sad. I've built a new set of faces for the unthinkable, a way to evaporate into relative invisibility when that serves, and to step forward cleanly when that's required.

Underneath the noise, I've relocated my original vow—why I said yes to the whole mission at all, to this life with all its intimacy. I touched the trembling heart that shows up when you stop pretending and actually care. A friend once said he feared only God and mediocrity. I pinned my mind to the place that only fears betraying the truth of what I know—while also knowing that ultimately, there's no way to ever really get away from that truth.

And then I wake up and want toast. I want warm water. I want a tree. I'm back at the sink with the brown, freezing water and the over-lit pink cinderblocks, and I still wish—desperately sometimes—for softness. But the stripping does its work. What's left is clarity, appreciation, light. And women being women: the toughest ones forgiving after a day, the outcasts getting adopted, the quiet hand that sets a cup in front of a newcomer with no cup.

There is no comfort here. That's the benefit. The distraction is gone, so the real consolation can show itself: a glimmer of sunshine at 2 p.m., a laugh you didn't expect, and the knowledge you feel in your bones that even in a fluorescent desert, people refill each other and keep going, just enough to keep all of us a shade lighter than gravity says we should be.

40

Advanced Practice

I spent the morning reviewing books and notes, ideas gathering and clarifying. That afternoon would be the first class of the meditation course I'd be teaching to the ladies of MDC. To be clear, it's an honor to be with the women here—fast, sharp, trickster-smart. Any "teaching" I'm able to offer in my meditation classes is both extra and essential. Extra, because their instincts are keen. Essential, because with even just a sip of practice, you can see them reanimate. It's beautiful and daunting. You can't underestimate them for a second or step off the post of perfect equality; miss the wink and you're out of the collective space.

The idea for a class didn't start with me. Weeks prior, fresh out of solitary confinement in the Special Housing Unit, Yilan came to me directly. "You meditate, yes?"

"Um, yes," I said, caught off guard. Over time, the women's initial incredulous reactions to Rach and I sitting in whatever quiet corner we could find had softened to curiosity. A few women sometimes pulled up chairs, imitated our posture, and tried it. But Yilan hadn't been there for any of that, and the rumors I'd heard about her didn't suggest meditation was her thing.

"You teach meditation class for all of us. We get certificates. Looks good for parole." She smiled in that matter-of-fact way that reminds everyone what's in their best interest.

I laughed—then realized she wasn't joking. "Certificates, huh?"

"All the ladies will go," she said. "You tell the administration, they give us a sign-up sheet. Makes it official. We get certificates."

And so it was.

These women have all the ingredients for excellent practice. Every interaction with authority, every repetition of routine, every moment of uncertainty could become a place of practice, an invitation to master attention. We live in extreme conditions here—questionable food, broken sleep, relentless heat and cold—and can use it all as inspiration. They could learn to regulate temperature, appetite, clarity, and energy from within. They could tap into and unleash the wild power within: the only force strong enough to drive someone all the way to enlightenment.

I feel like a kid on the first day of school. These are the women I live with, day in and day out. Prison walls, meant to separate "in here" from "out there," create a kind of compression on those inside. These women can smell performance. They really give attention, but they aren't angling to be the teacher's pet. They're either with you or not.

At 2:00, I walk into the gym with the women who are excited for class. The number swells well beyond the eight lines the administration allotted on the sign-up sheet they had posted four days ago in the dorm.

"That's twenty-two," Rachel whispers as we take our seats in front— well over half the dorm. No pressure. She grins.

"Okay," I say, as the room gathers itself.

"So, you're in prison. But when it comes to meditation, that's actually a good thing. Meditators in Tibet and Nepal go find caves in the mountains, alone, with less comfort than we have here. They are called cave yogis. These are top meditators, and for them, the bare walls, the cold, the simplicity are all benefits, so the mind has to face itself. You all are smart. You figured out how to get a meditation retreat without flying all the way to the Himalayas."

The few who'd heard this from me before chuckle, endeared to this crazy white woman sitting in front of twenty-two federal inmates, teaching meditation. Some are clearly there for the certificate. But Yilan catches my eye and gives an approving nod: *Keep going.*

"So if they're cave yogis, that makes us OG yOGis. 'Original gangster'—the part of you that's tough, real, unfuckwithable. And yOGi doesn't mean flexible; it means transformation. How little a shift does it take for the dorm to become an inner monastery for real change? It's routine, practice, structure. Shift inside, and the world shifts with you."

Luciana smirks. "OG yOGi. Okay, I like that."

Others aren't as sure. "You know what they can do to you here? They can lock you up in a little room all by yourself. You don't get any say in that."

"That's the threat that runs your mind," I say before I can temper it. It is true. I check Yilan's face—expressionless, watching me. "I'm not saying SHU isn't real, but you can transform it. Those cave meditators sit in the middle of nowhere, and to them it's the greatest place in the world because it helps transform their minds. Every woman here fears going into solitary. I'm saying, whether it's SHU or general population, it starts with a choice—choose where you are and put it to work for you."

"We're not saying you gotta take our word for it," Rachel adds, bridging the divide. "Just try it. Meditation isn't about believing the right thing. It's about having the experience for yourself."

She is right. It's not a debate about beliefs or religions. "When the Buddha taught, he used the word *ehipassiko*—it means 'see for yourself.'

Don't take my word for it or anybody's. Try it and see."

When I was preparing for class, I'd called my Lama to ask what to teach. "Teach them tummo."

"Really?" I was surprised. "Isn't that a little advanced?"

"They seem advanced enough." He chuckled.

We weren't going to need buckets to soak our clothes in like the cave dwellers of Tibet I've seen—the hyperactive prison A/C kept it cold enough that most women wore several layers under their uniforms in an attempt to stay warm. "Okay," I said to him, "let's try it."

I explain the practice—and its benefits. *Te pone caliente,* Mari translates for the Spanish speakers, to their delight. The women gather themselves, sitting upright in their chairs.

Rach checks her watch. "We'll start with ten minutes."

The practice works. Even the irritated women in the back uncross their arms and sit up, clocking how many around them had closed their eyes. The breath hold has several purposes, but for first-time meditators, it sharpens the mind, gives it something to do. The room quiets while the TVs in the other room drone on. A stillness descends.

We close with a word or two from each woman to seal the practice. "Love." "Peace." "Warmer." Royal offers grandmotherly warmth: "I'm just glad we can be doing something all together."

We pack up. Chairs scrape against the floor. Chatting resumes. Some talk about the class; others move on to the next thing. But I feel a shift—in myself and in the dorm. After nearly two months of being the odd curiosity, the two strange white women doing our own strange thing, the secret is out—and with it, an invitation.

41

Dakina

We're circling the indoor track when I hear birds for the first time in days. The rec deck is locked now because someone had been "fishing"—dropping lines down to someone outside and pulling contraband up onto the deck—but I can still catch a strip of sky through the wired window. In my head I'm humming a Bob Marley song, "Won't you help to sing these songs of freedom," and the birds feel like backup singers.

We were up early, like usual. But this morning has an unusual buzz. Nevaeh waves us over, rosary flashing white against her shirt. "Did you hear? Dakina was speaking Hebrew all over the dorm last night," she whispers. "I think it was an exorcism. Dakina doesn't know Hebrew. We took turns praying throughout the night."

"It's our minds playing tricks," I say gently. "Fear does that." She's not really listening to me, but it's 4:30 a.m., so I let it rest. The women here take dark spirits seriously.

There's a line from a teaching I love: Even when you're not sitting in meditation, treat every sound as part of the practice. Dakina's cries aren't random; they have cadence. I noticed it in the first few days after she arrived. She howls after disruptions, when the officers sweep through, when the dorm's fear spikes. If you listen, it's like a drumline calling our nervous systems to attention.

As the weeks passed, the blue half-moons under the women's eyes deepened. No one was sleeping. Dakina spent most nights running and howling on her top bunk. The women snapped: "Shut up!" "Enough!" Their voices mimic her sound. One morning, Claire stood by my bed with Luciana. "I'm done with this," she said through gritted teeth. Claire is not known for tenderness.

"Oh, you haven't figured out how it works?" I teased one morning. Claire rolled her eyes—then paused, listening. The next time Dakina called out, I pointed it out. "Hear the rhythm?" Claire's head tilted despite herself. "Notice when it starts. Always after the energy turns."

"Didn't clock that," she admitted, softening. She's tough, but she listens.

When officers file in for the weekly inspection—uniforms, bunks, corners—the dorm's atmosphere hardens like cooling glass. Dakina's cries get clipped, canine, as if she is a guard dog and a perimeter has been breached. The second the officers leave, she goes quiet. "Maybe she's our barometer," I say to Luciana. "Maybe she's sounding what we can't say."

But the tension kept climbing. The women who hover by the gate began to stake out turf. "Something's going down," Janiya warned.

One night at 3 a.m., I woke with a start. Dakina was standing by my bunk, staring. When it registered that I'm not Luciana, she drifted to Luci's bed.

"You got a Snickers?" she asked.

"No, Dakina. No Snickers."

"Any candy then?"

Luci got up, handed her a Hershey's bar.

"Can I trade this for a Snickers?"

"I don't have a Snickers," Luci said, and Dakina vanished.

Sometimes it takes some sweetness to soothe the ghosts. The next day I ask Miss Wu for a Snickers and leave it for Dakina. She takes it without a word. An hour later she pokes a finger into Rachel's back and says, "This is a stickup. Hand over all your candy," then grins. Playful, just for a second.

But the pressure in the dorm kept increasing. Dakina was loud in the night. Royal, despite all her pure-hearted love, couldn't sleep. "Back in the day you knew better than to mess with Royal," Nevaeh would remind us. I heard Royal's voice in the night, shaking with control. "Tamara, I gave her all my food. I asked polite. I'm gonna lose it." When Royal, of all people, walks to the officer's desk like she's turning herself in before something snaps, I know the wave has crested.

They took Dakina out on count. Four officers, one flaring body, a collective gasp. Then a few women clapped and whistled, and my breath stuck. How can you applaud? Over the noise, Miriam's gravelly voice rose up, clean and brave: "Y'all who be clapping, stop. That woman is no different than you. You are one break, one trauma away from being her. Or your mama. Or your sister."

Before I could think, I called out—loud enough to startle myself— "I'm with her." The room stilled. Maybe I don't have Miriam's street cred, but I can lend my voice to the truth under hers. My heart breaks at the way we treat our own pain.

Weeks later, Dakina returned from her time in SHU. The escorting officer told us she apologized for the noise. "Sometimes she's just in so much pain." Dakina was softer, a little. She shows us drawings— bold figures like Keith Haring's, alive with motion. Fewer women yell now. Miriam's words did something. When asked why she screamed, Dakina shrugs. "The pain." On her bunk were three notes in a childlike hand: If your back hurts, rub it. If your legs hurt, rub them. You do not have to yell.

So while I don't know that Dakina's episode last night was due to demonic possession, I can recognize that the women's extra prayers were an act of care for her as much as it was for their own sanity. And in the morning, they walk the dorm wearing their rosaries and saying their prayers. I teased Nevaeh that Dakina was more powerful than all of us at getting these women to actually practice religion. Nevaeh looked at me as if I did not understand the gravity of the problem.

Oh, I understand all right. I understand pain, and I understand the pain of confinement. I think to ask Nevaeh if perhaps we are the ones that Dakina is casting out rather than us her. And still I hear her over in the corner, now a bit quieter, her voice across the dorm, singing her song, running on her bunk as fast as she can, as if she might take flight, singing this song of freedom.

42

The Longer Game

The air before dawn has a rare clarity that reminds me of driving through New York City when it is still half asleep. My practice felt softer today. Less tension. More space. I stood at the bunk window and whispered a few simple prayers for protection and compassion while the sky lightened. For a moment I could swear I was looking out a window in Mongolia again. The edges between places are getting porous.

Then a pocket of old "junk mail" in my mind opened. The stuff I had pushed aside rather than face. I am getting better at noticing the little squeeze that pushes a thought away and, instead, letting it rise into open space where it can dissolve. I am also watching what wants to grow. Receiving is easy for me. I can accommodate a lot. What needs building is the channel that asserts, speaks up, and transforms. I have always side-eyed the personal development world because so much of it feels like wishful thinking dressed up as science. But the real thing is different. The real thing goes to the root. It meets the thought at the seed and says, like in a lucid dream, "I decide what you are."

I can spot certain thoughts coming now. I see them turn the corner like scruffy alley cats that want to drag anxiety into the house. It still feels like a miracle when I meet them at the door and redirect them. If one slips past, then all I can do is notice it, open, and let it move through. By that point I already bought the story. Even then, it passes faster. My inner core feels stronger, so fewer stray thoughts get access, and the ones that do are easier to usher out.

What I want next is a clean "bring it on" mindset. Not bravado. Competence. I want the part of me that assesses risk and spirals to be retrained into the part of me that faces the forest with steady eyes. Glad the thought showed up, because now I can turn its momentum into flow instead of blockage. I want the inner version of the cold-plunge person who grins and jumps, or the endurance athlete who runs toward the pain because they know how to work with it. I have the feminine side. I find my footing fast. Now I want the forward drive, like buffalo who head into the storm. At the level of thought. No freeze. No stunned silence. Go.

I am writing this down because I trust the desire itself. The right longing has a different texture than wanting a car or a boyfriend. It feels like the desire is calling me, asking my awareness to recognize it.

I used to pray for special abilities and then not know what to do with them. Or ask for light and then watch it activate some old pattern. Two things are different now. First, a humble boundary. I do not want a single ounce more than I can joyfully integrate. Like not eating past full, then taking a walk to digest. Second, I trust myself. My mind is anchored in the intention to serve. I can say, "I am ready," and mean it. Maybe that is what all the unread messages in the universe have been waiting for.

When I moved back to Harlem, I heard it plain as day. Harlem needed what we had to offer. If I wanted a real refuge, I had to commit and actually build all the pieces of Unconditional Freedom. I promised five years. The roots took. It developed and expanded—Free Food for those who needed it, a program for those struggling with addiction based on this same philosophy of dignity and humanity, teaching *The Art of Soulmaking* to people coming out of prison, struggling to get their feet back under them, programs for women to recognize their inestimable power.

It became clear, however, that this work is not tied to a neighborhood. It is tied to a population. Yesterday in the shower, I made a vow. It felt like a baptism. I want my post inside the justice world. All the energy I need will come if I commit to the long game. Twenty years. The vision is the same one I keep naming: Do for women, especially inside the system, what Malcolm X did for Black Americans. Not through branding. Through deep practice and real tools. I have tasted the gratification. I also know it will not always feel good. I used to marry every project on the first date, then wake up six months in and realize I was living with a dud. No more getting drunk on novelty. This work finally feels like the source of where women's power lives.

I understand why my friend Topeka started her nonprofit, The Ladies of Hope Ministries, shortly after being released from prison. Now, she's spent the last nine years on the road, advocating for women and girls impacted by the justice system. She has changed legislation, provided housing, helped women find jobs and banks post-incarceration. There are so many other things a person can spend their life working toward, shiny objects that offer fame and fortune. But the soul plays a longer game.

43

Light Returning to Itself

One woman was being transported to her "destination" this morning, which always results in some upheaval. Not bad, exactly—just the kind that opens the floor. In here, every woman becomes her for a moment. Hackles go up on some, others shrink like rescues being tugged from a cage, and a few of us stand at the edges, sending her off. The abyss of uncertainty yawns wide. Shackles. New guards with new rhythms. You don't know when you'll eat or where you'll land. All you have are sketches in your imagination of what the next place might be.

It takes a minute for the heart to catch up. First there's the clench, the braced breath, the hardness. Then warmth returns. On both sides. You hope the people receiving her can see what she is—a living creature, not a threat.

Later, I'm swapping cockroach stories with Royal. The women act tough until a roach appears, then they run shrieking through the dorm. Yesterday I opened the shower and a water bug, as big as my forefinger, stared me down. I tapped it toward a crack in the wall. Someone overheard and asked why I didn't kill it. "Because there are a million more behind that wall," I said. "Killing one just props up the illusion." I like to imagine it sent me a tiny blessing on the way home. Maybe that's naïve. Or maybe simple mercy is a kind of insurance for my own soul.

Threat is everywhere here, but I've never believed the world was otherwise. Now I'm on the side of the wall where the roaches live, and I'm not surprised. This is the underbelly doing what underbellies do—some people performing "big bad," some rebelling on cue, some hiding. We are united by circumstance even while we pretend we aren't.

I tell the women often, "There is no them." We love to fight, to stand in opposition, but most of the battle is in my mind: my projections, my stories. It makes me laugh how many women are sure *those* women are beneath them—"skanks," "rats"—as if hierarchy can't help but sprout even at the bottom of the heap. Down here, there's still a contest for "best of the dung heap." "Look at me, flowers are growing on *my* part!" I've been warned off nearly everyone by someone. "Don't talk to her." "Protect your energy." A nice woman like me should stay away.

What helps is remembering my center. "Unbreakable dignity"—that bedrock sense of worth no one can give or take. I practice sitting there, right in the hub of it all. If I can return to that seat, I remember what I'm here to do: offer. Location is irrelevant. Noise, doubt, even the arrows that seem to fly past your head after the lunch tray—none of that has to move you. The only way to lose your seat is to get up.

Several times a day, in my mind, I press my palm to the ground and ask the Earth to be my witness. It's a quiet gesture of faith: The world is here, and so am I.

If I'm building any muscle, it's faith—faith in what I've already seen with my own eyes. Miracles that would sound like exaggerations if I wrote them down. Kindnesses that arrive precisely when I've forgotten how to ask. Evidence that something in all this is *for* me, not against me.

When that faith opens, it feels like returning to a room I once knew well. Years ago, I stumbled into a place beyond words—a bright, motionless ease. I called it the Eternal Room. Years later, describing it to my Lama, he invited me to explore the idea of the mind as a mountain, to see life as light moving through form. I understood only enough to want to understand more.

This morning, I called on those merging memories and walked back toward that place. I could feel the layers that had grown over it—doubt calcified like mineral on a pipe. The work is the same as always: stay, breathe, soften, stay. Let the clench drain off until the warmth returns. Let the light notice itself again.

That's all I want, really. To keep choosing the seat in the center. To keep seeing past the categories to the creature inside them. To practice that unbreakable dignity until the room opens and the light, finally, returns to itself.

44

For the Woman in the Bunk Next to Me, Part Three

She tells me she wants to lose fifteen pounds before she gets out. The words I didn't say lingered in my mind: that I have marveled at her body. That I thanked God there are still women shaped as if sex itself designed them: soft curves, hips made for hands, breasts that look like, if pressed, milk would pour—sweetness for the drinking. I didn't say her round face is lunar, a tide-puller, a reminder of cycles and seasons and the invisible power that moves the world.

I didn't say it because we're in prison, where admiration is too easily mistaken for a come-on, and reverence for a woman can be misread as a proposition. But the awe I feel is the same awe I'd feel before a Renoir or any earthly abundance. It's the awe our culture learned to distrust during what I call the Great Impoverishment—when the experience of being a woman became too difficult, too thankless, too dangerous. The fix was to downsize us: less curve, less voice, less hunger. Become "girl" at best, "boy" at worst. No breasts. No life-filled belly. No threat.

We learned to starve ourselves into pre-pubescence so no one could accuse us of lording power over men with our pendulous breasts and swinging asses. We traded our nobility for a walk-on part. Behind him is the role. Stay small enough to fit inside his shadow.

Starvation or spinsterhood—those were the choices offered. Burn with hunger in an empty belly, or eat and burn with jealousy while girls—ever smaller, ever more compliant—take our seats.

So the priestesses and warriors, the thick-bodied women of Gauguin, the full-throated divas, Gaia herself, were all placed on a caloric deficit. We didn't just starve the flesh; we starved the sex, the voice, the vision, the wisdom. We made ourselves into dolls—easier for the male ego to manage. No need to rise in the presence of a queen if he can project a fantasy onto a vacant face: She loves it. She wants it. She's desperate for me. Sometimes he prefers the brat doll or the bossy girl simply for the thrill of subduing her. Wrestling with a little girl proves he's strong.

This can only happen in a sexless world where even the sex is projection—her vacancy is what he's filling. Not an actual woman with actual wants and hungers to interrupt his grim need to "bang one out" and be thanked for it. It's a double win: fantasy fulfilled, savior complex satisfied.

Her crankiness from emotional, physical, and spiritual anorexia reads as "cute." He pats himself on the back for being a good guy who can "handle" her. And desperate as only a starving girl can be, she apologizes for her appetite. Her tiny body becomes a billboard: Please don't leave me. I'm nothing without you.

It reminds me of that usual scene, sitting on a plane: The man holds the baby for takeoff and earns praise, but within an hour the woman is holding the baby, *and* the man, while trying to look slim and pleasant. You know the script.

I'm asking you not to step into it. You are perfection. You are only looking into funhouse mirrors. Choose older mirrors. Sacred mirrors. Those from centuries ago, when God wore a woman's face, and a woman's body was revered. Remember the time when it was assumed women wanted sex more than men—because sex was the source of our power.

Right now, the world feels upside down, ruled by children of all ages. We need women—adult women—nourished, strong, lucid. Men cannot grow into honorable equals without the erotic intelligence of women to shape and steady them.

We live in an era of war games and international tantrums, boys at podiums (not all), propping themselves up with girl dolls. We don't need smaller women. We need you whole.

We need you as Woman—fed, fierce, unflinching. We need your dakini warrior heart and the erotic fire that lives between your legs. That raw, radiant power is a compass. It turns us toward life. It points us to make love, not war.

45

Balancing Pose

Lately my mind keeps flashing to a stretch of Brooklyn by the apartment I stayed in during trial: the restaurant we'd go to for lunch on the weekend, the tree-lined block just past it, the clothing shop Emmett would point at and say, "You'd like that place." The intensity of the time burned even these simple details into my mind so that it comes back to me warm and whole, like a sunlit room I can step back into.

Harlem is blurrier despite having lived there for years. I remember the woman who sits on the bench on Lenox with her sand-dollar-sized rouge and calls everyone "hey, daddy." There are a handful of other flashes, but not the slow, underwater light from that short time in Brooklyn. I used to resist how easy Brooklyn felt compared to Harlem, like some workhorse part of me insisted things *should* be hard. Even this morning, doing breathing exercises, I caught myself layering difficulty on top of difficulty, as if strain made it meaningful. And in the moment I realized what I was doing, I caught a glimpse—brief but unmistakable—of a mind I could step into where the effort drops and the thing simply happens. I suspect that's closer to my natural state than the strained face I make when I'm trying to look like I'm working hard.

Today my mind feels like a messy room. These are the difficult days when my meditation and prayers and practice just feel fake. My mind mocks me, "an earnest person doing a weird little ritual." I keep telling myself, "Touch the desire for freedom," and I can feel the spark of why I practice, but then the mind scatters, rationalized, resigned. It's what a broken heart accumulates when effort never fully lands—like trying the same balancing pose for the 300th time and falling again. In yoga class, you can at least see someone else steady in the shape, proof that it's possible. Here, most people are on the floor.

A rabbi visited yesterday. He wanted Rachel to return to Judaism and leave "all that meditation and spirituality stuff." He turned to me, the Christian-raised, Jesus-loving, meditating spiritual adventurer that Rachel has traveled alongside for the last nearly two decades, waiting for my response. I told him it was her choice. He said, "The purpose of being in prison is to *fight*." Spiritually, of course. But I kept thinking about that all day. Maybe. Or maybe the point is to find a steady enough center that you can meet everything without turning into it.

In here, I can see every option on the nervous-system menu. Some women fight everything—guards, rules, each other. Others freeze, sleeping all day, faces turned to the wall, disappearing into their bunks. And then there's Dakina, our pure flight response, spending whole nights running on her bunk. Fight, flight, freeze—they're all on display in a forty-woman dorm. What I'm practicing is an inner steadiness that doesn't use any of those doors.

In meditation, most trouble starts in doubt: the mind that second-guesses, scrambles, splits. I remember being scolded for never praying for myself. There's a feminine distortion that says our worth is only in what we give, so we pretend we have no needs while trying to get them met sideways. Lately I'm letting desire rise without slapping it down. Not clinging, not dramatizing—just not vetoing my own wants.

What I'm not reaching for anymore is the costume of the martyr or the saint. You know the airbrushed spirituality that floats above money, sex, jealousy—above life? I'm over it. I'm just as over the glossy "Millionaire Monk" version that turns transcendence into a hustle. The truth I trust lives in the middle of all of it: wanting, losing, choosing again. Grown-up spirituality. Not vapor, not pose.

Yesterday we walked, Royal and I talking, Rach beside us taking notes. I'd told the women that their stories will be what dissolves the single story of how society thinks of women in prison. It's hard to project the face of an enemy onto a living, breathing story of someone's humanity.

Our conversation ventured into the area where I get in trouble. I told her I don't buy the story that women are broken and weak. A lot unravels when you start there. She said she's always wanted a tattoo that reads, "God made man," with the implied second line: *and woman made God.* I laughed. "I'm not sure everyone sees it that way." She laughed back. "No, baby. That's why these girls are in so much trouble—and why you and me are talking."

She is one of the greatest concentrations of love I've ever met. It humbles me. She talks about her father—the best man who ever lived—and the love pours out raw and unguarded. She tells me her ex got married while she was locked up, and that it destroyed her. She is an animal laid bare, no armor, and that nakedness is her strength. Next to her, my way of showing care through structure and action looks stiff. Maybe that's why she opens with me: We are equal and opposite currents, both unflinching in our belief in the power of women, both soft where it counts.

I feel moved by the smallest kindnesses. It makes me want to "hold" more cleanly: to keep enough structure and clear view that care doesn't turn into *idiot compassion*—the kind that comforts in the moment but leaves harm intact. Real holding takes backbone and warmth. It's a balancing pose: weight over the center, toes alive on the ground, gaze steady, breath easy. You don't force it. You stay, you adjust, you let the pose teach you. And then, very quietly, it holds.

46

Between Hope and Fear

The day was perfectly split: half hope, half fear. My mind ping-ponged between them until I realized the back-and-forth was the point. The tension wasn't a problem to solve; it was the current that holds the whole thing together. Something lands in the middle, a rumor or a piece of news, and two forces start pulling. Part of me fights. Part of me soothes. The work is to stand in the traffic circle without getting dragged by either car.

Then another layer showed itself: how eagerly the mind assigns meaning. If I look closely, everything I declare "good" or "bad," "secure" or "threatening," starts to dissolve. I remember once looking at someone I loved and seeing him as pure, neutral light, as if he reflected only what I projected. I hated it. I wanted a solid "you" over there choosing me of his own free will. Because if there isn't a fixed "you," then maybe there isn't a fixed "me" either, and what would I push against?

I thought I wanted truth. What I wanted was something to hold.

This morning I read a short Buddhist teaching called The Heart Sutra. It's a reminder that nothing has a fixed nature; everything is available for transformation. I could hear the cadence of an old chant in my head and picture the wooden clappers from the Zen Center I used to visit. I'd make the trip there before dawn, feeling as if I were making such a sacrifice driving that winding road so early, proud of my demonstration of spiritual dedication. Now I crave those hours for a simpler reason: quiet.

Something in me is ready to let go again. It's a familiar feeling, like a rocket warming on the launchpad. But letting go can't be muscled. It's finesse, not force. It means letting the tension be there, naming the discomfort and resisting the urge to fix it, and trusting that clarity comes on its own schedule. Cause and effect are still in motion. All there is to do is feel what's here, not manufacture wisdom on demand.

Royal asked if I'm ever afraid Emmett will leave me. "Not really," I said.

She laughed: "I'm so fond of you. You're so confident."

Some of that ease comes from his steadiness and generosity; he reassures me without prompting. But it runs deeper. It's a quiet faith in the road we've already walked together, the pattern we've made through a thousand choices. Simple. We travel together.

I don't carry the same fears that gnaw on most women day in and day out because the love I'm talking about isn't organized around the question *Will he stay or will he go?* My wish for him is that he be genuinely happy, however that looks, even if that happiness one day takes him in a different direction. I trust our connection because I'm not trying to trap it. I would never issue an ultimatum, and that absence of threat is its own kind of glue.

In here, women will lose their minds if someone so much as flirts with "their guy" at the gate. The whole dorm can tilt on one sideways look. Royal is trying to understand why I'm not living in that same constant panic. She thinks it must be confidence, or charm, or some secret move I have with men. But it isn't that I believe I'm so hot or smart or special that no man would ever leave me, although let's be honest, I like who I am. It's that there is a different kind of love that doesn't start with ownership. It starts with being *for* each other. I would rather free you than own you.

Emmett and I are loyal, first, to something bigger than either of us: a set of principles about kindness, honesty, and taking radical responsibility for our own lives. Our relationship is an offshoot of that shared loyalty. Part of the joy is watching how he lives those principles, how his devotion to them quietly benefits me. I know he has this same view of the relationship. When that is the ground, the question, "Are you afraid he'll leave?" doesn't disappear, but it loses its teeth. The real fear would be betraying what we most deeply value, not losing possession of a person.

It's the same reason I don't back down or scramble to convince people when the women confront me. Royal says I've got game, and I tell her I'm not sure she knows the game I'm playing. I'm not calm because I'm so tough or because I know all the prison rules. I'm calm because, as well as I can, I act in alignment with what I know to be right. My heart is clear. That is the concealed rule of this whole story: I'm not doing anything here that isn't available to anyone else. I'm just trying to live these quiet, stubborn principles, but when people live blinded by their fears, even that looks like I've got a trick up my sleeve.

47

Birthday

I woke with a kind of spaciousness that felt almost brave. Beyond sorrow, beyond even the effort to push sorrow away. Maybe because it was my birthday, I decided to invite all of it in—the fear, the grief, the ache I usually keep at the edges. I turned off the light that keeps the dark things out and let everything collapse toward the center.

It reminded me of that feeling in a meditation hall when no one turns on the lights—only the thin stripes of sunlight cutting through dust and the faint outline of a goddess statue in the corner. There's something tender in that darkness. You can stop being the warrior for a moment. You can let whatever you've been dreading finally enter the room.

I went to grab toilet paper and came back to a small miracle—a hand-painted card on my bed. Luciana had spent two days painting an image of Vajrayogini, a fierce, feminine Tibetan deity of wisdom, red and radiant. All the women in the dorm had signed it with tiny, careful notes—some funny, some shy, some beautifully raw.

They'd seen me. Women I didn't even realize had registered me— the quiet ones, the ones whose faces stay guarded—had written things about being touched, about finding calm through our circles. It was the perfect kind of birthday: private enough that I could cry freely, a small uprising of tenderness inside a place built on threat.

Later on, three of my favorite women sang me a doo-wop version of "Happy Birthday," Marilyn Monroe style. Miss Wu baked a cake from commissary ingredients and somehow made it delicious. She stuck an "Om Ah Hum" flag in the top—our makeshift blessing—and Kay-Kay, who speaks almost no English, stood beside her and chanted the mantra.

There was joy, absurdity, and ache all at once. One letter really undid me, an apology from a woman who had complained about our meditation class. Turns out, she had wanted a space of her own and was angry we'd secured a room. She wrote that our class had changed the temperature of the unit, that she could feel it. When I teased her— "Oh, you have to be the best at everything, even apology letters?"—she cried like a child who'd been told she was good.

That's what it felt like all day: the veils falling away. Naked heart is the only way to describe it, like standing in the open air with no skin between myself and the world.

At one point in my life, there was a quiet, persistent voice beneath everything I did, whispering, *I don't want to be here.* It was so constant I mistook it for truth. I read that this voice is one of the root notes of suffering, but I hadn't understood until I saw it clearly: It wasn't mine. It was like a song playing on the universal radio of the mind— everyone's station tuned to the same sad refrain. When I finally recognized it, I could unhook from it, like peeling Velcro apart. And since that day, I've wanted to be wherever I am.

Karma burns out faster in prison; the illusions come undone. Yesterday I felt that burn—the collision of opposites. A tenderness so raw it pierced straight through to the center of my heart, and beneath it, that ancient undertone again—the low hum of *I don't want to be here.*

Only now I could hear that it wasn't just mine. It was the collective cry of everyone who has endured the unthinkable—the moment when God seems to turn His face away. Or worse, when God becomes the punisher, striking at random, as in the story of Job.

I think that story exists for this feeling—the feeling that God is against you, yet leaves just enough air in the room for you to find your own way back. That's how it feels here. On the surface, the utter wrongness of being in prison. But underneath, the sweetest paradox: that within these walls lies a vast spiritual training ground, where the heart is stripped bare, and the holy work of remembering begins.

Still, I couldn't ignore the human ache—the part that keeps track, that whispers *why bother?*, that stares at the future with quiet dread. So I invited that into my heart, too.

My day ended with a young woman I worry about—sharp, wild, too fragile for this place— chanting softly near my bunk. I'd taught her a simple mantra by turning it into a rap: "Jo Rama Jo Rama Jo Jo Rama," and she'd taken to it immediately. She had come by in the morning, waking me up with it as well. My birthday was bookended by her voice—proof that something had taken root.

The next morning began like any other: I poured my coffee—made the night before so I wouldn't risk a guard's mood crossing the blue line for hot water—and sat with my dreams. One about a woman low on energy, one about a recycling center missing the letter A in "ATM," one about someone upset that a store wasn't in an apartment. Nonsense dreams, maybe. But I woke up feeling lighter.

I sat for my morning practice. I felt my breath move freely again, as if the lungs themselves had remembered they were elastic. And suddenly, without forcing it, the insight arrived: that thought of being punished or abandoned—it isn't personal. It's the collective voice of loss, of disbelief, of the ones who've lived through shock and pain. It's a story we all inhale. And I could finally exhale it.

I didn't need to replace it with new words. Just light. Just presence where the hurt used to live.

The dorm was still half dark as I bagged my laundry—Monday is laundry day for Row One—and washed my hair in the sink. The air was cold, the guards unpredictable. Some mornings they're kind, others curt. You never know until you're standing there with wet hair and a towel around your neck and have to ask for a hair dryer. This one was kind. I walked back past the women brushing their teeth, the ones just heading to bed after a night shift of worry. We nodded. The smallest gestures of kinship here matter most.

I sat down at the computer, still warm from that quiet morning light, and there it was: one message waiting. Just one. Usually I have more but I'd spoken to so many people on the outside for my birthday. The email had an update about a book signing that had happened at a Barnes & Noble the day before.

The work I do feels so often misunderstood. The idea of meditation and sexuality together, that there may be something beneficial to sex beyond procreation, recreation, or violation (the three limited categories society places sex within) can leave people bug-eyed. I know it can change. The same happened with yoga and psychedelics. First the world calls it dangerous, then they call it medicine.

Two years ago, I had explained the conundrum to my Lama who smiled and suggested simply, "Write a book. Call it *The Art, Science, and Spirituality of the Female Orgasm.* Write it with that doctor you mentioned." I'd rolled my eyes at the time—another impossible assignment from the universe—but I knew better than to ignore him. And so, we wrote it. The book had been published during my trial. Now my co-author was doing book signings while I was behind bars.

The thread of that life continues on as did the prayer of the woman I was in that life, that I'd plant enough seeds that they would sprout even if I wasn't there.

48

The Skeleton Key

I t was Monday, meditation class. I started with a story I'd heard from a Tibetan monk. When he was young he saw some kids throwing rocks at a puppy, beating it until it died. From that time on, he used that ache in the center of his heart—the unbearable empathy he felt—as his source of compassion.

It felt timely to talk about something more heart-oriented after they'd been so sweet to me for my birthday the day before. I mentioned the beauty I'd found at MDC, and Carla was not having it. In prison, things are divided along race lines, and it's hard to cross them. If you're white, you're assumed naïve, maybe oblivious. If you disagree, you're "ignorant," not informed. It can feel like sexism—being brushed off and dismissed. Here, the story goes, you don't know pain or the streets. Sometimes women would talk to me as if I didn't know what it was like to be in prison. I'd joke, "Oh, because my bunk is somehow more like The Ritz? Because my fungal rash and constant indigestion are fancier than yours?"

Carla started in on her argument, leaning on the credentials of someone who'd been locked up more years than she'd been free. "You have no idea. What you call beautiful? I call bullshit." She'd been a young kid from Cuba when she made her first trip to juvie at thirteen. Then, bounced through every kind of facility they could ship a girl to. By the time she was thirty-five, she'd lived in more institutions than homes, and she wore that history like a badge she dared anyone to question.

"You telling me your story," I said, "that was beautiful. That wouldn't happen on the outside." She cocked her head, granting me her listening.

"Okay, but you have no idea what happens in here," she said, like a coach had tapped her shoulder to keep fighting.

"You think I don't know about the opps?" I said, and a few women laughed at the fifty-eight-year-old white lady using the prison shorthand for "opponents." "You think I don't see the arguments, the bullying? You think I appreciate you because I'm duped? It's the opposite. I pay attention to everything. That's how I see beneath the drama to the heart that's still alive. I'm going to keep saying it, nothing is really the way it seems."

She conceded the point, then went for the knockout. "Okay, but you never been to solitary. People lose their minds in SHU. One crazy dude ate a light bulb. Ate it. First time they threw me in SHU was juvie. I was thirteen, locked in a box, didn't even know English yet. Years later, I spent five years straight in the hole. People smear blood and shit and howl like dogs. People crack."

"But it didn't get you, did it?" I asked.

She looked around, suddenly skittish. "Nah. It didn't."

"Because there's something inside you that refused to go down. And then you found something, right?" She eyed me like I was running a scam, then nodded.

"It's not so different from deep meditation retreat," I said. "Some people go alone into mountain caves for years—nothing but themselves and silence. Some never make it back. Encountering yourself is risky; it's the thing most people fear. But you looked yourself in the eye."

Another slow nod.

"Those hermits choose it on purpose. In some ways, SHU is easier by comparison—someone feeds you, there are others just like you on the other side of the wall, there's a toilet. And when scientists went looking for the happiest people, turns out those meditators top the charts. What looks like 'crazy' from a distance can be a kind of hard-won clarity."

Carla's not someone who goes down easy. She shook her head, but didn't push back.

I told the women in the class that soon we'd play a "concealed rules game." The kind where you don't know the rules until you start playing.

Nevaeh called out, "Like this place."

"Exactly," I said.

Désirée chimed in that she was in solitary for two years and that she preferred it. She has the softness of Janet Jackson in *Poetic Justice*. I've told her that and asked if she'd seen the movie. She laughed at me and said, "Of course—Tupac's in it!"

"And with two years in solitary, you found that secret too, right? You learned how to be fearless without getting hard. That's the name of the game." I pointed to the truth the women knew but hadn't put in words. Once you truly encounter yourself, you are fearless. Once you see that you're not the finite person you thought you were, you rest in something softer.

The conversation in the class opened. Suddenly meditation wasn't so theoretical anymore. It wasn't a course you take to get a First Step point. It wasn't something you do to be "good." It wasn't something you talk to your parents about to prove you're doing something with your time in here, even though you don't really meditate except on

Mondays and Thursdays.

Now it was real, applicable, and there was a secret. There was something that some of these women knew that made them, not immune to the conditions, but free inside of them. Carla and Désirée aren't pious women. They are women like the rest who were in the class that day, who cussed and had records, but these two had touched something. I looked to the other women in the room who I knew had done time in solitary: Royal, Yilan, and a few others.

"We're going to do a specific meditation today," I started again. I asked each woman to name something she was suffering with, the way that monk had felt for that puppy. It could be personal or global, like Gaza or Israel. Each woman chose to be vulnerable: missing their kids, not being there for their parents, the uncertainty of their future. The tenor of the room changed. That universal and ancient ache connected us as if a thread were running through the circle.

Next, I asked them to think of a memory, something that brought spacious joy. The moment of giving birth or seeing their child for the first time, the last visit with their family. A few tears started.

"Now," I said, "feel the heaviness of your suffering. Feel where it sits in your chest. Usually, we armor against that feeling. But we're going to do something different. We're going to breathe it in—fully. And then breathe out the feeling of joy you just named."

The sounds of the dorm faded. The crackle of dissent left the room. It was as if a thick warm blanket were covering each of us, all of us, equally.

More tears fell. Quiet. Brave women's tears.

We went around the circle one last time. New faces on each woman. Her before this place. Her before what brought her to this place. Original face.

I gave one more prompt: "One thing I want you to know…"

"I feel so connected to each woman here."

"I see you all but I feel like I've never seen you until now."

"I didn't realize that we all are feeling the same suffering."

"I am not alone."

The women lingered on the deck. The usual raised hackles were subdued by the only thing that could subdue them, the hidden rule, the skeleton key: compassion.

49

Diamond

Another Wednesday, another visit day. The usual scene in the dorm—women getting ready, whether anyone is coming to see them or not. Edges soft, lines blurred, even the tough ones a little more open than usual.

Hot combs are out, hair grease is shared, and mirrors are passed around.

Rachel's helping Diamond with a sweeping ponytail.

"Your family coming?" Rachel asks.

"My parents," Diamond says. "Every week. They don't miss."

They call our names and we fall into line. The hallway to the visiting room always feels cooler, the air charged with everything that might happen in there: joy, heartbreak, pretending, the performance of being okay.

Diamond walks between us, smoothing the collar of her shirt. "They're so excited," she murmurs. "My mom always brings news. My dad pretends he's not worried. They've never missed a single Wednesday."

As we approach the glass door at the end of the hallway, the one that never opens but that, if you're lucky, you can see your visitor walking from the other direction toward you, we see her parents on the other side of the glass door, her mother in her soft sweater, her father in a pressed shirt.

Diamond straightens like she's fifteen again.

"That's them," she whispers. "Oh—my dad got a haircut." Her smile trembles but holds.

We walk into the room and separate to our tables—Rachel toward Matt, me toward Emmett, Diamond gliding into her parents' arms.

From my table, as I eat my 'pizza' (it was a lucky day and the vending machine was stocked with the good stuff!) and Snapple Lemon Tea, I catch flashes of Diamond's mother wiping under her glasses and her father holding his hands together as if in a prayer.

The hour flies—too full, too fast—and then the CO comes around with our ID cards, signaling it is time for our goodbyes. Those final hugs, that one last squeeze. Everyone holding something together on their faces while everything inside comes undone. We sit in the chairs as the visitors file out, waving goodbye.

Then the usual drill: line up, walk into the search room, strip, bend, cough, get dressed, breathe.

Diamond walks with us again, quieter, carrying the warmth of her parents like perfume still clinging to her clothes.

"You okay?" I ask.

She nods, but her eyes stay forward.

"Seeing them…it lifts me and breaks me at the same time. They act strong so I don't worry. But I can tell."

Her voice thins. "My dad said the car got a flat last week and they didn't know who to call. He said, 'Without you, it's a lot.'"

There's tired pride in her voice—someone used to being needed, someone not used to being unable to help.

Rachel rests a hand on her arm. "They love you."

"I know," Diamond says quietly. "They're why I don't fall apart in here."

Back on our floor, the big metal door buzzes and we are back in the dorm. I feel the mixture of emotions, the women filled up from the love, some extra joy and also the sadness and heaviness, the longing, the reminder of what they are missing and who they have left behind. Relief at being back in the dorm, in the world they know better than the outside world at this point. The hallways always feel too bright after visits.

Diamond clears her throat, choosing her next words carefully, like the story requires gentleness, as we walk to make some tea.

"I used to be the one visiting," she says. "Every week. Hazelton, West Virginia. Me and his mom. I learned those mountains like the back of my hand."

I turn toward her. "Who were you visiting?"

"Lolo," she says, almost shyly. "My man." Diamond warms her hands around her cup. "You don't make that trip every week unless you're crazy or in love," she says. "I guess we were both."

Rachel leans in. "Was it love from the start?"

Diamond laughs softly. "From *his* side? Oh, he was convinced. From mine?" She raises her brows. "Let's just say I tried to escape him at least three times before we even started dating."

She starts where it's funniest—the CVS parking lot. "There he was, surrounded by boxes of all his stuff. He had asked a few days before when I would be his girlfriend and I'd told him we'd talk when he didn't have another girlfriend. So he left her! And called me for a ride, not telling me any of this till I showed up. I'm living with my parents at the time so I can't even take him in. I drop him off at his aunt's."

We are all laughing with the way she tells it.

Then she circles back.

"I was going through a divorce," she says. "I had this friend from the clinic where I worked. I'd go to her house to breathe. And her cousin, Lolo, kept showing up. She leaves the room one day when we are watching a movie. He comes in, locks the door, kisses me and says I'm going to be his wife. I was still married, he had a girlfriend, I was like, what is up with this guy."

She rolls her eyes, but affection glows underneath.

"He fixed up his aunt's basement, turned it into a one-bedroom apartment for us. He helped me with my divorce. My husband kept telling his girlfriend I wouldn't sign the papers. But I had signed, he was the one holding it up. She'd show up and yell at me. So Lolo went to his house, told the new girlfriend to bring my husband outside now so he could sign the papers and be done with it. He filed them for me."

She shakes her head. "I'd never had anyone take care of me like that. I was always the one doing the caring. I broke my toe one day and went to the clinic my sister worked at. Turned out they were short-staffed and asked if I'd fill in for three weeks. My last day of the temp job, I show up to find the physical therapist and the podiatrist arguing over me, they both wanted me as their medical assistant. I said, whoever give me the best offer, and started working there full time. I take care of people. Always."

She looked up as if to make sure we were still with her. We both were, hearts warm, taking her in and pouring out some love.

"Lolo's bipolar and schizophrenic," she continues. "I set him up with a neurologist. Made sure he went weekly. He didn't know how to read or write. I taught him. I taught him how to text on a phone. And he took care of me. Took a weight off of me. Helped with my family. He'd stop by my dad's job and visit, help my sister with things she needed. He never asked me for anything."

She sips her tea, then goes quiet for a second—bracing herself.

"Two thousand fourteen," she says. "Everything fell apart."

Her voice drops a level. We lean in.

"They raided our place. My parents' place. My sister's place. All of us lived in the same building." She places her cup down. "They put me on the floor. Put a gun to my head." She shows us the spot on her temple with one finger. "Screaming, dogs barking, officers everywhere. My dad—he was furious. And scared. I kept saying I didn't know anything. I didn't."

We were silent.

"They took Lolo. But before they dragged him out, he leaned over and kissed my forehead. Told me, 'Don't worry.'"

She swallows.

"I didn't even know what the charges were. I just...started working on his case immediately. Found him a lawyer. An investigator. Whatever it took." She dragged in a breath. "I did all of it. That's what I do. I take care of people. Even when it breaks me. I found this guy to work the case pro bono. He'd never done that before but he had a daughter with mental health stuff and saw how I was with Lolo. He said it melted his heart. He had to help."

She tells us about giving up her apartment, about being only twenty-seven and carrying everything. "At first I felt obligated. Then a year passed and I realized I wasn't obligated. It's just that...I loved him."

She shrugs, but it's the heaviest gesture I've ever seen. When she continues, her voice is softer, almost an exhale.

"One time, me and his mom were five minutes from Hazelton when a deer landed on my hood. Smoke everywhere. I said, 'I'm not missing this visit,' and drove the rest of the way with the car half dead, smoke coming out of the hood. Another time, snow was so bad the road disappeared. I thought we weren't going to make it. His mom is very Catholic. She said, 'God is watching out for us.'"

She gives us a small, tired smile.

"My parents ended up loving him. They saw what he did for me. They still pray for him."

She tells us about the appeal, how every lawyer said no. Then a jailhouse lawyer wrote motions for them that they filed and filed. "Denied five times. But the sixth? They appointed a new lawyer, and suddenly doors opened."

Her eyes soften. "He'd done seven and a half years when his dog died. He loved that dog. Two days later, Lolo's friend calls and says, 'Something has to die for something good to come. I'm coming over for a visit.' I go outside and...it's Lolo. I couldn't believe it."

Diamond lifts her chin a little.

"You know...I used to think being a giver was something I owed the world. But now I know—it's who I am. Something had to die for something good to come is right. My old life, my plans, the way I thought love worked...all of it."

She glances out at the rows of bunks, where Jackie is crocheting, Berry is writing a letter, Elena is lying on her stomach pretending not to cry.

"And still," she says, voice warming into certainty, "I find people to take care of. Jackie calls me Mom. I help Berry with her letters. Elena wakes me up when she can't breathe. I try to keep a small circle in here—but it doesn't matter. People find me. Wherever I go, I find something. I get everyone together. I'm always gathering everyone."

She smiles—not sad, not proud, but whole.

And the three of us sit there for a moment, warmed by the glow of a woman who has always been a hearth.

50

We Continue

Years ago, Dan Rather interviewed Mother Teresa. He asked, "When you pray, what do you say to God?"

"I don't say anything," she replied. "I listen."

He tried again. "Okay, when God speaks to you, what does He say?"

"He doesn't say anything. He listens." Then she added, "And if you don't understand that, I can't explain it to you."

At 7:30 a.m. in the women's unit at MDC Brooklyn, Luciana called me over in the half-dark dorm. The TVs that never turn off were running the story that Charlie Kirk had been shot.

We don't talk politics much at MDC—it's volatile enough. Every now and then there's a glance or a nod when we hear about Trump's First Step Act or a story about weaponization. Nevaeh told me that when she was in a county jail in the South—she's a Black woman who openly supports Trump—the vitriol from other Black women was immediate. They thought she was a traitor. She stood her ground. She may not have changed minds, but she earned respect.

I walked slowly toward the television. There was an aura around the group already watching, the kind you see around a family in a hospital that's just heard the doctor's solemn news—silent, protective, strong enough to repel any discordant energy. There was grief here. The illusion of permanence or guaranteed justice had shattered. The truth stood bare: In this strange life, bad things happen to good people. This is where spirituality starts—where Job's mettle is tested.

It was a poignant moment for the country. The newscasters, who so often feel cardboard and monotone in the name of "objectivity," looked visibly stunned. Three of Charlie's friends appeared on-screen—two young Black men and a woman. That said everything. His heart, true to conservative principles rather than conventional dogma, cut across stereotype. Many will speak of his legacy. For me it is simple: A man who preached a faith rooted in love and then, in front of all of us, lived it. He opened a door for that expression—especially for young people who were both sharp and kind.

I'm a fifty-eight-year-old woman who grew up in ultra-liberal California. I'm incarcerated because I worked to introduce a practice centered on women and sexual energy. I am not the person most would expect to be mourning today—to feel a blow to the heart I wouldn't dare express in a women's prison.

At its core, my case is about religious freedom. Through the prosecution, I've learned to recognize people of real character— neither the color of their skin, their party mascot, nor their holy book decides that. Some hold their beliefs tightly yet still see beneath surface distinctions. Those are the ones beholden to truth and freedom. Their arguments may live on different branches, but they recognize each other at the roots.

It takes fortitude to live at that depth—a moral compass that still points north in political storms and the churn of current events. Some people pick a crowd and rely on its consensus to guide and protect them. Others live by the truth of their convictions. Slowly, they gather a surprising, motley crew who love them. That love is deeper because it's born from recognizing each other at the core.

Charlie Kirk was one of the rare ones who offered himself to the fire—to be tried and clarified by his convictions. Across great divides he looked for understanding, not necessarily agreement, inviting people down from the branches to the roots of shared belief, honest discourse, connection, and, finally, the ability to love one another. Whether you agreed with him or not, you benefited from his presence. Those who can see that, mourn deeply.

The news rolled on. After offering condolences to Charlie's family, Fox News aired a half-hour segment on the anniversary of 9/11. Image after image: firefighters with heads in their hands, sobbing; women running through soot with babies in their arms; the tsunami of ash and flame pouring through New York City; the strained voices of air-traffic controllers—"We have a hijacked aircraft... we need some help."

Three of us sat on blue plastic lawn chairs. We were on recall— something had happened elsewhere in the prison, likely on the men's floors. Any violence, threat of violence, picketing, or riot, and we're moved behind the blue line.

Closed captions scrolled. A quiet Chinese woman sensed something and joined us, saying nothing. I saw her wipe away tears. The woman beside me, whose family is from Costa Rica, rubbed her eyes. Each of us tried to give the others privacy to grieve. We pretended not to notice the tears on one another's faces.

This, too, is America.

And the collision of three stories—Charlie, 9/11, and the four of us together—stirred something in me. A remembered vow to help change the world. The heartbreak at the senselessness of death, the scale of loss. Wounds heal, scar tissue layering over to cover the hurt. In the Buddhist tradition, it's said your strength can live in the wound itself—because it stays sensitive to suffering and fuels the will to make things better for those here now and those who come next. It's a reminder of why, even in hopelessness and helplessness, we persist: to lessen suffering and its causes, and to help others do the same. It's the flag we raise to honor damaged and lost lives. In their names, we continue.

51

Pressure Cooker

I got the news that a dear friend couldn't visit. She had applied and we hadn't heard anything for weeks, then got word that the BOP had determined my list of visitors was full. I let myself feel the sadness without numbing it. A sharp burn in the heart. I'd pictured it several times—my friend walking into the visiting room, getting a sense of this strange place, letting her in on my joke that I call it the Metropolitan *Dakini* Convent of Brooklyn. I imagined the two of us eating snacks and drinking Snapple from the vending machines, talking about what it's like to be in here, what it's like to not have me out there.

But there are some experiences you simply can't ever fully explain—pilgrimages, LSD, prison. Everyone thinks they can imagine, and no one can. They're what I call "primary number" experiences: indivisible, irreducible, everything else in life an iteration of them.

This place is like that. Like those cartoons of what people think meditation looks like—someone floating on a cloud, smiling beatifically—versus what it actually is: being roasted alive in the fire of your own mind. That's prison. A slow, relentless cooking.

I made simmered fruit, a recipe from Louise, because we'd just gotten our once-a-month kiwi and our every-six-weeks plum. I wanted to make something special. I cooked them down with cinnamon (a precious commodity here), sugar-free honey that tastes nothing like honey, and a few dates as shriveled as raisins. The real recipe calls for a Dutch oven. We made do.

I spooned the compote into a tortilla and shared it with Nevaeh, who shared it with Lyric—the pregnant woman here. She'd recently arrived and we'd never shared with her before. That kind of sharing is an initiation; it can go either way. Lyric yelled across the dorm, "Hey, this is *goooood!*" and that was it. We were friends.

We've become known for our desserts. Jingyi commented in her quiet way, "You never let us down." I took it as the highest compliment.

This place teaches you the art of simmering—everything boiling down to essence. Inside each of us, everything extra gets cooked off. Some women get their lessons in the dorm; others need more heat and end up doing solitary in SHU where you're only allowed out for an hour a day, if you're lucky.

Every day, steam rises. Agitation releasing, frustration venting, pressure building and breaking. Dakina drives people to distraction. Me? She doesn't bother me. Dakina's not drowning anything out; she's letting something loose. Her body is a brass section. Sometimes she stands in the middle of the gym track, howls, shakes, flings her head until I worry for her neck.

Luci asked her once, in a lucid moment, why. Flight is the only thing that makes the yelling in her head stop. She's gotta fly. Now she just runs in place as if she is trying to get liftoff. Luci thought the howl was the engine but we don't know. But if that isn't the sound of women grounded against their nature, I don't know what is.

Yesterday there was a fight. Rach and I were midway through our nine-mile walk (that's 288 laps) when we heard it. We paused, but the guards—two women, both firm and kind—handled it. We kept walking. It's safer to stay out of the storm of "sides" that always follows a blowup.

Sometimes I want to shout, *We are the least of our problems.* The real fight is with our own internal doubts, and those doubts are like invisible forces that keep us divided. Ignorance loves a distraction. You're going to war over some guy you've never even seen?

I go back to walking. I walk until my body aches, then crawl into bed with sore hips and a clearer mind. That night we celebrated Carla's birthday—a loud one, even by MDC standards. She's an OG, which means her people made sure she felt it. Their laughter boomed through the bunks.

By the time I lay down, I knew I wouldn't wake at my usual 4:00 a.m. But that's okay. Sundays are slower. We have to stay in the bunk area, on recall until 7:00, an hour longer than the weekday schedule. I can still find silence before the phones start ringing and everyone starts yelling their grievances to the outside world on speakerphone.

Cooking down. That's what we're all doing here.

The politeness, the posturing, the illusions of control—they all burn away. What's left is essence. This place is life stripped of window dressing, the chance to face what everyone else avoids with bubble baths, naps, or locked doors. Here, you can't withdraw. You can't repress what's boiling. If you try, it explodes.

So you learn real-time emotional skills or end up in SHU. Even the women who just stew in silence eventually reach the breaking point. Yilan once came to me, furious, saying she didn't know why she was *so angry* all the time. I told her anger means she's close to the bone, and inside the bone is marrow. She rolled her eyes but came to meditation class the next day. She left after fifteen minutes, but it was something.

The beauty of this place is that the illusion of control is gone. And yet, without that illusion, you meet life directly. You realize that the things you once called "rights" were human agreements, not

219

guarantees. Death teaches the same lesson: When it comes, you surrender everything man-made anyway.

Here's the assignment: Live with no idea what's coming next, in a volatile environment, stripped of all control, and try to stay balanced. Bonus points if you can maintain your basic sense of calm. Championship level if you can keep your joy.

Eventually, you discover what most people only suspect: There are only two things that really matter—your ability to connect with something larger than yourself, and your ability to connect with people.

The second one is underrated in most spiritual traditions, but in here it's everything. You can't survive without it. If one person acts up, everyone is punished. The illusion of "them" dissolves fast when you're all in the same boiling pot.

The pressure gets so hot that the surface layer—the skin that separates "me" from "you"—melts. The blessing is that the fire we spend our lives trying to avoid is the same fire that purifies. We call it suffering. But really, it's alchemy.

There's a famous spiritual teacher Ram Dass who once said, "It's not that you want too much. It's that you don't want enough." I think about that a lot here. Before prison, I was always managing the heat—trying not to blow. But that same management kept me from dissolving. It kept me separate. Maybe the real problem wasn't that life was too intense. Maybe it wasn't hot enough to burn through the illusion of otherness.

I take nothing for granted now. I came in with years of practice under my belt—muscle memory for staying steady—but what keeps me sane isn't meditation or philosophy. It's connection. Not friendship exactly, but that deeper kind of care that arises when you know you're here *for* people.

That's the sanity: being for everyone, so nothing becomes personal.

There are sixty assaults on my preferences every minute—the sound alone is enough to drive anyone mad. No one walks across the room to talk; they just shout. Thirty-five women shouting at once.

But in the chaos, I find a strange kind of peace. Before coming here, I learned the precious truth of "we're in it together." Out there, it was abstract. In here, it's literal.

I used to joke, "Just us chickens in here." Now I *am* a chicken in a cage with other chickens. Turns out, my hypothesis was right. Whether in the vast plains of Mongolia or an over-lit dorm in Brooklyn, it's the same thing: life in a pressure cooker.

Different scenery, same lesson.

The only thing to do is what there's always been to do—be with what's here. Love the people you're with. Right in the middle of the fire.

52

Luscious Stewed Fruit

I n the ninety-five days we've been at MDC, we've only been given kiwis a handful of times. It's always exciting when that happens because it's an extra boost of vitamin C. For fruit, we're typically given apples (red, which are very pulpy, and yellow, which are crunchy but nearly impossible to cut with a plastic knife, though we make do and find our way).

Today, on this glorious Saturday, a miracle of miracles happened, and we were given plums in main line, so we decided to test out the Luscious Stewed Fruit recipe Louise had sent us.

Prepare to have fun and to get messy and sticky along the way. This recipe is simple, delightful, and as always, meant to be shared with friends.

Serves: 8 (as a snack)

Prep Time: 15-20 minutes

Cook Time: 5 minutes for fruit + 3 minutes per tortilla

Ingredients

- 2 kiwis
- 2 plums
- 2 red apples
- 1 banana
- 4 Jozev Medjool Dates
- 1 sporkful of Colonna Ground Cinnamon
- 2-3 healthy squirts of HoneyTree's Sugar Free Imitation Honey
- Walnuts from a Jozev Deluxe Mixed Nuts Salted bag, crushed. If you run out of walnuts, be bold: spill your deluxe mixed nuts out on the table, and if you can't find any more walnut pieces, use almonds. You can break up the walnuts with your fingers, but almonds are trickier, so put them in a bag and crush them using a lock or shoe, or crush them in the door.
- 2-3 Mayan Farm Tortillas
- 7 small packets of Lucky grape-flavored jelly from main line
- Topping from the coffee cake you get in your breakfast tray

Supplies

- 2 plastic knives
- 2 plastic sporks
- 2 lids from the main line trays
- 1 Tupperware container with lid

For this recipe, there are ingredients you will want to save if you happen to get them earlier in the week, for example: kiwi, coffee cake, plums, and banana. If there are ingredients you're missing, you can always ask a friend or bunkie. We didn't have any cinnamon, but the wonderful Miss Wu let us use some of hers.

1. Prepare the fruit.

I recommend having two people helping on this recipe since there's a lot to do. First, cut up your fruit and dates into small pieces—the size you'd want for a tuna salad. While one person is doing that, the other can crush the walnuts. You want them in pieces, not dust.

As you cut, add all your ingredients to the Tupperware, including the walnuts. Then, sprinkle your cinnamon over the top. Start with a little and increase as needed. Add 2-3 squirts of HoneyTree's Sugar Free Imitation Honey to the mixture. Once you've gotten the perfect amount of cinnamon and honey-syrup, stir everything lightly, taking care not to smush the fruit.

2. Cook the fruit.

Once everything is coated well, take your Tupperware to the microwave and cook it for five minutes. This timing is for the ancient microwave here, so for those of you on the outside with newer models, keep your eye on your fruit—it may take less time. Everything should be lightly cooked, not overdone, and any liquid should be thick, not runny.

3. Prepare the tortillas.

As your fruit is cooking, take out two or three tortillas. Work with one at a time. Put the first tortilla on your tray top and evenly spread about three packets of grape jelly onto it. Put your tortilla in the microwave for 90 seconds to warm it up and let the jelly cook into it.

Add a few hefty sporkfuls of the cooked fruit inside the tortilla, then roll it up like a crepe. Add one third of the topping from the coffee cake, then put it back in the microwave for another 90 seconds. Be mindful that the jelly and fruit may leak, so take care as it is hot.

Repeat this until all the crepes have been made and cut into pieces, then share with friends.

53

Fed Baby

On the track, Rach and I are logging miles—five to ten a day. Thirty-two laps make a mile. Darla, who left last week and runs marathons, once did fifteen miles here. We were inspired. We talk a little, mostly we churn the wheels of insight. Nevaeh and Lyric stroll in their lane. I overhear Lyric saying to Nevaeh, "That's how you do it," pointing to us. "Look, they don't even talk, they just walk. Fast." Mind you, this shifted their walking not in the least. They are there to go through the motions of walking that serve as a backdrop for their ongoing conversation that needs to change sets every so often, from poker to betting on the football game, to lying on Lyric's bed.

We pass the two of them on the track freeway and do the equivalent of a light honk. Lyric's ass is round, her tits are round, her moon face is round. And her belly is round. She's seven months pregnant but is more active than the skinny 22-year-old who doesn't wake up until 7 p.m. and then glares at everyone that they would dare make noise prior to that. As we pass, I ask Lyric, who is so fluent in "hood" language that she could hold a Hood Linguistics Ph.D., "Is there a slang word for 'inmate'? I'm playing with book titles."

"Jailbirds?" she suggests.

"I like that," I tell her. "Flight."

Lyric brightens, her smarts shining through. Around here, compliments are suspicious; attention is a rare currency, and it's almost always transactional. I keep it moving.

The truth is, really *seeing* another woman takes a kind of wealth most in here don't have. The women here are used to the fake version of that attention—the kind that's a setup, not a gift. A compliment isn't kindness; it's a currency exchange. It means: I want something. A favor, a shortcut, a little safety. "Your hair looks nice" sounds less like affection and more like a car salesman trying to close a deal.

Lyric stands out here, and not just because of her pregnant belly protruding through her prison uniform. She reminds me of an inner-city honors student at a crossroads—the question is, which game does she want to play? But here, in a federal prison, the options are different. The choice isn't between the familiar and an Ivy League scholarship; it isn't a choice in your external circumstance. The question is whether you want to play *any* of the "outer games" or whether you want to master the inner game. Lyric's got a grade-A game and outside these walls it could get her whatever man and whatever security or diamond jewelry he offers. The trouble is, she's bored.

"Don't be number one at the number-two game," I tell her. "The number-one game is inside."

"That's a million miles from here," she says, but she hears me.

On our next lap, she grins, still turning over possible book titles. "*Fed Baby.*"

"What's that?"

"Means you 'made it to the feds, baby.' Big-time now. Not just county or state."

"I like it," I say. "Let me think on it."

By the next lap, Lyric and Nevaeh join us and after a few times around the track, Lyric and I find ourselves paired off. Up to then I'd mostly *heard* Lyric; she travels with her own laugh track. We trade ideas back and forth; it turns out we've watched all the same strange and esoteric Instagrams and podcasts, had all the same fascinations with them: "Oh, you haven't heard the Telepathy Tapes? You gotta check it out." Cities build public squares so people can bump into each other and cross-pollinate. This is ours.

She tells me she's worked as a stripper and, to her surprise, I have too. She says she's been with a lot of men, "But I ain't a ho, if you know what I mean."

"I am," I deadpan, letting her peek behind the polite-housewife façade. She cackles. A door opens.

The story spills. "Yeah, I got pregnant by another guy. My guy's here—got arrested before me. I met someone else. I don't even like him. Thought I was pregnant, test said no, then I get here—test says yes. I can't tell my man; his mama just died. We gotta go to court together soon—maybe I can hide it." The belly that leads us around the track suggests that won't be an option.

"You have to tell him," I say, too pragmatic for the moment.

"Yeah, but...his mama..." The sentence trails off. In here that usually means: *I'm afraid of losing him*, but no one says it directly. Softness is dangerous. You have to shine like you have options, money, a plan.

A few days later, she calls me to her bed—an honor. She wants to show me a photo. Not her boyfriend. Not the baby's father. A *new* guy she met through means we won't discuss. He's cute—waves, dark skin, all coyote. Knows his way around a woman's body and the money game. I pray she meets a man who is, as they say in here, *for real*. I don't know he'll be found inside these walls, but who am I to say?

Three days later, they scheduled a bail hearing for Lyric. It feels like a miracle; the women cried in sympathetic joy and relief with her. She's due in two months. Nonviolent crime. Already served real time. They have to send her home on confinement. There's gratitude for the many prayers made by all the inmates here for this to happen. And, still in her womb, Lyric's baby is present in the dorm with us. Blessed by the hope of forty women. This baby's already made it to the big times—not county, not state, this is a fed baby.

54

Bittersweet

Walking out of the craft room turned meditation room one day, we see Jingyi at her usual spot in the puzzle room, the place where I'd first met her. Although today instead of just one table, she has three which she pushed together, arranged in a loose horseshoe, as if she needs space for the mind she's using. One puzzle is spread wide, pieces turned the same direction like fish in a current. Another is half-built, the image still hidden, only geometry showing. The third is new—its border already complete.

She doesn't look up when we enter but I can tell she feels us. She's the kind of person who registers those slight changes in a room. From a distance, she can read as untouchable. A composed beauty: the moon-round strength of her face, hair down her back like a dark ribbon, her steady eyes. People have called her "stuck up." I've learned that's what they call women who don't leak themselves everywhere.

Without looking up from her puzzles, she says to me, "People say you're a feminist. I do not understand feminist."

"I would hardly say I'm a feminist. I'm too feminine for that," I joke.

She looks up, studying my face, unsure of what I mean or if I'd understood. "I think feminists are wrong," she says. "Woman is not a good man."

"This, I agree with," I say.

She looks relieved and moves on to something else she's been wondering about. "I have a question about your meditation class. I don't like lazy spirituality. Some people..."

"Oh, neither do I," I tell her. "Sometimes people do use the spiritual to avoid life. But, practice can also be the opposite. Not escape. Contact."

Jingyi's gaze holds for a beat longer. "Contact," she repeats, as if letting the word settle inside her. She turns back to her puzzle and Rach and I head back to the dorm.

A few days later she comes by our lunch table. "What is the word," she asks, "when you wear something...so nothing can touch it?"

If it had been anyone else, I might have turned it into a joke. With Jingyi, I don't. Her questions are so gentle and revealing.

"Armor?" I say.

She nods. "Yes. Armor." Then, quieter: "But not hard metal armor. Soft armor." She touches her own chest lightly, like she's indicating a place beneath the ribs. "I wear it on my heart. I don't talk emotions."

"Rach and I are careful with our emotions too."

"I am sad," she says. Up close, I see what I'd missed at a distance: her eyes are swollen from crying.

"Do you want to talk about it?" I ask quietly.

"No, thank you," she says with her quiet politeness.

I gesture for her to sit down and she does for a few moments. We all sit in silence, a warmth between us.

"Wait here, I want to show you something," I say to her. I go back to my locker and grab a picture I have of White Tara. "You remind me of her."

She looked cautious. "Why?"

"Because you are so still. Quiet. Peaceful."

She nodded. "Wait—I think I read a book in Chinese." She returned with a book, finger marking a page. "This her?" White Tara stared up from the paper.

"Yes." I smiled. "You *are* White Tara—peaceful," I said. "Luciana is Green Tara—activity."

Jingyi flipped through her book. "Her?" she asked, pointing to the page.

"Exactly. One leg out—ready to move."

Luciana, hearing us talk about her, walked over from her bunk and beamed looking at the page, approving of her representation.

"Yes. I feel peaceful with my White Tara." Luciana grinned, taking Jingyi's arm. "Come on, White Tara," she teased.

"Okay, Green Tara," Jingyi echoed back, as they walked off together. And for a moment, clear sky broke through the prison ceiling.

One morning, I find a carefully folded card on my bed, Chinese characters on the front. Inside, in neat handwriting:

Thank you for your kindness.
-Jingyi

Later that day, while in line for lunch, she asks if she can join us for meditation. At 2:00, she comes with us to our humble little room. We've long since abandoned the fantasy of floor cushions and taken to sitting on the hard plastic chairs. Jingyi walks in, takes one look, and immediately sits on the floor in full lotus. Rach and I look like we are wearing emotional football gear next to her simple elegance. Vastly American.

We sit for forty minutes. She does not move—not even the flicker of an adjustment. In our practice, we visualize White Tara surrounded by light, sitting on a lotus. Jingyi is a better version than anything I ever pictured. The feeling in the room is so strong and clear. Everything feels washed, as if through the kind of fresh, clean scent a lotus flower would have if prison had lotuses.

When we finish our sit, she says quietly, "My mother was a nun. She got pregnant as a nun. When I was born, they took me from her and sent her away. The nuns raised me. My husband was the son of a wealthy businessman," she goes on. "He is not coming home. I find out. I do not like the material either."

Here she was: a woman whose two great gates—love and faith—had both been slammed on her. One world took her mother. Another took her husband.

As we make our way back into the dorm, Dakina is in rare form. She wants to show Jingyi her drawings. People kept coming to the table asking to see, but she wouldn't let them. She stands between them and the notebook, like a wall. But the minute she sees Jingyi, her whole face changes.

In fact, Jingyi is the only person I've ever seen Dakina give what I think of as her *pre-face*—the face she must have had before whatever it was that so profoundly disrupted her nervous system.

Jingyi walks over slowly, her compassion pouring out as she takes on the role of an art collector eager to see her favorite artist's work. She slows to a stillness that quiets the whole area, including Dakina.

"Dakina," she whispers, "Dakina, this is beautiful work."

Dakina beams. She holds her pen in midair, hand frozen in reverence.

The exchange feels ancient: an offering from a shattered soul, a blessing that does more than just restore. It's as if some invisible lineage—teacher and student, mother and daughter, patron and artist—flickers to life right there between the plastic tables and the humming TVs.

That night, across the dorm, right in the middle of her nightly percussion—shouts, song fragments, sudden laughter, constant running—Dakina calls out:

"Jingyi!"

Jingyi calls back quietly, "Yes, Dakina?"

"I love you, Jingyi."

In that moment, it feels like the favor has been quietly returned.

55

Adapting

Two signs tell me I'm adapting a little too well to prison. The first is a "you'd have to know me" thing, but if you do, you'd say I've transformed in here.

My whole life has been tuned for call and response. Out there, I always knew the right note to hit. In here, officers issue the call and I deliver the precise, calming reply that gets us all to the visiting room—or through the dorm—without friction. I'm a thoroughbred learning to play jazz, not just the clean classical line but the notes between.

I have attorney visits more often than most, and the trek to the visiting room feels like navigating a field of tripwires. Once, I opened the door to hug Rachel's attorney, unaware that it was as grave an offense as opening mail from the Unabomber.

"Get down!" the officer bellowed. I hit the floor like a scolded dog.

The same duo escorts me once or twice a week: a sweet Latino officer and a woman whose face reads, *Try me*. I don't. Though, apparently, my mere existence does. I put on my invisibility cloak and aim for neutral-to-pleasant. I like the grumbly ones.

Each visit she asks, "Do you have your card?"

I nod.

Then comes her mystery follow-up: "You aren't trying to bring any lip gloss down, are you?"

For the record, I do not wear lip gloss to the visiting room. Or anywhere. Is this a common contraband? Does she think white women are lip-gloss obsessed? I drop my gaze and say no. What else is there to say? Still, it eats at me. It's so odd.

Then one day, I was ready.

"Do you have your card?"

"Yes," I said. "And I don't have any lip gloss either."

We stood in front of the elevator, all of us equally stunned. I had disrupted the pattern, played in a way I hadn't before. They say the longest distance is from zero to one. In that moment, I covered ground. The night before, when I wasn't sure I could go get ice during recall, Miriam told me, "Fear don't get paid." I suspected that meant, "go get ice." I got paid the next day at the elevator. We're all a little better for it. They don't have to ride down with Casper the Friendly Ghost, and I don't have to keep answering that question.

That's sign number one. Number two might make my mother worry about my new friends—though she'd probably be as charmed as I am. They're definitely rubbing off on me. I can't help but smile when I hear Royal's booming, "Hey, baby," the kind that makes you want to be that baby because it means you're that loved. And then Nevaeh: slow, authoritative, with a wild streak. If she gives the invisible thumbs-up, you're in good company. She vets hard and since we passed, she's offered the kind of protection that can only be earned.

Most often, my inner Magic 8-Ball lands on yes. When it does, I offer whatever support I can to help someone step into their greatness, whatever their lane. I don't care if you're Christian, liberal, pro-Trump, anti-Trump, Jewish, Black, Asian, feminist, vegan (the last two can be a challenge). I care if you're here to heal the world. If that's true, we'll figure out the rest.

Nevaeh reads the books I give her with a pen in hand, filling the margins with notes and questions. I'm moved and honored. And then, as often happens here, she delivers the tat for the tit. Nevaeh's not doing all the spiritual reading if we don't do our part. Hood books. A whole genre I hadn't known existed before prison. I'd overheard many a conversation in the dorm about them.

Royal reads them nonstop and often barrels over to Nevaeh's bunk— two down from mine—like a field reporter talking over explosions. Sometimes even in the middle of the night.

"I can't believe it, baby! I was pissed till the last chapter when she said, 'Now what you gonna do? Huh? Huh, motherf—, now what you gonna do!' And that little girl finally stood up to him. Nevaeh!"

"I know, Royal, I know," Nevaeh said, more composed, pulling the blanket over her head. It was 3 a.m., and while she loved *Kiss Kiss Bang Bang*, she was not up for a debrief.

We each get a book. Rach gets *Kiss Kiss Bang Bang* and I get *Diary of a Street Diva*, from Nevaeh's private library. My first hood book. Fifteen pages in I was hooked.

Cease is in court. Remy, the only woman his thug heart ever loved, and her unborn baby are dead. Cease is being accused by his ex. And he finds the memoir Remy left behind. Cease and I read it together, discovering that Remy's hard past makes her even more ride-or-die.

There are those flashes, the sudden moment that changes your direction like a lightning bolt of purpose that sets you on a path you can't turn from. I'm not sure what the hood-book equivalent of that lightning bolt is, but when I told Royal, "I started the book and…" she gave me the same look my old teachers used to give me, the "yep, been there" look.

On visitation day, I told Emmett all about my new book. He informed me the genre is called "urban" on Amazon. I laughed. *Urban* sounds clean—skyscrapers and sleek lobbies—unless you tack on *jungle.* "Hood" tells the truth about where you're headed.

When I finished it, I was gutted. Nevaeh and Royal warned me—"Just wait till the end"—but nothing could have prepared me.

The story toggles between Cease reading her journal, the courtroom where he's on trial for her murder, and his thoughts in the margins of that love. God, Remy. You can't help but love her. She's been carved by pain and still chooses the Code. In theology they call it *unio mystica*—a felt union with the divine. In hood books, the equivalent is *ride or die*. Remy does both. Fierce heart in equal parts.

Hood books read fast—like hood life, I suppose. Between my practice and our marathon walks in the gym, I only have an hour or so a day to read. I still finished in three. For those three days, Cease walked on one side of me and Remy on the other.

"I love those characters more than some people I've lived with," I tell Royal when I return the book.

"I know," she says, already holding the next one. "Makes you *fuckin'* cry. Sometimes I read and I just *fuckin'* cry."

"It felt like they were still walking around with me after I closed the book." I move closer so she can see my eyes.

"I know, baby. Gets you outta here for a while, don't it? Those books are ad*dictive*," she says, leaning on the last syllable the way only Royal can.

I'm happy to share anything with her. There's something about recognizing a common purpose in another. There's no need for chitchat. You can be naked there. The conversation starts at the marrow.

Royal tells me that back home she liked to get high and read. A friend once asked, "Who gets high and reads?" She shrugged. "I do." Junkies recognize who else is as hardcore as they are—whether it's for truth, drugs, sex, or prayer. Who's under the table early and then who's still awake at sunrise. For better or worse, I'm a sunrise girl. So is Royal. Maybe that's why we love Remy: the three of us love hard, each in our own way.

There's a kind of love that leaves romance and sex looking like dots in a rearview mirror. That's how I love Royal. The way you love the moon. You don't need to possess it; you want to be moved by it like the tide pull, the quiet authority that makes wolves howl and women go a little *luna*-touched.

I don't love her in spite of her history; I love her with it. When her mother left when she was a girl, she asked her father when Mama was coming back. He didn't lie. "She's not, Royal. It's you and me now." Then he told her he loved her to infinity. Years later, when Royal got a dog she adored—"so *fuckin'* beautiful I love that dog so *fuckin'* much"—she named her Infinity.

56

For the Woman in the Bunk Next to Me, Part Four

For my soon-to-be-former bunkie, who's leaving our little sanctuary and reentering the world: a non-user's guide after leaving the Metropolitan Dakini Convent.

I worry about you. Silly, maybe—but true. Others are celebrating, certain you're ready. Their version of "ready" is simple: Don't come back here. They treat freedom like a change of conditions. And yes, you'll be outside these walls and out from under the officers' schedules. But the world out there has its own chains. It worships the pile you're standing on—money, fame, followers, the corner office. On top of the heap you can charm, buy, or command your way through. You can perform relaxation while scrambling inside to keep your place.

You can fake nearly anything but one thing: being at one with your life. From day one I've told you—don't be number one at the number-two game. You have a gift: You can adapt to any room. That's a blessing when it's rooted in generosity. It's a curse when it's fueled by hunger to be special, untouchable, "above" what others endure. That choice is the difference between a mansion and a beautifully designed doghouse.

There's a story I love. The Dalai Lama once stayed at a hotel where no one knew who he was. Each morning he took the elevator to the conference. No fanfare. No title meant anything to the staff. But by week's end, housekeepers and janitors gathered at the elevator to wait for him. They just wanted to feel how they felt in his presence. That's power. That's the number-one game.

Positions, titles, and applause are rented. People will love your role; they'll worship the access it gives them. Lose the role and they'll climb over you to reach the next one. The number-two game runs on jealousy and scarcity. It's all chutes and ladders.

The number-one game looks soft by comparison. "Kindness is your religion"? Really? But remember—after the climactic moment on the cross, the story says Jesus returns as a gardener. Humble. Useful. Alive.

I tell people that sometimes you're brought low because you did well enough to be trusted with humility. The only power that lasts is the way people feel in your presence. That's portable. Take it anywhere and the room shifts, whether people know your name or not. Humans or no humans, even among plants and alley cats, you can serve. There's a joy beyond walls and headlines, a deep steadiness that doesn't need a stage.

I wish that for you.

I worry when I hear anyone say happiness is "over there." That's the root of separation, and separation is the root of suffering. It leaves you hollow and hustling, seeing people as obstacles or trophies. You start climbing over your own heart, one body at a time. Praise from "above," flattery from "below"—none of it satisfies for long. The more you get, the more you want.

And the "above" will try to buy you. They'll spot your gift and recruit you to their team. They'll hand you treats—passes, perks, proximity— just enough to keep you a step ahead of your peers. Meanwhile, someone's doing the same to them. It's a pyramid with no top. The flag just reads: GREED.

Those "below" will do their own dance—people-pleasing, threats, sudden withdrawal when they don't get what they want. Same game, new costumes.

Freedom isn't granted by the people we try to impress above us or the followers we collect below—it's decided by our peers. The people who drive you crazy. The ones you can't avoid. The ones you had to find a way to live with. Us chickens. The question at the gate is simple: How did they feel around you? Did they feel seen? Unhurried? Like you turned off the machine that's always going somewhere because *they* were where you were meant to be? Did you use your position for their benefit? When something needed doing, did you just do it—no scoreboard, no points?

That answer will match a deeper one: How good a *you* did you become? Just how my friend Ed said he became a pretty good Ed after his fifty years of meditation practice, the assignment is to become a pretty good you. You always know when you're off it—beneath every excuse and rationalization is that clean yes/no. When the light is on, it shines as generosity. It's one of the few binary things in life: either on or off.

You will have chances to go against the stream, to represent who the women in here really are. You might not be popular. Popularity is often just the number-two game in a new outfit—renouncing what you were, selling a cleaner version, joining the transaction parade.

A hard truth I once heard: Only one percent maintain true north. They keep going through terror that roars, delights that seduce, doubts that say give up and join the crowd insisting nothing real exists. They settle for the antidepressant version of life, trading wonder for comfort and constant complaint. They believe there's always someone to blame and a shortcut to buy. They join the "top-secret"

241

clubs. The secret the top keeps is that there is no secret.

The relief is this: People who know can recognize others who know—cab driver, nurse, imam, priest, grandmother on a stoop. Feeling can't be faked. Free people want other people free. They see your maneuvers and your masks, but more than that, they see your intention. If you live on the plane of generosity—*no matter what*—you are never without help. The invisible workers show up: the ones quietly healing the world. Like gaydar, they have kind-dar. They can spot their own. They won't do your work for you, but they'll slip you what you need to do it yourself. Tools. Allies. A nudge at 3 a.m.

Before I left for college, my mother gave me two slim books—how to boil an egg and sew a button, how to open a bank account and change oil. Stereotyped and perfect. I used them like bibles. I could feel her wanting me to have what I needed when she wasn't there.

Think of this letter that way—a non-user's guide for a user's world. Like the Passover egg: a reminder to soften. Meat softens when cooked; an egg hardens. Let this be your reminder to stay soft. "Slow and kind" may not win the race everyone's running, but they get you *out* of the race and *into* the only place you truly want to be—the joy that has no opposite.

When you go, I'll keep my funny morning rituals. I'll do them in your name. I'll sit the way I taught you to sit. I'll pray that you carry the light into rooms that have forgotten it. Remember the hardest thing: The most precious gift is already yours. It matters more to be good at who you *are* than to be good at what you *do*. And there's an army at your back—seen and unseen—hoping you find freedom and help others find it, too.

Godspeed.

57

New Dawn, New Day

A bird got into the dorm before sunrise, which in the language of prison superstition means "somebody's going home." It shouldn't happen. Of all the windows in the dorm, only two open, one an inch, the other just a few inches, and they all have tight metal grates. And still somehow, a sparrow managed to enter. Most of the women are not from places with much nature. So there was some shrieking as the bird circled overhead.

Luciana was up, getting ready for an early court appearance. Release was possible, not promised. She told us her parents had stayed up all night praying at home. Rach and I joined in the prayers, sitting up in our bunks in the near-dark, repeating mantras. Out of the narrow window slat by her bed, a single warm city light burned, bright as an autumn moon.

Later that afternoon, the room hums like a backstage dressing room as everyone prepares for visitation day, trading mascara, smoothing hair, giving last-minute pep talks. Rosa's late, which means three women are doing her hair while she balances a compact mirror and wonders aloud how her six-year-old became a diva. We all try not to smile.

News in here gathers more than it arrives. First a ripple—looks, whispers—then a swell you can feel under your feet. Sometimes it breaks clean into joy. Sometimes it drags you under. You learn to stand in the swell without bracing.

Across the room, I spot Rach on the phone. She listens, then hands it to Claire. When I reach her, Rach whispers, "It's Luciana."

The swell lifts a little higher. Hearing the news is always a big wave crashing down. Emotions I never anticipated having because I never imagined that I would be in prison, developing relationships with other inmates. The tiny tug of feeling how I'm going to miss her. The sense that the dorm is now shifting like a kaleidoscope. Collisions of hope and fear throughout. Hearing a woman is going home, celebrating, and then having her return at 7 p.m. exhausted from having been put in shackles and made the big trip, only to be denied.

Time thins. "Luci?" I say into the receiver as Claire hands it to me. "I'm going home," she says.

I want to pour every reminder into the line—live what you learned, stay in the depths of who you are—but she belongs to her people now, soon to be breathing first-night-out air and being served mozzarella, basil, and tomato.

"I love you," I tell her. "Go be with your family."

I ask Rach if we can tell the unit. In here, silence breeds stories, and stories breed trouble. She nods, turns, and lifts her voice for the first time since we arrived.

"Everyone!" The room never goes quiet, but it softens. "I just spoke to Luciana. She's gone home."

Faces flip like a shuffled deck—joy, envy, relief, fear. It's as if a tree we all leaned on got pulled up while we were out; the ground still trembles where the roots were. That's the crest. Then comes the undertow: the practical, hungry questions like "Who gets her bunk?"

already tugging at ankles.

A CO starts calling last names from the gate. Visitation. Two currents at once: one woman going out into the world, the rest of us walking toward the small world downstairs.

We line up. The dorm exhales, then inhales again. I smooth my shirt and follow the tide to the visiting room.

The visiting room is dim and bright at the same time. Emmett rounds the corner like a headlamp in a cave and hugs me like a soldier in a train station. I remind him—softly, again—that this isn't the place for grand gestures. In here, visible warmth gets you trimmed like a tall poppy. You learn to draw it all into the interior and remain beige like your uniform on the exterior.

We sit and swap stories: Royal, Nevaeh, our "marathon training" on the track. We laugh and the laughter lifts us into collective flight where we are out of this environment for an hour, but in that space, it is an eternity.

Later, back upstairs, the dorm swirls like a street scene in a musical—newsboys, chairs scraping, everybody narrating. Row One—"Religion Row"—rearranges: I move into Luci's old bunk against the wall; Rach slides in next to me. Nevaeh jokes she's now sandwiched between Christians and Buddhists. (She does ministry calls on the unit phone; I hear her telling women to try ten minutes of meditation a day. Our little practice is sneaking into her repertoire.)

"You know there are Jewish Buddhists—'JewBu,'" I say. "You're on your way to being a Crew-Bu."

She gives me the big laugh, the contagious one.

Right then, and I feel her before I see her, Jingyi comes over, eyes wide. "Dakina...she's been a little wild. Is it my fault? I'm worried they'll take her to SHU." Yesterday she'd taken a break from talking to Dakina, overwhelmed by the chaos.

"I don't think it's anyone's fault," I say. "Her flight is just a bit more turbulent. She's a reflection of the dorm. Luciana left, things feel a little less steady. If you want to reflect, do it—but feel remorse for six seconds, see what there is to see, and let it go. Anything longer just feeds the ego's need to be the villain, the victim, and the savior."

She scrunches her nose. I explain: We fixate on a single thread in the fabric so we can feel in control. The giant open sky of reality is scarier than our tiny story of blame. In here, that fixation is a sport.

I know we need a stabilizing force. Rach and I go walk the track, my mind churning. We are on lap two hundred sixty when I realize, it will be Miriam.

I think back to how at first, I hadn't been sure about her. She had such big energy and was loud. But, time and again, she'd stood up in places others hadn't. Telling the women to stop cheering when Dakina was taken out, putting her foot down when women were getting up to something she knew would be no good.

Right after the first meditation class, Miriam pulled me aside. "I don't do that," she said. "I'll explain later. But I respect what you did. Half the unit was actually quiet. Keep going." Praise from someone honorable hits different.

A couple weeks later she had come to me again, quiet, Bible-underlining Evelisse in tow. "Would you be willing to meditate with us but not with everyone else?" Evelisse was looking at me with those big eyes, pure warmth. I picked up on what Miriam was saying: Some people are almost too pure for the world. "She is having experiences she wants to understand. But not with everyone else, if you know what I mean."

"I know what you mean, just tell me when."

Turns out, Evelisse was having experiences that happen in the minds of advanced practitioners. She didn't think she was going crazy so much as she worried that other people would think she was.

"You're right, you are not going crazy," I said, as was once said to me. "You are going sane." The next morning, the four of us sat in a row, as if one thread were running through us.

Now, with the dorm in some upheaval, I know I needed to say it plain: Miriam's the stabilizer. The weight is real; she should know she won't carry it alone.

Rach and I walk over to the table where she's sitting with Evelisse. I want to tell her I know the weight is real, I want her to know she won't carry it alone. She looks up slowly, sun-warmed.

"There are four reasons I back you," I tell her. "One: You shut down gossip without igniting more. Two: I saw you with your man—I know who you are under pressure. Three: The day with Dakina, you stood against the room to do the right thing. Four: You walk a clean line with the guards—no boot-licking, no avoidance. You see we're all in the same boat, and you lead with—"

"Respect?" she says.

"Respect. I'll put my chips on that number. I may not look like it, but I have a lot of chips."

She doesn't show her hand, but the light in her eyes gives her away. She nods. I nod. Evelisse glows. Rach smiles.

It's a new dawn, it's a new day in our little corner of the Metropolitan Dakini Convent.

58

Mandalas

T he invitation is always the same: Take your seat right in the middle of where you are. In the mess and the mercy. In the bad lighting and the voltage of intimacy that rattles your ribs. Every place is its own little world—a mandala—with visible rules and hidden codes. I've met them all: pilgrimage trails in Mongolia and sidewalks in Harlem; the tight duet of only child and mother; the machinery of work where I try to stitch dignity back into vulnerable places; my (probably too) subversive itch to swap out the artificial flavors of "girls-rule-the-world" feminism for the real thing; and the silent, electric trek through my interior, hunting words for what I see.

A mandala is a world with a center and a surround. They are easier to sense than to explain. Most days we install *ourselves* at the center and treat "out there" like a pantry to raid so we can fill a hole "in here." In the Tibetan tradition, you play with that habit. You swap the small self at the center for something wise and generous, then imagine a world that matches—one designed for peace, courage, clarity, or right action. In other words: If you're going to insist on a "center," make it a source, not a vacuum. And if you're going to see a "periphery," treat it like a community, not a colony.

That's the question I bring to every system I land in—activism included. How do we shift from ego-activism (me proving I'm right) to compassionate activism (us ending the causes of suffering, right now, for *these* people in *this* moment)? First I locate myself: Where am I? How does this system actually work? What's the most sacred, life-giving vision embedded here? What knobs and levers would bring that vision into focus?

It's mandalas all the way up and down. Back when I did psychedelics, I remember being rocketed through layer after layer of worlds—each one a self-supporting city of meaning hanging weightless in space. I moved too fast to explore, but it was clear: If I stepped off on any floor, a complete reality would be waiting.

Held this way, the world becomes "play" in the best sense. I'm consciousness, dropped—*plunk*—into a specific scene. Each second is its own "world," stocked with memories and beliefs that pretend to have a past and future. Sometimes I imagine there are infinite versions of me doing this at once: some tired of being here forever, some begging to never leave, all of us learning the same lesson—again.

So I "come to" wherever I am and check the instruments: Okay, this mandala is a federal detention center in the 2020s. I'm a woman in my late-fifties, healthy. The small woman—she prefers "petite"—is my friend across the way. Rachel. We share a lot of overlapping scenes. I'm Buddhist; looks like I'm serious about it. My mind is strong. I appear as white and upper-middle-class; I stand out. I'm a writer. I'm sturdy, not combative.

The aim of the game is intimacy: Dissolve the sense of alienation without betraying your character. It's the ultimate improv. You draw your character card and—"Go." Pro tip: If you tell everyone around you that you think it's all a game, you'll sound unwell. The only way to show it is to sit down in the center, let the scene move you, and respond honestly.

And then, sometimes, the whole mandala dissolves—the set melts, the spotlight turns to soft daylight—and you carry that knowing quietly, like a jewel in your pocket.

59

Rules of the Game

The first rule of MDC is that there's no one to explain the rules of MDC. Break them and the consequences are real—anything from discipline to a trip to SHU. The guards treat new questions like gnats. Most women aren't exactly rule-obsessed, either. They'll violate a code, get scolded, apologize, and do it again. Their method is basically: "Mess around and see what happens."

There *is* a manual—faded type, written by whoever writes those Ikea guides that always leave you with extra screws. It answers maybe forty percent of what you need. The rest is like one of those ridiculous obstacle-course shows where you never know what is coming next: You're climbing a rope net with a dog bone in your mouth while surprises launch at you from off-screen. Ready? Go.

That doesn't include the "not a good idea" list your lawyer mentions *after* you've done the not-good-idea. Cue the 3 a.m. spiral: Did my attempt at being a good Samaritan look like I was trying to influence people? Add time to my sentence? Meanwhile, I keep thinking about Ye's life-as-level-ten video-game analogy. Sometimes I want to tell him I've found an even spicier level. He can compare notes with Diddy two floors up.

There was an additional note in the morning howling I woke to, less volcanic than Dakina's, more a loud, tearing whimper that carried across the dorm. I follow it to the computers and find its source: a brand-new arrival. Carrie is with her—Carrie, who used to be deeply religious, used to be a counselor, used to be a lot of things, like so many of us in here. The chaplain here recently reminded me, "You're not here to be somebody." It stung—and it helped. Another invitation to be known by how people *feel* around me, not by a title or a role.

Picture a stock photo: a deeply distressed woman and a deeply steady helper. In the photo, Carrie would be wearing a white coat with a look of deep concern and the patient would have the expression of a howling ghost. Here, they are both in tan uniforms. The new woman's face is a storm—tears, snot, panic. "They told me I was going to a mental institution. I can't do this. I don't process things." It sounds practiced, like a line carved by years of being told her condition.

Carrie's voice is a whisper you'd use with a skittish cat: "I know. It's overwhelming. I understand." The new woman begs to call her husband. It's too early; no one's in the office yet.

"Right now you are okay. You are with us. You are okay." Carrie's expertise comes from years in the field. I whisper to her that she is very good at what she does.

I take over as Carrie walks toward the door to laundry. I don't think the woman registers who is here and who is not. Because in a profound way, she is not. There is a merry-go-round of rumination and she is riding it. Even if there is a momentary light of recognition, it dims quickly and she is drawn back in. I watch any hope of a presence that could cope with this moment fade. Then, as if a new shocking horror at where she was arose, she repeats.

"I don't know what's happening. I don't process things. Can I call my husband now?" Louder. Tighter.

"Are you safe *right now*?" I ask, trying to find her eyes. "This second—

anything hurting you *right now?*" She shakes her head. "Okay. Just this moment, it's you and me. And you're okay in *this* moment." A small nod. That's how you do it here: inch by inch, moment by moment.

Miriam clocks what's happening and slides in. I head to the office to see if anyone's arrived; she steers the woman to the TV tables, distracting her with what she likes to watch. That's also how we do it here. Over the sea of women drowning in exhaustion, meds, or the churn at the gate, there's a quiet handful with a "we got this" mindset. We do what needs to be done. We mop when the ice machine floods and ninety-nine percent of the dorm steps around the lake and the stench. We answer screams at 3 a.m. in our shower slides. We make gentle suggestions before inspections—because these women do not like being told what to do, and they have ways of making your life unpleasant if they feel ordered. Some are grateful. A few you do not cross. Miriam, because she's a real leader, thanks us for helping even while she's shouldering the same load.

"Teamwork," I say. "Makes the dream work," Rach finishes the couplet.

Later in the day, the new woman drifts to our table like a ghost. "I can't do this," sobbing again, her face melting in front of us. "I'm going to hurt myself." You can hear the echo of an old therapist saying: *If you're going to hurt yourself, you have to tell us.* I motion for Rach to get an officer. Some things you escalate immediately.

Rach returns with the instructions to bring her to the office. They've called Miss Nelson, the therapist who runs the shame class—the kind of person whose heart is too loud to ignore. Later, at count, we're one short. "She's on suicide watch," someone says—moved to SHU for monitoring. Pain is everywhere in here; it shapeshifts, and the tools here are limited. It's like trying to do surgery with a butter knife. No one here can save you. Those of us with surplus love pour and pour. It's not enough. It's what we have. So we use it. And we keep going.

60

Lyric

The night before Lyric's bail hearing, we all gathered to say goodbye. Nevaeh led a Loving Tree, an exercise from *The Art of Soulmaking* where one person receives love, in the form of reflections, from others. The women shared their experience of Lyric—her brightness, her laugh, her humor, her perseverance in carrying her baby through trial, through months in prison, and now hopefully to freedom. All the favorite prison dishes, from cakes to nachos, come out for the party. When one woman wins, every woman shares that win with her.

But at 7 p.m. the next day, Lyric walked right back into the dorm. A cold wave of horror rippled through the dorm. She's due in nine weeks.

"You okay?" I ask as she passes.

"No. I'm fucked up," she says, rare emotion cracking the mask. She crawls into bed and disappears under the blanket.

The next day, she explains the situation. She was denied for home confinement but there's still one last chance; she *might* get into a pregnant-women's facility, but there may not be one near her family in New York. It may not even be possible until December, when the baby's due. If she delivers inside, they'll take the baby.

There's no way to show her how my heart breaks without making it worse. This isn't a hugging place. I try to send what I can through my eyes, careful not to stare. "Oh, Lyric. I'm sorry," I say. She hears me.

"I don't want to lose my baby," she says, tears rising to her eyes. "It's the system. They're trying to help—but this is messed up." Her words tumble out, so I have her slow down and breathe.

Here's the clock, the way it actually runs: Lyric is twenty-nine weeks pregnant. Once she hits thirty-six weeks—November 5—transport is off the table. She gets sentenced on October 15 and then after her sentencing, the Bureau of Prisons' designation center in Grand Prairie, TX, usually takes six to eight weeks to place you. She needs it done in three to four. There's a program called MINT—Mothers and Infants Nurturing Together—that could keep mom and baby together, but only a few sites are operating, and she has to be designated and moved in time. If Grand Prairie doesn't move quickly, she'll deliver at a hospital and the baby will be taken.

Now I got it. This is what I call the impossible glitch: not bad people, just bad timing inside a rigid machine. The story that outsiders love is that officers are cold; what I see most days are people with their hands tied, trying to help through glass. For all of the "family values" we hold as a nation, the federal carceral system is still lacking. This woman is in prison for fraud, which is no small thing, but it is not violence. That this child might be born motherless breaks my heart to no end.

"I'm trying to get someone at MINT to reach the BOP directly," Lyric says, wringing her hands. "Sentencing guidelines say zero to thirty months. I've already served six. I just want to be with my baby, Han."

I was there the day she chose the name—she wanted royalty and reverence in one breath: Han Christian D.

Han, for an emperor. Christian, for faith. D for her family line.

So this is my prayer, right here in the noise and too-bright light:

Han Christian D, may it be that you spend every minute of your early life in your mother's arms. May you know how loved and precious you are and the lengths that you, a child whose mother considers a miracle, were granted the miracle to be raised by her. That is my prayer.

Until then, we hold Lyric steady. We walk the track. We braid her hair. We sit with the clock. And when her switch flickers, we lend her our light.

61

Let's Talk

A friend once texted me, "We need to talk," and my whole
body clenched. There are few phrases that strike more fear.
We laughed about it later, the way women do to keep from
crying.

Between lover and fighter, I'm a lover. I'm Sicilian; we're stubborn
about love and humor. History kept conquering us, so we learned to
keep laughing. Turns out that's the real victory. Humor and love are
subversive technologies. In here, they're survival skills.

After Luci left, Tamara became my head bunkie, which means she
was in the row behind mine and the tops of our heads faced each
other. It's an oddly intimate position. You hear everything. I know
when she gets up to pee in the night. She knows when I'm conked out
and snoring. When she does "readings" for people with the cards or
goes through her rosary, I try to put up a protective wall for privacy.
When Rach and I chant or do other practices in our bunks, I feel her
trying to do the same. It's a clear and deliberate non-intrusion.

A few years back, I was staying in an Airbnb in the Hamilton Heights
area of Harlem. It was hot. Dirty, humid, city hot. My mom and I,
in a rare turn of events, had gotten into it. I'd gone on a few dates

with a guy and her hackles were up. Something about him rubbed her the wrong way. He was too fast. Too smooth. I didn't like her snap judgment. I did the eternal daughter's protest: "But Mom, you have to get to know him." She did the mother classic: "You only need to know one of those guys." Long story short, she was right.

I went for a walk, the great panacea. Unless it's 100 degrees. I instantly regretted my decision, but I was committed at that point.

I wasn't altogether familiar with the area. There was a much higher concentration of Dominicans than other parts of Harlem. Spanish writing on the awnings. Guys in long jean shorts and white socks. Photos of Dominican seafood in the windows. Heat fumes were coming off the sidewalk. My mind felt like a dry mouth, thoughts stuck, yet I had a grim determination to make it to 125th Street.

Suddenly I heard, "You need to come inside." It came from a woman dressed all in white.

I looked around. She was looking at me.

"You. You need to come inside," she repeated. I glanced at the window filled with candles and crosses, images of Mary. The awning torn, dirty. A Santería store.

Santería, if you haven't met it, is a Caribbean religion that blends Catholic saints with West African deities. It lives in back rooms with candles, rum, cigar smoke, and prayer, and it can be as healing as it is risky, depending on who's handling the power.

I was not up for the task. My Latina friend who inhabits the depths of that secret world once warned me, "Keep your eyes on. We are the cleanest and the dirtiest of 'em all. Not knowing the difference can get you in a heap of trouble."

I was not in the mood to decipher.

"Your mother does not want to argue with you. She wants you to come in and listen to me."

Okay, now it was getting personal. I looked around again as if someone who knew what had just happened with my mother was signaling this woman. Except no one knew what was going on with my mother other than me.

The air in the store was cool. The lights were out. It was a space out of time built only for these conversations. It was very clear there was very little commerce. My mind, like melted wax that was now cooling, reformed. There was a sharp clarity, like pristine reality breaking through hot smog. She handed me a white rose from a vase of roses. I remained cautious. She laugh-smiled as if she'd seen this response a thousand times.

"That's it. Keep this. That's all I had to say," she said.

I reached toward my bag. Clearly this was her gig: Call people in, give them something for free, and they feel inclined to give you cash. Give her the money and go.

She held her hand up in a "keep your money" gesture.

"She loves you. Your mother loves you. That is all. I serve the Mother." She pointed to an image of Mary on the wall. "All mothers." And then she let me go. I say "let" because I was suspended there for those few minutes. I was retroactively humbled, a bit embarrassed at my suspicion. She read this too. Smiled. Nodded. I turned and left, walking down 145th with a white rose.

Tamara makes me think of this woman. The keen eye. She can tell that I am somewhat wary. The profound softness.

There is a mischievous quality to Santería women. You can sense the legacy of women, back rooms, rituals, candles, and secrets. Tuning in, tapping into things not all of which should be tuned into, and if they are, the person turning the dial had better be skilled at both knowing what she is calling in and how to handle it when it arrives. It's rarely of this world. It's not always light. It's clear Tamara has wrestled with more than a few night creatures, and that when she calls the light, it picks up the phone.

259

It was another "game recognizes game" instance when we met: the cat-circling of encountering someone in a different game, gauging the ethical distance between the two, the priorities. She was quick to say she had no fear of the darkness but that the light was her home. I said, "Same, same. If you fear the dark then the light is just a hiding place. But if you're not afraid to enter, you find the hidden light inside the dark." She liked that. Gave me an "I'll think about that" look.

"You know I get exhausted back here sometimes," she said. "I take in a lot of dark in this place. Do my best to cycle it through for the ladies, but sometimes it just knocks me out."

"I know a few practices, if you're ever interested, to transform that energy."

Again, the "I like that" look and a nod. Needless to say, she had been the first person to sign up when our meditation class sheet went up.

She has a charming habit of moving her mouth with yours when you speak and murmuring back what you say. It establishes a rapport, a sense of one current. Then she'll throw her head back and laugh as if to break the spell, because all spells must be broken, and go on her way to her job mopping the dorm.

I keep my eye out for her. She does go down often. I tell her, "We need you," meaning the love, the light, the care she brings. A mother at fourteen, two boys and a girl with severe autism. You see both the care woven into the fabric of her nervous system and a lifetime of never enough sleep. I try to wrap her in mantras, try to send a field of safety around her. I invite her on the walks which, more often than not, she says yes to, but when it's time she's wrapped in three blankets in deep sleep. This place is, for some, the first time they ever rest.

She's my age. We talk about "codes." I try not to sound like I'm scolding a younger generation, but she's right: A lot of folks in here never learned any code beyond impulse. I caught her talking to a few girls after a blowup at the gate and gave the talk: You don't put a man before your girls. Loyalty first. Things calmed for about five minutes. We were stuck on recall—count was off again. Someone was miscounted so the whole dorm freezes while they redo it. Xi-yen is often the culprit as she speaks no English and will be in the kitchen happily cooking her fourteen-minute congee. We will hear all the Asian women at once: "Xi-yen!"

Tamara was close to Carla, the woman who had called "bullshit" on the more generous perspective of prison I had tried to share in meditation class some weeks back. Carla was not, shall we say, an easy woman. She was walking, talking prison slang. "Hard time make a bitch hard" was one of her favorites when someone would ask her to lighten up. Never before have I witnessed the "opposites attract" reality as I did with Carla and Tamara. Most women here are close to one person at a time, vacuum-sealed, then wake up and start hanging out with someone new. But those two somehow got along through thick and thin. Where everyone else bristled, Tamara just giggled over Carla's insults.

As much of a shit-kicker Carla can be, that's exactly what you need when shit goes down. She had defended us more than once, first when Isabella refused to let us into the room where we were supposed to hold meditation class, and again when Lisa accused us of stealing her bottle of pink oil the Black women use for their hair.

"The fuck you think these rich women need your hair oil for? They not bald, ugly bitches like you."

Okay, so I did not say it was a sweet defense, but it worked.

Having spent the better part of her life in prison, and solitary, you see it in her eyes. One half can't be messed with and one half has been touched by something deeper, moved by an otherworldly force.

"Didn't read, didn't get high like everyone else," she said when I asked how she got that strong aura. "Just sat and listened in the silence. First in juvie SHU, then every hole they threw me in after. You sit long enough, you hear more than your own bullshit. Even longer and you hear more than angels even. At some point it's not even you hearing no more."

I tell her that in meditation that's called meeting yourself. That's when we did as close a version to connecting as could be done with her. She winked at me. "I feel ya."

What I want to give the women is ten minutes a day to meet themselves. Distraction is the devil, and the prison installed two additional televisions, an amenity designed to keep you from hearing your own life. Or that silence. A woman who meets herself is ungovernable. She doesn't need saving. She starts changing things.

Without that inner compass, people get blown around like leaves in the fall. Week to week, enemies become ride-or-die and back again. That's why codes matter when the wind picks up.

Eventually, she would be transferred, and she'd leave me her plastic soap holder. "Your soap is important in here. You gonna get sick if you don't take care of it." And I'd know it was her version of a warm hug.

Now, back on recall, Tamara, Carla, and I compare street codes to the bodhisattva codes in Buddhism. Can you be someone who dedicates their life to helping others wake up and suffer less?

Carla says, "Look, I am sweet as candy. Don't fuck with me, I don't fuck with you. I'd do anything for you until you cross me."

I laugh and say, "See, that's a bit like karma, or like the buddhas and bodhisattvas. You do no harm, you relieve suffering, you're honest about the price, and the wish-fulfilling jewel is yours. You cause harm, that boomerang hits hard. What matters is that you live by a code and know the ride you're getting on."

We've had some wins. In between practices and walking, Rach and I have started minding a little corner. People show up at our table for sun burgers and quiet. We run unofficial office hours: say mantras for Nevaeh's daughter who applied to a master's program, or Kiki's nephew whose girlfriend was in a car accident. It's for the mothers in us. Jingyi studies notes from meditation class and comes by with questions. Rach whispers, "I could die happy right now," which in here means this moment counts.

There are other wins too. A group of women who used to blast the TVs at jet-engine volume all night have agreed to use headphones after 9:30. The TVs are a whole saga, but nothing compares to the phones where the women leave notes and times they've arranged calls. It will read "Diamond 1 p.m., 6 p.m." Or "KoKo 12:30." Sane. Civil.

Except for Isabella. She keeps one note above the phones that reads "Bella." As in period. As in she can come in any time and say she needs to use your phone.

She has seniority and relationships with various guards, so while the rest of us are on recall, behind the blue line, she will saunter over to the phone, call her wife, and put her in her place. Mind you, it is in rapid-fire Spanish, but the tone is universal. You can sense that Bella's wife has been conditioned to her voice. Rumors travel, of course. That the way her eye slightly wanders is the result of her wife finally fighting back. That the three scars on her face are where her wife's nails dug in. We do know that no one knows her wife's name as anything other than "bitch." That "bitch" has a way of making Bella whisper into the phone, cry sometimes, plead sometimes, and slam the receiver down often.

"Bella's wife is fucking around with a man. Pregnant. Bella found out from her ex-wife of all people. They say she went crazy on the guy," Janiya whispers as Bella, with her square muscular body, nearly shaved head, pants worn like Ben Davis, strut-slinks back to her bed after one of the desperation calls.

Dakina howls in a different tenor when Bella gets in these moods. I swear she voices what people can't express. They have one of the

263

odder bonds in the dorm. Both have a quality of unreachability, untouchability. And big, tough Bella is surprisingly tender with Dakina. She seems to have very little for commissary but always buys Dakina something. They've been to places others wouldn't dare go. They are not like the cute little Nicki Minaj-style fraud girls who are going to get out, catch the first flight to Vegas. They don't use words like "baddies."

Lately, though, there's a low rumble, some tension between Isabella and us. She rolls her eyes at me like I'm a substitute teacher but aims something sharper at Rach.

There was the library incident. The library is prime real estate in here. One of the only relatively quiet places. It's small—as in three bookshelves and one table small. Isabella sits in there like, well, like a crime boss. Whatever deals or conversations she needs to make, she makes them in there.

We'd worked out a meditation class, reserved the room.

Isabella does not take reservations. Rach was charged with setting up the chairs. It was one of the rare occasions when Rach was unable to break through with someone. She came over to the bunk and said only, "I think we should do it on the rec deck." Something smelled funny.

"Um, there is an endless catcall conversation on the rec deck. I'm not imagining we'll do a lot of dropping into silence," I countered, questioning her logic. She just stood there, speechless, wide-eyed.

"What?" I prompted.

"Isabella said she's not moving."

"She's not moving?" I looked across the dorm and saw her through the library window, sitting, legs spread open, leaned back like she should have a cigar in her mouth. Ah. Got it. I walked over in my super-bouncy tennies and little grey sweatsuit, trying to look as intimidating as I possibly could.

264

"Yes," I said, way too chirpy, walking into the room. "We signed up for this room. We need to have a class. You're welcome to come. You might like it. But we need to set up." I think my total obliviousness caught her off guard. Silently, she got up and skulked out. Use everything you've got. That I am capitalizing on looking totally oblivious, after the initial shock, strikes me as funny.

Then came the cold war. Literally.

Didi was moving to her designated prison. She had the coveted "fan control" role. MDC is most certainly a hell realm. We alternate from a Death Valley desert dust storm to a frozen tundra igloo. There is no middle ground.

She who controls the fan controls, relatively, the temperature. She who controls the temperature controls the torture. She who controls the torture controls the dorm.

Didi was extremely fair, dealt with more than her fair share of complaints. The fan is big and loud and could knock a car off its course. Women like it on at night for the white noise. Well, they like it from 3 a.m. when they go to bed until 4 p.m. when they wake up. But they also like it to modulate the dorm weather. I cannot emphasize enough how the dorm revolves around this fan.

Didi thought it would be a good idea to pass the baton to us. We were not in a turf war and would not use the fan as a weapon. What she did not take into account was the fact that we are not in here for gang violence, as she was. This means people do not fear us. People would kill for that fan unless you look like you're carrying a shank. Rach and I do not match that description.

Isabella is always hot, a side effect of her medication. Not only does she need the fan on twenty-four-seven, but unlike most of the other women, she wants it facing the beds. It was Isabella and the women she hung with, maybe six, against the rest of the freezing-cold dorm. I take my ethical position very seriously. I wanted to be a good representative of everyone.

"Bella not about you," Janiya whispered to me. "She or he or what the fuck ever don't want you fucking with her fan no mo'."

I must have looked like a receptionist. "It's not her fan, it's everyone's fan."

"You smart but you dumb. You gonna end up brawlin' if you not careful," Janiya said with a protective love.

"We will not be brawling," I said, the definition of stiff.

One morning I wake up and Rach is trembling. I can't tell if it's fear or anger or both.

"Keenan told me to turn the fan off at three in the morning. I did. Next thing I know, Bella's passing by me saying I better watch myself. Goes over and turns it right back on." Keenan is an officer. A right-on one at that.

"Did you tell Keenan?" I ask.

"No, I just went to bed. I didn't want trouble."

"Fair and smart," I say, trying to calculate our next move.

I find my answer in about twenty minutes. We are next to each other near the sink. For a minute I'm, as they say in Buddhism, between this and that. Isabella has a certain charm. There's a way she's so real, so direct, that you want to be on her good side. When she smile-winks at you (which she has not done in a very long time with me, and only once), it has the same quality as a rock star singing to you onstage. I think that is why women collect around her. And why they are so loyal to her. You really want to be on her good side because the good is so good and the bad is so bad.

I feel a lot like a perky cheerleader next to an asshole football player. That attracted/repulsed feeling I thought was reserved for high school. I have to be very conscious of that deep groove of conditioning that wants very much to flatter or seduce my way out of this. I have no plan whatsoever when my mouth decides it's a good time to open.

Looks like we are going to ride this one bareback, I think to myself, and go straight improv.

"Let's talk," I say in a voice that sounds like it should end with "young lady!" For a moment I swear I see her wince, almost like a dog that pulls away fast when you accidentally step on its foot. She recovers.

"Yeah?" she says, continuing what must be the longest tooth-brushing in the history of teeth.

"Yes," I say, thanking the gods that I did not go into a long explanation.

"I can't talk till later. I got an appointment."

I don't dare say, 'An appointment? This isn't the outside. What are you going to do, get a manicure?'

"Good. Two?" I say, smartly.

"Two it is," she confirms.

I hear her name over the loudspeaker. A guard comes for her. Attorney, court, or medical.

But at 1:45, I look up and she's standing at my bunk. When she catches my eye, she sits down on Rachel's bed across from me. It's disarming. I've heard an expression, "circle of fear," that criminals and true spiritual people have one common quality: they get into your circle of fear. I've had challenges here because I am so accustomed to keeping that gate open; in the ordinary world, only spiritual people enter that gate, and there aren't many. Most people don't like that much intimacy. It's a kind of close where I feel like I can feel her body heat or hear her heartbeat. She's suddenly profoundly human. It's unnerving.

"Yeah, okay, so my bad. I fucked up," she begins.

Well, that was not how I expected this to go.

"Fucked up?" I ask.

"With Raquel. I didn't mean to scare her. It's just...I'm drenched at night. I can't fucking take it sometimes." This is going much better than planned.

"Raquel?"

"Yeah. Yo girl," she says in a tone that intimates she means "my girl" in the same way the song does.

"Oh, Rachel? You think she's my girlfriend? She's my co-de," I say, using our prison slang for co-defendant. "We've been friends for twenty years." I smile. Everything is a negotiation. I don't want her to think I think having a girlfriend is bad, but I don't want her to think Rachel is my girlfriend. It's a common experience in here to navigate tightropes like this.

"Okay, well yeah, her face look like I killed her mother when I pulled that chain. I can say when I done wrong."

I'm down for the count. I'm a sucker for what Janiya calls a gangster apology. She says, "When a thug apologize, it hit deep." And it really does. It's far from the girl in L'AGENCE Jeans and freshly done nails cutting in front of you at the smoothie bar with her clickety heels, "Sorry, sorry."

"You know," I say, in typical Nicole form, "in Buddhism they have what are called dharmapalas. The toughest ones turn into the greatest protectors. You have a lot of sway in this dorm."

Dharmapalas are those fierce-looking guardians you see in temple pictures, the ones who look like they'd beat the shit out of you and then tuck you into bed. I'm telling her she's that. *Dharmapala.*

She looks like she likes it. "Domo-pomo. I like that. I got anxiety real bad. Like bad bad. Sometimes all I can do is sit in that library and try to not lose my shit. I haven't always been like this, you know. My fuckin' wife. She's killin' me. Fifteen years and now she got a kid. All while I'm sick." She hangs her head in a way that looks soft, feminine. All the bravado melting away.

"You're not well?" I ask as gently as I can.

"Nah. That's why I'm here. I get transferred to Carswell in a month."

She means the medical facility. "I'm advanced. They don't know."

I don't ask "advanced what." I can guess. And it doesn't matter.

"My hormones all fucked up from the meds. I'm all fucked up."

"I'm so sorry. I imagine that has to be terrible in so many ways."

She looks up and into my eyes. We lock for a minute, as if we've known each other forever. We are meeting in a place that only deep love or deep pain can bring you to. She's letting tears fill hers, which means everything in this place.

"Can we do this?" I say. "If you want anything, just ask. We can talk directly."

"Yeah. Yeah, I can do that. You know you and Raquel, you're alright, you know. I mean what you're doing is alright."

"Thank you. You're alright too," I say, smiling. In the chilled environment of a federal prison, that's the equivalent of a bear hug. "I'm happy to hear it. I'm always looking for more peace in here. It's better for the whole dorm. And I am serious. If you need anything, you tell me. I have friends who work with people in your situation. I am happy to help."

She looks at me with the warmest smile. "Girl, you crazy. I fucked with you. You don't owe me shit. We good. I need to show you around. You gonna get yourself in big trouble, you be nice to the wrong people."

"I know I don't owe you anything. I want to. Okay?"

Now it's gone too far and tears are really coming. She wipes her nose like a twelve-year-old boy. Looks at me like, *I gotta get out of here, you understand,* and turns and goes back down the aisle.

In case I needed final proof, that was the last pin to fall: a shift from loving the unlovable to coaxing love out of the unloving. It's simpler than it sounds. Give a little room. Everything is trying to move toward love if you let it, not just to be loved but to love. Because in truth there's no such thing as unlovable.

62

Truth over Team

I once watched a grainy film from the 1950s: a prim, pearls-and-aprons kind of woman sitting beside a clinician in a white coat, pencils lined up in his pocket. Machines hummed in the background. She looked into the middle distance and said, in a breathy Princess Grace voice, "It's just...so...I can't explain it. It's so beautiful. We are—there is no separation—you are me. Oh yes...I am you."

She'd been given LSD in a supervised setting. Whatever she was touching, language couldn't hold it. But you didn't need words to know something was happening that ordinary life rarely lets through.

I used to show that clip when I taught. It was my "finger pointing at the moon": You don't have to take my word for it. There's more to reality than the skin we live in.

If I ever got a tattoo, it would be *ehipassiko*—the Buddhist phrase I love that means "see for yourself." It cuts against our armchair culture: people who feel like athletes on Sundays as they watch football from the couch; spiritual spectators who mistake reading about God for being in relationship with God; do-gooding at a safe distance that never risks a heartbeat. White-glove spirituality stays clean—and brittle.

I invited people to taste honey by putting it on their tongue. Don't watch someone else live. Be the person others can't look away from because you're actually here—unmediated, unedited, alive. To be able to answer from your own bones, not theory, the question: "Is that true?" That is raw, trembling power.

Here, five televisions pour out "true crime," a genre that suggests the world has Prison Envy. It's a kind of safe-distance thrill. You get the charge without getting your hands dirty. Alan Watts once joked that we try to keep the "bad half" of life while saving only the "good," as if you could split a coin and keep heads without tails. The only way to avoid the bad is to avoid life. But life—real life—gets your white gloves dirty.

Ancient practitioners understood this. They'd meditate in *charnel grounds*—open-air burial sites—on purpose, to face death and imper-manence head-on. It wasn't morbid. It was honest.

I'm saying there's a life hidden inside this life—more real than the "real" we perform—and it's most visible in unlikely places. Step off the painted backdrop and you'll bump into it: in a hospital room, a new love, a cell block, a funeral. Your guard drops, reality slips in. In here, in the middle of the charnel ground, there's no escaping it. Miracles and grief take turns. Synchronicities wink. In a world where most people shop for identity at the Beige Store, women here dare to be jeweled.

Take Alex: black hair to her hips, everything turned up—lips, laugh, courage. She walked out of Venezuela, dodged bullets at a fence when there was no water or power, and still cracks jokes like a court jester. She makes jewelry from yarn, makeup from watercolor paint, and her shorts quite a bit shorter with a roll and a grin. She catcalls me down the aisle and I whisper to Rach, "That's why I love sexual women— they're rich enough to play." If most lives read like *Reader's Digest*, the women here are Dante.

271

Every night when Rach says, "I could die happy," I tell her that's the title of her book. Because that's what these flashes are: die-happy moments. They don't erase the hard; they climb on top of it and sing.

The other night news flashed: James Comey, former head of the FBI, indicted. Mari translated for Rosa in Spanish—"la, la, la, Comey"—while eyes flicked between the two end TVs. Women clustered at the middle screens. They waved me over to interpret the circus: What's true? What's payback? What would justice look like if it healed instead of just feeding the machine? I choose truth over team.

If an artist renders a subject, she hopes the subject would nod and say, "Yes, that's me." That's how I try to think through these public bonfires—hug the hairpin curves, respect the whole spectrum, and still tell the truth. In plain terms: I believe people are fundamentally good. I believe everything in us leans toward freedom when given the right tools. And I believe ignorance—often dressed up as virtue—can hijack that process.

That puts me at odds with our national origin story. On the surface, we talk like we believe in original sin: bad seed at the center, best-case life is a lifelong project of problem-chasing—crime, disease, defects— instead of soil-tending. We build whole industries on the assumption that the heart is a hazard zone. But go deep enough and people don't report finding darkness at the core. No one comes back from the depths of their heart saying, "I found hatred." They come back saying, "I found light." My own field test says the same. You don't have to take my word—see for yourself.

The problem is, we're not a nation of depths. Our cultural soil is packed and dry, so weeds that grow fast—dogma, outrage, spectacle— take over. Power brokers make their living guarding you from a monster inside you that, on inspection, isn't there. If you discovered your core wasn't a crime scene, some experts might have to trade the podium for a paycheck behind the counter. And people do love their pedestals, especially the ones built on fear.

I used to think "justice" meant balance, scales, and gavels. Now it feels more erotic than legal—by which I mean: full-contact, embodied, unafraid to be touched by what's true. It isn't about watching from the bleachers while the "professionals" play. It's about taking the field. It's seeing for yourself.

I still believe in laws. I just no longer confuse laws with justice. Justice starts deeper—in the place where you can't lie to yourself. It starts the moment you stop being a voyeur of your own life and step into it with your whole body. It grows when you decide to test the story you were handed about who you are and what lives at your center.

And when you do, you might find what that 1960s housewife found, what women in this dorm keep stumbling into between court dates and casseroles made in a microwave: not a theory, not a team, not a TV show—just the bright, undeniable fact of being alive together, without the glass between us and the guards watching over. See for yourself.

63

Tricksters and Bandits

In the 1960s, there was a Tibetan monk named Chögyam Trungpa who wanted to bring meditation to the West. He traveled to England, attending Oxford to study the religion, history, and philosophy of these odd and interesting Western people. Standing out in his maroon robes, he was a curiosity himself, and different scholars and rich, educated people would come to discuss philosophical topics and learn meditation. But these were not his people.

So, he gave up his robes. He went to bars. He went to parties. He met the rowdiest of them with a smile and a wink. These were his people.

There's a story about the Buddha from his lifetime just before becoming enlightened. He was a monk walking through the forest and came upon a starving tigress and her cubs. Drawn by compassion, he nursed them, offering blood from his own body until they were strong enough that he could offer his entire body to them. I never liked that story. It seemed gruesome, unnecessary. Are you supposed to go around throwing yourself to the tigers and wolves and bears? But this morning I felt it: the joyful self-offering. Not martyrdom. Placement. Give yourself where you benefit beings most.

Sitting by the small window, feeling my body come alive after an easeful morning practice, watching the yellow light filter through the slats, I feel a pure, unadulterated joy. It's one of those moments when you realize who you are is exactly what is being called for. I look around the dorm and feel the water source seeping into the soil. Dakina, who is called "crazy," was profoundly sane when Luciana met her with kindness. Where others felt intense aversion, Luciana showed tenderness. She'd have conversations with her in her clearest moments and wake up in the night to give her candy when others just yelled at her.

Seeds of kindness sprouting. These moments are what I live for.

And here's what surprised me: I had no idea how fertile the soil would be. I thought it would be filled with tough women who didn't give a shit. In fact, these are some of the most pure-hearted women I've ever met. It's painful to see the cruel joke. It's not that these women are bad and need their power removed lest they hurt someone. It's that harm came as a result of their power being so miscast.

One woman who comes and sits with Rachel and me for our afternoon meditations is going home soon. On the phone she told her sister she actually wished she could stay in prison; she was nervous to be back outside. I promised we could spend more time together meditating so she'd have tools she could take with her. This is not charity. It is an honor to be with these women.

We had meditation class the day before, now a regular part of the weekly rhythm in the dorm. The women came with questions from last week (if they hadn't already pulled me aside in the days between classes) and took pride in their increasing breath-holds during tummo practice, warming their bodies enough that they've started leaving off layers of clothing.

As class started, I tried to explain what I see: They're Lamborghinis; I'm just offering GPS. Compassion, animal instinct, limbic connection,

275

single-pointed focus—these women have engines powerful enough to get to where meditation is meant to take you. They have the potential to change the world. They need only a mirror and a map. The metaphor resonated in the room.

"The labels we put on ourselves—or let other people put on us—that's the trap."

In here, identity is a contact sport: who is friend and who is foe, whether you're wearing an inmate's uniform or a guard's. I hint at another way, a third option where you neither bow nor assert. You know who you are outside the bounds of cultural ascription, floating above the boundaries they draw on the map below.

I pointed to Royal, who was nodding, for confirmation. She has enough years inside to have seen labels get stuck on and eventually peel off again.

"You can be invisible and not need to be seen. Revered and not get inflated. You arise according to the needs of the time. Like tofu, you take on the flavor of whatever you're steeped in." That's the holy grail—not a chalice above us, but a ladder that allows for seamless motion into any realm. "If you really want to bring benefit, you have to be able to say two things: There is nothing you can do that will scare me, and nothing you can do that will make me not love you."

I often call myself a surveyor, exploring wild realms where brand-name companies won't dare to go, offering what I have. Most people are different from me. I'm too wild to be "good" and too good to be bad. In, but not of. There's a one-percent club—spiritual transients who don't abide anywhere but connect the dots wherever they land. They are my people. Some of the women here are those people.

"Just how does meditation work?" Nevaeh asked, looking to tie the pieces together.

"It gives you access to a whole other game. It's fifth-dimensional chess—no other game like it—and only for real ones." They like a challenge.

Years back I took a tour of a Zen convent. There was a painting on the wall, a figure sitting in meditation, blue sky stretching behind him. My Lama said it was Samantabhadra, a buddha whose name translates to "Universal Good."

"Patron of tricksters and bandits, criminals and the wild ones," my Lama added with a grin. "We like him a lot."

It was love at first sight. It's easy to do the kind of spirituality that looks good, benefiting the needy and the poor. But who takes care of the hard cases? Black-diamond spirituality doesn't leave the prostitutes and junkies at the door and then congratulate itself for giving a cookie. It goes straight to where society piles the bodies it doesn't know what else to do with and sets up shop. Shouldn't there be a heaven for the bad boys and girls, the wild ones most people root for in movies and TV but forget to include in their prayers?

These women—forgotten and tossed aside by society, the ones most would only try to control and restrict—have the greatest potential I've ever known. I made my vow decades ago, and I can see its trickster finesse and how it carried me precisely here. This is where the road has been misnamed and misunderstood. These women are dying to drive, to let their engines roar, to see what happens when they finally get a clear stretch of runway instead of a cul-de-sac.

Sitting in that early morning light, it hit me that this could be my post for a very long time. Bonkers in terms of justice, righteous in terms of service. I think often of the dignity Malcolm X sought to bring to the Black men he was incarcerated with and the potential he saw in them. That's what I want for women, but through dharma, not dogma: each woman waking up to her unique power so she can carry out her unique calling, her unique flight. I give myself over to where I am of most benefit. The greatest joy comes from the place of greatest contribution.

I don't pretend to know how it will unfold, but I give myself to it wholly.

64

The Rupture

bove anything else, the threat of disconnection is tantamount
to death. For women, connection is how we know who we
are and how we know we are safe. It's also the basis of
our power. For decades, I taught women's empowerment through
sexuality, but the key was always this: True intimacy cannot exist at
the expense of connection. Without her sisters, a woman is left to be
devoured by the wolves.

The truth is, you don't know who someone is until the rupture.
Anyone can be warm and sweet and generous on the calm side of
things. But can you stay with it as the storm brews, as the ominous
clouds gather, as the sky claps in thunder? Through the torrential
rains, the roofs lifting off houses, all the way to the first break of
sunlight, to the rainbow that hints at renewal.

I'd learned early on that the dorm we live in was a pressure cooker.
Alliances shift fast in here. One day you're family; the next it's an
opps day and no one remembers how you were ever friends. I'd seen
it with Janiya and Nevaeh, best friends one day then suddenly on
opposite sides of something I certainly couldn't name. In a place this
compressed, things don't need to be true to become real. They just

need to take hold.

So when someone I wasn't close to found and read the pages I had printed to share, pages the printer had jammed on and then quietly released later, it didn't really matter what was on them. What mattered was that they were words, detached from me, stripped of beginning and end, context and consent.

In here, rumors are like California superfires: It doesn't take much to ignite when the air is this dry. There is very little "rain" in a prison dorm—very little softness, nuance, or patience to slow the spark. A few words, a few misunderstandings, and the whole hillside goes up.

These women know what it is to be flattened into a single story, one in which they are seen as dangerous, defective, disposable. They know what it is to have the world decide who they are without asking. They believe there is a vendetta against "our kind," that you survive by hook or by crook. But a few—my kind—stay through the turbulence long enough to watch division melt and the lie of "other" dissolve. If the devil is a liar, that's his favorite lie he whispers to you: "We are not the same." That lie tells you to hoard what's in your heart to protect yourself and get yours because no one else will.

For two days, the dorm's mood shifted around Rachel and me. Conversations stalled when we walked by, then picked up again in a lower, tighter register. Eyes skated past us like we were made of static. Even Royal's usual, "Hey, baby," sounded like it was coming from another floor.

Kiki slid up just close enough to talk without looking like she was talking to me. "They're preparing to lynch two white women," she muttered. "That's you and Rach."

My stomach dropped.

"They found some pages," she added.

The clouds that had been gathering now had a target.

That afternoon we were in the gym, walking the little track that circles the room, doing what we always do: pray with our feet, breathe, pretend our bodies still belong to us. The officers were nowhere in sight.

We saw them coming.

Seven women. Nevaeh, Royal, Carla, Isabella, Lyric, and two women I'd never spoken to who had clearly come along for the ride. They sauntered in, not rushing. They moved like a single body with a single purpose, cutting across the gym floor toward us.

"Well," I said to Rach, feeling my mouth go dry, "it's a good day to die."

Everyone has heard the stories of women getting jumped in prison so I won't pretend I didn't clock the details and feel relief. No pillowcases full of soap to beat us with, no wild running start. The danger was real, but inside I felt oddly still. I once heard two race car drivers describe the same track: The one who kept coming in second said it felt insanely fast, like he was barely hanging on; the champion said it felt like sitting on his living room sofa. Same speed, same curves, totally different experience. In that moment, I knew which game I was in.

They encircled us at the edge of the track. A chair scraped. Carla, who had naturally taken the lead, dropped into it like a foreman about to conduct a disciplinary hearing.

"We need to talk," she said.

The other women tightened the circle. It felt like a basement scene in a mob movie, only with harsh lighting and cheap sneakers.

In meditation class, I had told these same women to treat what is true like gold: burn it, scratch it, rub it. Until then, you don't know what it's made of. And while I am not the Buddha and there are still impurities in my nature, I was, in that moment, one hundred percent clear about the nature of my intent. It would be ridiculous for me to paint these women as evil or ugly when I am one of them. I am far too Sicilian for that, both in the way I live in the "us" of things and in my refusal to make an ugly portrait.

They had been gentle with us so far. True intimacy means testing.

Carla held up the crumpled pages. "People been saying you writing some kind of hood book about us."

They waved the pages in front of me as proof of my malintent. That I was pulling one over on them, as if I had been sent into their midst like an embedded journalist, observing the wildlife to send reports to the outside world.

"It's part of a write-up of a conversation," I said, my voice steady even as every cell paid attention. "I printed it to share." I looked at the women I knew, the ones I was close with. "I always share my writing. You've read pieces before."

But in a place like this, intention doesn't protect you. Stories move faster than truth.

They started naming their fears. That people on the outside would read this and judge them. That their kids might see it. That some prosecutor or probation officer would use it against them. That they'd be frozen in these pages as exactly what the world already thinks they are.

I could see what they were saying. If I believed my story might be taken and weaponized against me, I'd be nervous too.

The air was thick, a living thing pressing in on my skin. This wasn't a theoretical threat; this was seven women in a room with no officers, telling me they felt betrayed. Seven women with limited information and limitless imagination. Seven women who could be dangerous if crossed. Steadying yourself in the face of that force is no small thing. To receive it, let it move through my body, and turn it into a steady explanation instead of a counterattack—that was my task.

I was neither afraid nor fully competent. In the space where a certain fear used to live, a clean determination rose instead.

These women wade through the swamp of disappointment daily. The nurse who promises to come and doesn't. The family member who promises to visit and doesn't. The court date that promises to end this nightmare and instead pushes it further down the calendar. I had wanted to be a glimmer, enough of a flame to ignite something in here. Now even I was being doused.

They took turns.

"I was disappointed..."

"It made me feel played..."

"I thought you were different..."

They said they were going to report me to their attorneys, to MDC, to anyone who would listen. That they wanted nothing to do with this book. Take their names out. Take their stories out. It was clear they were getting ready to ostracize me and Rach. They called Rachel a snoop and a spy. We had gone from "we got you" to "we're done with you" in under ten minutes.

A strange, awful, beautiful thing: hearing women use the "I" statements I had taught them in meditation class to give me a more emotionally responsible dress-down. Threat in one hand, tools of emotional literacy in the other. I was wired and very much alive, and I was proud. Proud because, in this dry place, they were doing their best to practice an uncommon maturity instead of just swinging. This was them testing the gold.

Mixed in with the accusation I could feel the ache of women who did not want to be disappointed one more time. I tried again.

"I would never publish anything about you without your approval," I said. "I always share what I write. I want you all to read it. Read every word I've written. Let that speak for itself. I can't convince you, but the words can. For me to try to take someone down is against who I am and what I'm here to do."

But trust had been broken. Threat hung in the atmosphere, both sides breathing the same air. But there was also something else present, like a low current underneath: my Lama's voice, talking about the freedom of a pure intention. The deepest fear is exposure. When you no longer fear being seen, you operate differently. If everything in you is oriented to bringing benefit, the person who looks most threatening becomes, potentially, your greatest ally. They are the one who will test you thoroughly enough to prove what you're made of.

What I didn't know until later was that this was the scaled-down version. Originally, the plan had been a full Town Hall, the whole dorm taking turns coming for my head. An officer who had proven, in small ways, to be both wise and humane had put a stop to that. "No," she told them when they marched into her office demanding blood, "only a group."

She even sneaked in a quiet check-in with Rach. "You alright?" she asked. Rach nodded automatically, good-girl reflex. The officer held her eyes and said, more firmly, "No. I mean it. You alright?" In here, that's a glimmer in the tunnel, someone charged with being the big tough authority giving you the smallest wink that you are being watched, and not just in the surveillance way.

I owe that woman—as my friend Ed would say—a deep bow. We've maybe exchanged thirty words, four of which were, "Where is your uniform?" But that one boundary she drew on our behalf mattered.

Back in the gym, the circle stayed tight.

In Buddhism they talk about the confrontation with the adversary on the threshold, your own private hell, custom-built for your ego— the last test before you slip the gravity of your old story. I have to hand it to whoever designed this episode. Seven women in prison, no officers, confronting me over something I had intended as benefit. A mischaracterization I could not simply explain away. A misunderstanding I could not just make right. Hopelessness, helplessness, powerlessness. Check, check, check.

In the middle of my talking-to, two parallel thoughts rose clear as bells:

We will make this right, no matter what.

And:

How could I love you more than I do right now?

Royal finally spoke, her voice cutting through the heat. Royal, the self-described OG of OGs.

"You know what, Nicole," she said, "you got game. I got more game than anyone I know, and you got game."

"I do," I said, smiling with a confidence I hadn't yet let them see, "but I'm not sure you know which game I'm playing."

She looked at me with suspicion and curiosity in equal parts. Royal is smart. I knew I could leave her with that question and she would track it.

There is an order to this game, the kind you can sense even when the rules are still hidden from view, but it isn't a game she'd seen before. I know the feeling. I had it with my Lama. I couldn't understand how he could pin me every time until I got on the same wavelength as what's called *bodhichitta*, the aim to bring benefit. When that is your aim—when you've glimpsed the desire to transform every last drop of self into the ending of suffering—the person who looks the most threatening, the one who might expose you, becomes your greatest ally because they not only see you, they see you through the eyes of love. When you change your address to that street, things look very different.

I was, of course, disappointed. It looked like the end of something beautiful. I am very clear that the only way to correct public perception is to present so many human stories of the women in here that they wash out the "animal" story that's out there. These women were forfeiting that. On one level, no skin off my nose; I could keep writing this book as a story of practice inside these walls. On another, the color and life would be drained. And most importantly, the greatest weapon to combat hatred—the very stories of the hated— might no longer be available.

As the conversation unfolded, lines were drawn. Some women made it clear they wanted out of the book altogether. Others left the door cracked, willing to read more, to decide later. It wasn't a tidy resolution; it was a crime scene, with yellow tape in my mind that read *do not cross*.

But years of practice had trained a reflex in me: Let go. Like a well-trained dog with a bone, I unclenched my jaw to let it drop. All the hours of meditation, all the teachings about renunciation, had been for this moment. Do not convince. Do not chase. Do not keep trying to write a woman's story if she doesn't want it told. Great idea, great vision, and if they say no, let it go.

That room was fire.

And as much as they saw me and Rachel, I could now see them. I could see who was fanning flames for her own agenda, who just wanted to keep her ass out of the heat, and who I'd choose if I were building an army for unity. I could see the rawness under the anger, the history under the suspicion, the sliver of courage it takes to walk up to someone and say, "You hurt me," instead of just taking her down.

This is what rupture does when you stay. It shows you what you're made of—and what everyone else is, too.

65

Stay for the End

Rachel and I returned to the dorm buzzing from the mediation. Our nervous systems were set to fight-or-flight. We'd seen who had caught a glimpse of what we'd been pointing to, of what was possible. And whatever had shifted in that room hadn't settled yet. The air still felt charged.

The dorm kept its hackles raised. Through the afternoon I could feel its eyes on us—some direct, some side-eye, a few soft. Rachel called my name from the kitchen and I moved toward it at a measured pace, full-body radar on. The kitchen lights were out. She stood there with four women. "You have to hear this."

Mari. Ramona. Alma. Jingyi. Mari had welcomed us on arrival, she'd broken through her shyness to teach yoga classes. Jingyi had opened up to us in her quiet way and her White Tara self smoothed Dakina in moments, offering something to the whole dorm. Ramona and Alma speak mostly Spanish; Jingyi speaks Chinese and is learning Spanish to talk with them. They aren't in the mix. Some call them "stuck up" or "superior." I've been scolded for doing yoga with Mari or meditating with Jingyi—violations of the invisible boundaries that line the dorm.

Alma was one of the first women to arrive at MDC after Rachel and I did. The experience of my own arrival was fresh in my mind and I had wanted her to feel held, the way you hope any new woman will be held when she lands on this planet. You're coming out of one life and being born into another. Who you were no longer exists. And then you get dropped into cinderblocks and pink paint—hell's own palette.

Alma's eyes had a stunned, saltwater sheen that day. Caramel highlights, chic glasses, a rosy tan. There was nothing I could fix, but I wanted to let her know there was someone here *for* her—even if all we can trade are *"Buenos días"* whispered across the divide, the extent of our sustained connection these past months.

Mari had been our own ferryman—the first person we met in the holding cell. It made sense she'd be here again after this death and rebirth. She's the woman of the in-between. She reminds me of Mary Magdalene. My friend Ed sends me images of Black Madonna from around the world and I always share them with her.

Ramona keeps a perimeter around her that only this group of women have been allowed in. People said all kinds of things about her—jungle, guerrilla, don't mess—but in prison, stories grow like vines. She could just as easily have been a nun. I'd only once ventured across the line she holds, offering a small, sad prison cake Rachel and I had made for her birthday. And as we had stumbled through our Spanish to sing *"Feliz Cumpleaños,"* she had let us in with a smile.

In the dark kitchen, Mari translated while Alma spoke, their voices soft. "She's saying," Mari translated, "to put her in the book. She wants to be in your book."

I looked from face to face. "We want to support you," Mari continued. "We all want to be in the book."

"Nic, they want you to write about them," Rach translated the translation for me; I think I was in shock.

This is why non-attachment is the bomb. Not because you get so holy you float above your life on some cloud of detachment, but because there are forces at work that are simply wiser than my little gripping mind. Clutching is what jams the gears. I used to say, "My God loves me too much to let me keep going down the wrong road." In that moment, when I was actually able to loosen my fist—to stop insisting it had to be *these* women, *this* outcome—almost immediately a crack opened. In walked women who were not only willing, but genuinely excited to be written about. It reminded me of that cheesy cartoon I used to roll my eyes at: Jesus asking a little boy for his torn-up teddy bear while hiding a big, new teddy bear behind his back. Corny? Sure. But in that kitchen, it felt exactly right.

Jingyi added, "We will translate to Chinese." Alma—through Mari—added, "And Spanish." I lifted my head and finally met Ramona's gaze. For a second, the veil dropped. Her face held so much concentrated mercy I could barely look at it.

In that mercy, I let my own face be seen—awkward, awed, newly innocent. The kind of tenderness that comes to get you out of hell, lay a cool cloth on your head, and murmur, "There, there. You're all right."

The world is full of hidden light—and when you ask, one face of that light steps forward. That's what it felt like in that kitchen. The face stepped forward.

Tamara had been gone at court while the mediation happened. She came back in the evening, bone-weary, her eyes looking like someone painted the rims with red eyeliner. She'd missed the excitement. But the "dorm phone"—our name for the sweep of gossip—had already brought the headlines to her.

Even in her exhaustion, she rolls down the sheet that separates our beds and provides a little privacy. As she does, I hear her say, almost to no one, "Put me in it."

"Huh?" I ask, through the hanging bedsheet.

"Put me in it. If you're writing it, I want to be in it. I like being seen through your eyes."

"Tamara," I say quietly.

"I told 'em, I know who you are. Knew the first day. People don't always recognize light."

I turn over and peek at her bed. We're both a little shocked to see the sadness in the other's eyes. She does what we do when it gets too honest: makes a joke.

"The only thing...can you make me ten pounds lighter in the book? Maybe it'll carry over into real life."

"Happy to," I say.

Later that night, after count, heading off to sleep, I say, "Tamara?"

"Yeah?"

"Thanks."

"No problem," she says, like a customer service agent who's just cheerfully accepted a return.

You don't know until you know. And you'll never know if you leave before the miracle.

That's the punchline, isn't it? A woman walks into a life full of difficulty. She agrees to sit down in the middle of it. Terrors and tremors arrive. A few delights. Some scary faces. She keeps sitting. The sun breaks through. The rainbow laughs: "I've been here the whole time. Thank you for waiting for the clouds to pass."

There, in that raw intimacy of stripped-bare nakedness, you find yourself reunited with the one and only lover—in love with life.

You don't know until you know. And you'll never know if you leave before the miracle.

66

Born Free

My mother still tells the story of coming home to *Born Free* blasting from the TV, her daughter glued to the screen, tears streaming.

"You cried every single time like it was your first," she says. She learned not to put dinner on the table until Elsa was free. I'd sing between sobs: "Born free, as free as the wind blows..."

I grew up in Los Gatos, a tidy suburb that would later become part of "Silicon Valley." I've mostly lived in cities, but the wild has always tugged at me. Some days I felt like a big cat trying to be polite in a living room.

In *Born Free*, a lioness dies defending her cubs. One orphaned cub—Elsa—faces cages and keepers, except for the one keeper who refuses to mistake instinct for savagery. With stubborn love, she helps Elsa remember what her mother couldn't teach: how to hunt, roam, belong to her own life. Because someone trusted her nature, Elsa runs.

I once watched a video about a black panther named Diablo who paced his cage with a violent edge. He had attacked his caretaker. The man—never afraid of animals—now wondered if Diablo should be shipped out or put down.

An animal communicator spent time with the panther and reported what she sensed: He missed the cubs he'd protected, hated his name, and felt unseen—nobility treated like a circus act. The caretaker listened. Diablo became Spirit.

The pacing stopped. Spirit stepped out, long and calm. The caretaker cried. Recognition changes things.

That wild nobility is why people were surprised that I gravitated to John, a straight-laced Buddhist teacher known for strict precepts. I'm the supposed wild child. He's the rule-follower. We worked together for more than a decade.

"I just don't get it... John?" friends would say when I packed for retreat. It didn't help that I was visibly moved by him. "What do you see in him?"

It was what he could see in me. He saw the part of me the world labeled dangerous. He knew the difference between power and threat. In a Bay Area spiritual scene that could be prim about anything to do with sexuality, his steadiness was oxygen.

On retreat, I finally found a way to explain it. I was furious during a session where a woman said any mention of Chögyam Trungpa—my favorite Tibetan teacher aside from my Lama—needed a trigger warning. Yes, Trungpa drank, he married a woman half his age. He broke decorum and defied expectations. He was undeniably wild, but that was exactly his brilliance. I told John I was in the wrong place and should go home.

"No," he said. "Your voice is needed here. Come to the session later. If you still want to leave, you can."

I walked into a circle of misfits: a woman who couldn't stop talking, another who drew while listening, another who had to stand. This, at a center where the "good kids" sat with perfect posture. One by one the misfits said John had saved their lives. He had made room for them.

In my one-on-one with him after lunch, I asked how he understood us—the Bad News Bears.

"I'm a big-game animal, too," he said. "There was no place for me either. I realized my work was to be the keeper of the wildlife refuge."

"But then you have to be so straight," I said, stunned by what that would require.

"It's my honor," he said, with a small wink of gratitude.

He's a better man than I am. I try. It takes a very wild refuge for me not to be the wildest person in the room. MDC does the trick. I joke with Nevaeh that here I pass as a "housewife." The part that's hard to explain is this: The wildest you can be is the wild that's yoked to something greater than yourself. Otherwise it's just recklessness— more collisions, less freedom.

People love the feeling of the edge. My friend Kate once went to a concert with a world-class violinist. As a soloist herself, she's hard to impress. "I thought she'd snap a string every second," Kate said. "She hugged the curve of every note and never fell." That's the real wild: knowing the rules so well you can play with them—and playing for the right reason. The only rule worth keeping is compassion. Play for the benefit of all. If that's in your pocket, you can find your way anywhere.

I know it can sound preachy—*be compassionate*. That's not it. It's practical. When your intention is clean, your action is clean. No guilt, no remorse, no schemes. You don't need to hustle when you've touched the place in you that already has enough. Why would you want to "get over" on anyone?

That's what makes you hard to rattle. The world feels like it's at your back. Obstacles don't disappear; they just become material, giving the path shape and meaning.

So when the line of women marched into the gym toward Rachel and me, it could have ended everything. My private nightmare had arrived: The people I love and respect saw me as the enemy. A breach of trust. Even as cold fear climbed my spine, I couldn't cut myself off from them. This was the wild—what happens when a group feels threatened and moves as one.

And it was an obstacle tailored to my most tender nerve. A dorm full of women seeing you as a threat will rattle anyone, especially here. Most of these women aren't in for nonviolent crimes.

For some women, the pressure turns inward; for others, it leaks out sideways. For days after, it felt like walking around after surgery with the stitches missing—every step a flinch, nerves on the outside. Eyes followed me across the room. Dakina went from restless to untethered. Her rhythmic hoots and howls grew more intense and paid no mind to the women who yelled at her to shut up. When she wasn't running in place on her top bunk trying to take off like an airplane, she scratched at her arms and legs until they bled. It was like watching the dorm's nervous system discharge through one body. The officers finally did the only thing they knew to do with a woman who won't come down: They came and hauled her off to SHU. One less wild card in the room; one more woman alone with her mind.

Who you are in the intensity of the unknown, flying far from the ground, that's who you are. That's the point of the whole story leading up to now. As Miriam says, don't leave before the miracle.

67

Getting Back Up

The shamans say that becoming a medicine man begins by falling into the power of the demons. The one who pulls themself out of the dark place becomes the medicine man; the one who stays becomes the sick person. Even the worst things you fall into are part of an initiation, because you are in something that belongs to you.

In the days that followed, everything in me wanted to stay down. Don't get back up and you can't get hit again. Stay in the corner. Take the loss. In that corner was survival. Every last pattern—escape, avoid, hide, quit, justify. This was beyond my capacity. I was a raw nerve. Whatever makes your hair stand on end was alive across my whole body. It felt like walking over scorpions, naked, being tased in front of people jeering—just to cross the dorm to the restroom. I cut back my water to the bare minimum.

They say pain makes you a narcissist: Get a toothache and try to think about anything—or anyone—else. Your first confrontation in prison is like a toothache in your survival instinct. Everything becomes a siren of self-consciousness. Your ears ring. Those people laughing in the corner? They're laughing at you. The person who used to make eye contact and won't anymore? Now an enemy. The whispering that runs rampant in prison? It's all about you. Someone being called to the office? Must be a complaint against you.

And then, being in prison, there is no escape. The cute spiritual line about prison being the ultimate place for transformation, where you finally wake up because there's really no hope of escape suddenly wasn't cute anymore. I was walking around wrapped in an electric fence, with no way out. The dreams I had of a different kind of incarceration, meditation classes and real training for the women I still believed had the power to change the world—now felt like just *dreams*.

What the women had shown me, the love that still makes itself available in the worst circumstances, that these are the women who, every day, shoulder that load and are able to make the best of it—if this meant anything, then it had to mean something even now.

Somewhere under the noise, a small voice kept repeating: *Get up.* So I did.

I gave the whole book to Royal. And when we spoke after, I felt that shared lift that's possible between women. She has a depth of love most people never get to. Under the layers, she has what the world needs. She has everything but the mirror that says, *You are that.* I've been some version of her—needing someone to reflect my own knowing back to me. Shame is the cloak women of power learn to wear until they start believing it's their skin.

I often think of the story of the prodigal daughter. The son spends his inheritance; the daughter never claims hers. She begs for scraps of approval she doesn't need. Her story of redemption is to come home and finally enjoy what's hers.

I had the jewel and didn't know. Royal wears the crown and doesn't know. We hold mirrors up for each other so we can finally see ourselves truly.

A friend once told me that maybe I'd been cancelled because people needed to see me go down and get back up, so they'd know I wasn't born made of steel. To see that it is possible for you to get back up. In the aftermath of my cancellation, relationships weren't "as good as before." They were better. We find out who we are when the bomb goes off. Those are the moments when intention can't be faked.

The same was happening here, now. "I know you for real," Miriam confirmed. "Nobody gets back up after a hit like that unless they got power behind them. And nobody got that power unless they're for real." My walks with her had sparked an idea in me.

Nevaeh joined her. "Just remember—people who fuck with you, they fuck with you. They got you." In here, that's love.

I wasn't all the way back. But I was walking again.

68

Little Miracle

As if we got the same memo, Miriam and I doubled down on our walks. Our warrior turned power-walker—lap after lap, like we could get the wheels turning again. We dreamed out loud: her house when she's home; her nonprofit where wrongs are made right; most of all, her ministry. A world inside the world. An engine inside the dorm. We were yoked by a single want—to see these women rise.

We shared. I talked about how I'm fifty-eight. Also, an introvert. How this is not usually a "making new friends" era of life. But here we were. There'd been no other way. Miriam shared from her own life, her dream of becoming a minister, the church she hoped to build, the wisdom she'd gained from her time inside, the sermons she played out in her head, waiting to come out.

"Like what?" I asked, sensing the burgeoning creativity. "You ever write them out?"

"I know, I should," she said, shaking her head, like trying to clear a fog from in front of her. "It's hard, who would want to listen to them? I just keep doing my Bible study groups."

An idea began to percolate in my mind.

Lyric joined us. Eight months pregnant, wrapped in a head scarf that makes her look like Mary. Even swollen-bellied, she set the pace and we kept up.

"Finding out I was pregnant on intake was crazy as fuck," she said. "Before I got locked up, I thought I might be, so I took my ass down for an abortion. I knew I couldn't have a baby with that dude, not the life I was living. They did the pee test, the sonogram—said I wasn't pregnant. Said I was irregular from birth control. So I kept going."

She shook her head. "I get locked up and they tell me I'm four months. You gotta be kidding me. The nurse called psych 'cause I was crying so hard. I told her, 'I ain't crazy. I'm mad.'"

We laughed because she wanted us to.

Then her voice went low. "Looking back, I feel different. There's a reason I came to jail. A reason my baby hid that long—from me, from the doctors. He was meant to be. He's my little miracle."

We went quiet—pin-drop quiet. Lyric has presence. She can make you laugh till you wheeze, then bring the room to stillness. In that moment, the only thing to see was the miracle. And we did.

"I prayed my whole bail hearing," she said. "Judge slammed that gavel—bail denied. So I started looking for other ways. I'm the type who doesn't dwell on the bad. Yeah, I was tight, but I try to keep spirits high. I got my sentencing pushed up four months. I had a shot at a program where I could keep my baby. I didn't even know that existed—being locked up with your baby."

She swallowed. "Then boom. Government shutdown. Programs shut down. Now I wake up scared my water's gonna break and they'll take him."

We all went a little green—roller-coaster stomachs. In a dorm like this, under constant uncertainty, empathy concentrates. We don't just hear stories; we live them. For a minute, we were all Lyric—carrying a miracle that might be taken.

"I still got hope," she said. "I picture staff walking in and saying they'll drive me to Seattle. I'd even risk a flight—anything to keep my baby. I put in a pardon app. Wrote to Al Sharpton. I'm trying everything. Don't take my baby." Her eyes broke away. "But sometimes you gotta lay down and stay down…"

The silence returned, but heavier. I saw Miriam's lips moving—prayer. Rach and I traded a look—our turn to hold the thread in our way. Nevaeh moved in beside Lyric with the kind of steady that doesn't need words.

The five of us, bunkies on Religion Row, walk the track together in silence, circling, powerless to fix what matters most—yet still holding to a miracle after so much defeat. That is its own miracle.

The voice in me said a single prayer: Let this baby be born free.

69

Good News

We hear applause from the dorm—howls, screams, the kind you'd mistake for a rowdy sorority party. Rach and I look at each other. We round the corner fast; the room is buzzing. What could make everyone this happy?

Then we see her.

Royal sits in one of the awkward prison chairs, only she's sitting tall. Grey hair, head wrap, beige jacket over the matching uniform—cool the way Tupac's mother is cool. Picture a grandmother at a club being adored, except it's all women, sworn "opps" and besties alike, circling her. Tears stream down her face.

Royal was born to lead. Her voice carries clean across a room and lands in your chest before you have time to think. By the time you process it, you're changed.

"And Mr. Rubin said—God, I love Mr. Rubin, he's been so good to me—he said, 'Miss Royal, I couldn't wait to call. The prosecutor dropped the major charge.'" She pauses, lets it hit. "And he said it's possible I'm going home. Soon."

Her laugh booms, and the room answers, laughter flocking in. We make our way through. Royal stands and hugs each of us, one by one.

When a miracle shows up in prison, everyone wants to hold it. She wants that, too—that her joy might be catching, even for a minute.

"I don't even know how to feel," she says, a little dizzy. "I don't know what to do. I'm just so happy." She does know what to do, better than most: Let it be felt. Let the tears come where "cool" doesn't cry. Let us laugh and cry with her.

Hours later, I'm at her bunk.

"Nicole," she says in her usual way, punctuating her sentences with the name of their intended recipient. "Nicole, I need to tell you. I don't wanna go back..."

I blink. "Back?"

"I don't wanna go back to the streets. I was good for twenty years. I wanna be good. I wanna be there for my grandbabies. For my kids. Nicole, I never known nothin' but the streets, my whole life. But I wanna do this different. I get a new life, Nicole."

That, I can hear. Everything in me wants it for her.

She takes a breath. "But what am I gonna do? What skills I got? I've had two heart attacks and a stroke. I got no house. I can stay with my mother, but how I'm gonna take my grandbabies shopping?"

Hope drops into my stomach. The confetti feeling from the dorm gives way to the math of rent, jobs, health.

"I don't know, Royal," I say. "But I will give it everything I have to help figure it out. The world needs to know you. You're rare in a way you don't even know. These women survive on what you give. We'll find a path."

She studies me. "I'm starting to believe you, Nicole. People talk a lot of bullshit in here, but I'm starting to believe you."

A seed lands. I picture a room full of people listening to her the way I have—how her voice would steady them. Then something precious seals it: a woman who's met more defeat than most deciding to trust, even a little, that a new start is possible. I would do anything to be worthy of that trust.

Royal reaches up and moves a strand of hair from my face. It's the most tender moment I've had in here—two women, strong and tired, lowering their guard, each trying to make the other's life a little easier.

70

Yilan

A month previously, there had been a fight in the dorm. Rach and I heard shouting and ran in from the gym. Officers stood in the aisle. Janiya was being led out. Yilan, too. Each off to their own individual cells in the SHU.

Things constantly shift in here, but this was a voltage drop. It felt like someone had hit the stun gun on the unit. Janiya was our circulation. Not a gentle heart—more a smack-talker who could start something and still keep the blood moving. Yilan was a different fixture: our collective heartbreak turned to heat, the cartoon cloud with steam out the ears. "I won't start it, but I'll finish it," her posture said.

At first, the quiet felt like relief. Then the absence opened a hole. You don't know what a person holds up until it's not held.

Nevaeh—who used to be driven bonkers by Janiya—asked after her the most. "She grows on you," she'd say, or, "She's an acquired taste," softening the edge each time. It was her way of marking a change.

Now they're back, fresh out of thirty days in solitary confinement, and Yilan has questions. She was the one who'd suggested we start the meditation class, after her last trip to SHU. As if she'd known there was something she'd learn for her next round. Rach brings her over to my bunk. She remembers me saying in meditation class that anyone could talk to me about "this stuff" anytime.

"I wasn't there and I wasn't here," she says, still standing as if still floating between the two worlds. "They turn off the lights in SHU. It gets quiet. I'd wait for lights-out, because that's when it would happen. Is this crazy?"

"It's not crazy," I say.

That's all the permission she needs. She's been holding it in. Her eyes keep flicking between mine—*please tell me I'm not crazy*—and the wall, like she's tuning to a frequency where the memory is still playing.

"I'm always scared of what people think," she says. "And I'm always angry. I've been angry my whole life. I didn't know why. Now I do. Now I'm not angry. Because of what I saw." She's breathless, half laughing. "Now I get why you say meditation isn't a religion. There's something there. No one can tell you different. What was that phrase?"

"*Ehipassiko,*" I say. "See for yourself."

"Yes. That. You don't have to believe—you really see for yourself."

She searches for words. "There's no...'me' the way I thought. Everything I thought I was...I'm not. And I'm happy. I didn't need anything. I didn't even need to eat. Is that crazy?"

"It's not," I say. "Sometimes, when the mind goes very quiet, people feel fed by the world itself—like the air is nourishing. It's rare, but it happens."

"Yes! People keep saying I changed in SHU, but I can't explain it. If someone else came back and said these same things to me, I'd think they were nuts. But I know what I saw. I feel like I can't be mad anymore. I don't need anything. I have everything. I don't have to take your word for it. I didn't before. But now I know for myself."

She's glowing, innocence braided with certainty, her eyes bright but soft. Looking into them feels like looking out at the ocean.

"I'm not even mad at Janiya. I want her to see it too. I used to want more stuff. Now I think people just don't know."

"It's the game with hidden rules," I say. "Once you spot them, you can tell who knows and who doesn't."

She nods. "You don't have to be sad or mad, because you don't have to be *here*," she says, tapping the room—meaning you don't have to live only at the surface level of this place when there's sky available. "I get what *free* means. In SHU, I kept hearing you in my head from class, talking about us being 'unfuckwithable.' I thought you were crazy then. Now I get it. They could lock the door, turn off the lights, take everything—and they still couldn't touch this."

"That's why I say freedom is possible in any condition," I tell her. "But I need to say this part, because it's important: You found something precious. Protect it. It will guide you, but you have to listen. It will ask you to be brave where you used to be scared, to be kind to people you don't like, to let others think what they think—because now you know who you are."

She nods, a satisfied grin. "Yes. Yes."

"No one can take this from you," I say, "but you can lose sight of it if you don't care for it. That's why I keep a daily promise to myself." I open my locker and pull out the vows taped inside, ones I learned long ago at the Zen Center. And I've kept them, my simple commitments to keep helping, to keep clearing confusion, to keep learning, to keep going. I read them quietly. She listens like someone warming her hands at a fire.

Beings are numberless; I vow to save them.

Delusions are inexhaustible; I vow to end them.

Dharma gates are boundless; I vow to enter them.

The Buddha Way is unsurpassable; I vow to become it.

"You said that in class," she says. "I thought it was crazy. I was

306

terrified of SHU. Everyone is. Isolation. You kept talking about turning everything they use against us into something for us, about that being the way to be unfuckwithable. You told Carla that SHU could be heaven. That nothing is the way it seems. I thought you were out of your mind. You kept saying it's where we can finally meet ourselves. I didn't want that. But I get it now. You talk about flying. SHU is where you can take off."

"Exactly."

We sit on my bunk and watch the wall for a while, letting the silence between us do its work.

The day after I learned I'd been indicted, I stood in a field of yellow flowers in Mongolia, one of the flowers tucked behind my ear. Sitting on my bunk with Yilan, in this prison in Brooklyn, I feel dropped back into that location. The words of the divination reading from the head monk I'd had that evening echo in my ear: "It will be difficult but you will be born into supreme happiness." We sit there, letting a little of that happiness drip back into the room.

Officer Flannery walks into the dorm. "Snickers for Dakina?" he asks. Mari asks when Dakina's coming back from SHU. He shrugs. "Not sure she is. Seems to like it in there by herself."

Yilan and I exchange a look and smile. We know what it's like to find calm in the last place anyone expects. May she fly to the Supreme Happiness that knows no opposite. May we all become the jewel in the victory crown.

71

The Rapture

Nights got quieter as the mending process continued. Not silent—prison never is—but the air didn't bite as hard as those first days after the pages of writing were discovered, after the confrontation in the gym. The collective hope and concern for Lyric's baby and her upcoming sentencing occupied many prayers while bright moments like Royal's legal win glowed too, a reminder that prayers do sometimes come to pass. Even so, I could feel the tug: something unfinished, like I'd written my thesis and hadn't stood to defend it. The bond was repaired enough to walk on, but not enough to carry weight. In time, memory of the rupture could start to fade into the mottled history of the dorm. But fading away wasn't the point.

I lay on my bunk and let the room's low thunder roll—the never-ending gossiping of the women, the shouts across the room, the TVs droning, the industrial fans blowing. I thought about how these women survive on each other's shared good news: somebody's daughter turning three next month, somebody's appeal hearing set for spring, somebody's first clean night of sleep in weeks. I thought about my first day here, the vow I made to the quiet part of myself:

See them as they are—wild, brilliant, misnamed. And how I wanted them to see it too, until the world couldn't look away.

The idea I'd had percolating on my walk with Miriam remained half formed, lingering at the edges of my awareness, the creativity that wants to burst open, like a seed ready to sprout. I felt it as a pressure behind my sternum, asking for release. The kind of pressure that promises an explosion and then...doesn't. I've heard the universe began as an infinitely dense point—a singularity where all potential compressed until, in a flash, it expanded outward, birthing stars and space in a cosmic boom. It felt like that: The potential and pressure were here; we were just waiting for the spark.

When it finally arrived, it was plain. Not bells or visions. Just a clear sentence, like a paper slid under a door: Put her on a stage. Not just Royal, not just Miriam. All of them. Let them tell the world who they are. The picture clicked into focus so hard I sat up. I could see it—metal bunks as a set, picnic tables as props, a spotlight landing on one woman at a time. A chorus of voices breaking the single story that had flattened us all. It sounded crazy and true in the same breath.

Then the fine print scrolled in my head like a drug ad: This may not happen; this could be a lot of work for nothing; you can't do it for them; they have to choose; it might look like you're overreaching; it might be rejected. No promises. Not one. And that was right. They don't need "promises" from me. They need an invitation and room to choose.

I decided to risk it. Make an invitation and give room for the women to decide how they wanted to do it.

I invited the women who dressed me and Rach down that day in the gym, Mari—who gave us the courage to keep going—and anyone else who wanted to come. Same place as the confrontation—same scuffed floor, same humming lights. But this time, a different offer.

They trickled in: Lyric, Yilan, Nevaeh, Mari, Diamond, and Janiya.

309

Friendlies, and a few still unsure. Miriam moved her chair out from the others to make room for her six-foot-two frame. Carla found her way in, bringing several with her, offering a quiet nod before she took her seat. Royal came last, on purpose, letting the room register her before she sat, the signal that we were ready to start.

I stood where I had stood two weeks before—same square of floor, new reason to be there. I looked out at the audience: Black, white, Asian, Latina. Women from opposing sides of the "opps" line who wouldn't be caught dead speaking to each other. Some will call federal institutions home for the rest of their lives. A couple have "bodies" in their indictment—someone died. The snooty ones say "they only got me for fraud." The fed babies and the fed OGs who have done enough time in the system for royalty status. This isn't a crowd that would choose to come together, but who of us would have chosen any of this? The question left is: What do you choose when you have no choice left?

I started. "You can trust me or not trust me; it's up to you. I can't make any promises. I'll share what I see and you let me know what you think."

"I want you to imagine," I continued, and the room leaned in, some with arms crossed, some with hands open. "We're on a stage—picture Broadway, or picture our bunks right here turned into a set. This is the last scene of a play you've built. You've each told your story. Nevaeh has guided the audience through the maze. Scene changes happen when Royal walks the aisle and says what she says every morning: 'Hey, baby.' People laugh and cry because they recognize themselves. And before the curtain falls, we read a letter together—a letter to the country about who we really are." I let them see my hands. Empty. "That's the dream."

"Two things," I said. "First, I can't promise anything. Not Broadway. Not a publisher. Not a bus ticket. If nothing comes of it but each of you having your story told the way you want it told, then that's what we get. Second, this is a choice. No one can do it for you. You say yes or you say no. Whichever is the right answer for you." I felt the old thrill of falling with no parachute and remembered the lesson: There is no ground. Might as well fly.

They watched me like you watch a high-wire walker. Will she wobble?

I didn't. "If you want to try," I said, "we'll meet here Tuesday at six. I'll walk the gym with you, like I did with Miriam. Rach will follow and write the words as they come. We'll draw out the shape of your story—its spine, its breath—and you'll get to keep it. If nothing else happens, you'll walk away with that." I paused and looked toward Miriam. "And tonight, so you can see what I mean, we're going to end with a sermon she wrote. It's what happens when a voice is given a mic and room to stretch."

As the women began doing the math—risk on one side, possibility on the other—Miriam stood up.

"Alright then." She carried the gym like it was a chapel. "Since I'm tonight's exhibit, I'm gonna testify." And she did. The sermon she had written poured out of her. She raised a flag over the day, called it good, and told us what it takes to grow wings under low ceilings—gratitude as throttle, pain as runway, the stubborn knowledge that the One who made you doesn't do throwaways. Her voice moved up and down, drawing each of us in. By the end of it, the dorm had settled into the quietest I had heard it.

"You put in the dedication and the Lord is ready to carry you on the wings of your belief. You make the choice and you watch it work." As her sermon filled the room, the same image filled each of our minds: Dakina on top of her bunk, arms outstretched, head down in focused determination as her feet stomped up and down, the turbines coming to life. The deep howl that reverberated through her being, echoing through the dorm, reaching for the sky she so desperately longed for. "You believe and He does the rest."

No one clapped. We didn't need to. We all just sat there inside of the experience together, our faces expressing it all.

We ended by going around the room, each woman responding to the prompt: "I'm leaving here with..." One by one, they spoke. A sentence each, sometimes two.

"I'm leaving here feeling light," Mari said.

"I'm leaving here with a plan to stop hiding," said someone I hadn't heard speak all month.

Royal waited until nearly last. "I'm just so happy," she said, then laughed at herself because tears were coming. "I'm grateful we're all in this room together. Your color don't matter. Your group don't matter. I would do anything for you women. You might not know that, but I would do anything." The room exhaled like someone had punched us and healed us in the same breath.

There it was: Liftoff.

72

Dear America

ear America,
I challenge you to live up to your promise—where it
matters most, in the belly of the beast: our justice and
carceral systems. When the roots are poisoned, the fruit will be too.

From inside the "worst of the worst"—MDC Brooklyn—I can tell
you we treat prisons like toxic waste sites. We pretend there's an "over
there" where we can dump people without consequence.

I believe that anyone who signs up to serve as an officer in this
institution was called. And yet they live under constant threat—more
than the human nervous system can bear and still function in a way
that can offer simple human dignity to those around them. I have
served alongside these officers, in different capacities of course, and I
have watched them overcome unnecessary difficulties day after day.
The system neglects all of us equally: the officers standing in the same
freezing dorms, dealing with the same neglected plumbing, navigating
the same impossible bureaucracy. Their uniform in no way inoculates
them from what we endure.

Most of the time, they don't have real authority to do what is right
and humane at the most basic level. If someone is profoundly mentally

ill and having a breakdown, if someone is going through withdrawals and can't stop vomiting and the whole dorm is "going through it with them," if the place is flooded and we are walking through sewage to get to the legal room, the officers on the ground still don't have the power to carry out the calling of stewardship and guardianship of this precious resource: women who, if they had the means, have the power to change the world. These officers can and should be heroes of our society—and many are—but they live and work against the odds, because we don't supply them with what they need. To be clear: There are officers who use their own paycheck to buy cleaning supplies because the dorm reeks, or puzzles and art materials so women can engage their attention in something other than watching true crime on TV. These stories are greater than the stories of the officers who, under untold duress, buckle and fall to a lower common denominator of humanity by violating ethics or being cruel.

Inside, the only tools widely on offer—for officers and incarcerated women alike—are the ones that make things worse: sugar and junk food for numbing, endless TV and sleep for escape. Crochet class substitutes for meaningful skills. Communication breaks down. Hope is scarce. And where hope dies, aggression thrives.

In this form, prison is a dehumanizing machine. Responsibility— the engine of real freedom—is stripped out. Yet the potential here is enormous: Train people in ethical responsibility, train officers in noble stewardship, and train government to pursue truth and justice for all.

We are wasting human power by walling it off. People are reduced to a conviction, as if that were the sum total of their lives. With no shared purpose, the days collapse into gossip and survival. The system funds compliance, not growth.

This isn't a small corner of America. We cage hundreds of thousands and supervise close to a million more. We spend tens of billions to maintain the machinery, while families absorb hundreds of billions more in lost income and cascading costs. Every dollar poured into warehousing is a dollar stolen from healing, education, and community repair.

This is your report card, America.

First, face the truth: The incarcerated are human—those wrongfully convicted and those rightfully sentenced alike. In the program I built, we aim at real rehabilitation: tools to make use of time, to uncover purpose, to contribute.

We've all heard "the meek shall inherit the earth." The original Greek word, *praus*, described a battle-trained horse—still wild at heart, now directed. That's how I see the women here: untamable in spirit, generous with little, waiting for a worthy rider—truth—to guide that power. Without it, they buck against the narrow lanes of "acceptable" life. Ignore their strength and we all lose.

There are encouraging signs. The First Step Act is one. People here whisper about it like a weather change—the giant is learning to walk, not just stomp. The mentality of warehousing is cracking. A different future feels possible.

Let's go further. Responsibility is the ground of freedom. In our dorm, it's common wisdom that if a woman blames her crime on a man or her childhood, she'll get a lighter sentence. But that training breeds dependency, not liberation. Rather than rehearsing blame, what if we trained women to recognize their power—to channel care into contribution instead of numbing it with romance, food, or intoxication? When a woman claims her inner freedom, others around her begin to unshackle, too.

Here's my vision: Take two of our most underused resources— women and prisons—and build centers for inner liberation. Keep the buildings; change the purpose. Gut the aimlessness and install structure: quiet, focus, healthful food, real education, and the hardest curriculum of all—human dignity and responsibility. Partner with universities to teach cutting-edge skills, from environmental repair to AI literacy, alongside the essential technology of a free life: integrity, attention, service.

I believe, as the Dalai Lama has said, that Western women will transform the world. And I see how. Our prison system is America's weakest link. Strengthen it, and we strengthen the chain. It is not that we want too much when we dream of a mere lack of recidivism; it is that we do not want enough.

My aim is to do for women at the root what Malcolm X did for people of color at the root: Break mental slavery. I write this after a day in shackles; I don't say this lightly. No woman is free until all are free. Physical release is not enough. Train inner freedom, and recidivism falls on its own.

To start, we must end the trilogy of hopelessness, helplessness, and powerlessness. The key is human dignity. Punishment alone is shortsighted. It breeds a cycle of compliance without change. If we cultivate people at the roots—those inside, those guarding, those prosecuting—we restore what's been lost: shared values, shared humanity, shared future. I ask you to set our systems of incarceration up for success and watch the miracle happen.

Dear America, let us become great here at home, deep in our roots. May we take the poor, huddled masses in our own backyard and transform them into a national treasure. And let us dare to be great in the domain where few dare to tread.

Epilogue: The Vision

Early one morning, as I neared the final edits of this manuscript, I sat on my bed watching the yellow light of the sun rise through the slatted window. A bright, rich vision of what had sparked on that walk with Miriam came to mind, fully formed.

I'm in the back of a blacked-out SUV, pulling up to Madison Square Garden with a convoy so long it looks like New York decided to do a dignity parade. Escalades, matte-black Range Rovers, mysterious sedans with midnight tint. Someone says there are five hundred vehicles.

This is the Love Army—every type of person who has ever fought for freedom from the inside out. Presidents whose shoulders look heavy. Rogue reporters who'd crawl through sewers for a story. Ministers, lamas, rabbis, activists, the spiritually curious, the practical, the skeptical, the ungovernable. A real family reunion of people who rarely agree on anything except that human beings deserve to live free.

Out front is a brand-new Freedom Wall: a huge slab of white Italian marble split down the middle, like the world finally cracked open on purpose. All the names of everyone who supported the stories from the inside are carved into it—letters, prayers, protests, small acts of human decency.

Families are everywhere—Rosa's girls in bright scarves, Nevaeh's kids bouncing in excitement, Diamond's parents and sister holding an unnecessary but heartfelt bag of snacks, Alma's husband and children, and Royal's whole family, taking up space the way she always said they could. Everyone looks more themselves than I've ever seen.

And when we walk inside, it hits me what all of this is for. We've come to the special finale performance of the Broadway play, *Jailbirds in Flight*. The show ran so long and so wildly on Broadway that they moved this last, celebratory performance to Madison Square Garden.

The ushers guide us to our seats in the sold-out arena. Celebrities are tucked into seats like slightly bewildered houseplants—Mike Tyson, Lil Wayne, Lindsay Lohan, Angela Davis, Gucci Mane. The Kardashians, Joe Rogan, Charlamagne, political leaders, Garchen Rinpoche. I even spot the Italian Prime Minister in the balcony.

The lights dim. The curtain rises.

And there we are.

The play tells the women's real stories, no embellishment, no smoothing. Just the truth: messy, fierce, hilarious, holy. The audience laughs at the right parts, gasps at the hard ones, cries openly when tenderness sneaks up and grabs them.

Watching it feels like sitting inside a heartbeat I know by name.

When the curtain falls, the applause hits like weather.

Then the cast waves us, the women of the Metropolitan Dakini Convent, forward and we find ourselves onstage, holding hands. Topeka is the MC, crying through her mascara, thanking everyone for making this the most attended Broadway production in history. She announces—with the casualness of someone reading a lunch order— that the play has just won the Nobel Peace Prize.

And finally—the officers: Officer Santoro, Officer James, Officer Smith, and all the rest. The whole theater stands. They are honored not as guards, but as Guardians. Gucci outfits, Chanel makeup, and— for once—everyone smells like real soap.

And then a soft montage of "what came next" came into focus.

Royal becomes the Ambassador of Love, welcoming leaders with her signature, "Hey, baby," and dissolving tension wherever she goes. She walks every morning to stay strong for her grandkids, who somehow end up with lifetime Jordans.

Nevaeh becomes Executive Producer of all things Jailbirds—books, media, the channel—while Darius stands beside her, making sure she has fun while she runs an empire.

Miriam launches *Real Deal CBN*, broadcasting weekly from a transformed prison cell she redesigns into a sanctuary. Her husband now has AI-bionic bones and walks beside her like a gazelle on their backyard track.

Diamond heads the medical transformation for the entire system, caring for people with the tenderness she once saved for family. She cries joyful tears at least once a day.

Mari becomes Head of Yogic Arts nationwide, teaching women how to make any room a jewel, any life a practice of liberation.

Lyric chairs the National Foundation for Incarcerated Women, ensuring no mother is ever separated from her child again. She's also a quiet celebrity with a truly loving husband.

Janiya opens the Tina Turner Nam-Myoho-Renge-Kyo Center for Freedom, tagline: "Be you." Her graduates change the world through music, humor, and unabashed joy.

Dakina has her own 747 stocked with unlimited Snickers. Officer Santoro attends every performance just to cheer her on.

The final image flashes across the backdrop. It's MDC Brooklyn, but the sign now reads:

METROPOLITAN DAKINI CONVENT

Inside, a woman stands on a bunk, arms spread wide, practicing flight. This time, she rises. Not metaphorically. Not symbolically. Just rises.

Acknowledgments

My deepest gratitude for all those on the outside who fought along the way.

Naomi Aeon
Arthur Aidala
Lucky Angel
Cris Arguedas
Dave Asprey
Ramani & Louise Ayer
Debra Bailey
Francheska Barrientos
Rev Michael Bernard Beckwith
Bill Berndt
Dr. Stefano Bertozzi
Jennifer Bonjean
Darren Breeden
Ken Brown
Nanci Clarence
Celia Cohen
Ashley Cohen
Reverend Joanne Coleman
Jill Conklin
Loni Coombs

Lama Mike Crowley
Richard Cruz
Meghann Cuniff
Michelle Dacus
Beverly Daedone
Andrea Davis
Jay Davis
Alan Dershowitz
Teresa Diaz
Paul Dietrich
Cléo Dubois
Kiki Dunston
Todd Eagan
Harry Eccles-Williams
Jack Elias
Juda Engelmayer
Craig Engle
Summer Engman
David Ephron
Mark Faucette
Kate Feigin
Bryn Freedman
Hon. Judge Karen Friedman
David Friend
Alejandro Garcia
Gil Gilbert
Angel Grant
Samuel Gray
Brian Hack
Laura Hahn
RJ Hauman

Ezra Hermann
Jim Herriot
Amy Hertz
Brian Hill
Joan Hoeberichts
Sophie Hollander
Alice Howe
Mike Howell
David Hutchison
Emma James
Marie Jones
Van Jones
Rhodessa Jones
Emily Kaplan
Adam Katz
Sheila Kelley
Judy Kern
Isabelle Kirshner
Margot Koch
Lisa Kramer
Jenny Kramer
Dan Kriegman
Schuyler La Barge
Ezra Landes
John Lauro
James Lawrence III
Duncan Levin
Jennifer Lewis
Kelly Lin
John Liu
JoAnn Lovascio

Hon. Connie Mack
Doug Mackey
Kelly Madrone
Andrea Marz
Christine Marie Mason
Joseph Massey
Ian McCaleb
Rev. Dr. Luzette McDonald
Dr. Robert McDonald
Christin Medvec
Chloe Melas
Fred Mitouer
Sofia Moazed
Reverend Kahli Mootoo
Amy Moreno
Karla Morgan
Dream Mullick
Trace Murphy
Gabi Myers
Nazim
Susan Necheles
Elizabeth Nolan Brown
David Ord
Eric Osborne
Michael Pallares
Walt Pavlo
Paul Pelletier
Jhody Polk
Marcie Prohofsky
Corinne Ramey
Jigme Rangdrol

Drew Rayman
Nicole Rittenmeyer
Michael Robotti
Ippolita Rostagno
Craig Rothfeld
Donna Rotunno
Bob Sabado
Michelle Sabado
Salomé, Rocco, and Ziva
Vivian Siegel
Ira Silverberg
Robert Simels
Malidoma Patrice Somé
Jeff Stoddard
Shawn Sugarman
Ron Sullivan
John Timpone
Meghan Tobin
Aaron Turner
Tholyn Twyman
Kiki Tyson
Paula Van Vleck
Marc Von Musser
Tyler Walton
Ken Wapner
Beth Wareham
Courtney Waybright
Louisa West
Omari West
Alexandra Whiston-Dew
John Whitney

Seth Wiener
Rick Wiley
Emma Woollcott
Mike Zimbalist

May we all find freedom today!

Jailbirds in Flight Trust

Nicole Daedone has irrevocably transferred the copyright and the rights to all proceeds from the book and any related rights to the Jailbirds in Flight Trust.

60% of the trust proceeds go to a group of women who were incarcerated at the same time as the author. Some of their stories inspired portions of the book.

40% of the trust proceeds go to the Prison Monastery program, an initiative of Unconditional Freedom, a 501(c)(3) which runs the popular Art of Soulmaking and Guards to Guardians programs.

This book is published by Soulmaker Press.

www.ingramcontent.com/pod-product-compliance
Lightning Source LLC
Chambersburg PA
CBHW070054030426
42335CB00016B/1887